tasteofhome
GRILL IT!

12   230   88

tasteofhome
B O O K S

REIMAN MEDIA GROUP, INC. • GREENDALE, WISCONSIN

97

201

taste of home

A TASTE OF HOME/READER'S DIGEST BOOK

© 2010 Reiman Media Group, Inc.

5400 S. 60th St., Greendale WI 53129

Editor in Chief	Catherine Cassidy
Vice President, Executive Editor/Books	Heidi Reuter Lloyd
Creative Director	Ardyth Cope
U.S. Chief Marketing Officer	Lisa Karpinski
Food Director	Diane Werner RD
Senior Editor/Books	Mark Hagen
Art Director	Rudy Krochalk
Content Production Supervisor	Julie Wagner
Design Layout Artist	Catherine Fletcher
Proofreaders	Linne Bruskewitz, Susan Uphill
Recipe Asset System Manager	Coleen Martin
Premedia Supervisor	Scott Berger
Recipe Testing & Editing	Taste of Home Test Kitchen
Food Photography	Taste of Home Photo Studio
Administrative Assistant	Barb Czysz

THE READER'S DIGEST ASSOCIATION, INC.

President and Chief Executive Officer	Mary G. Berner
President, US Affinities	Suzanne M. Grimes
SVP, Global Chief Marketing Officer	Amy J. Radin

International Standard Book Number (10): 0-89821-766-0
International Standard Book Number (13): 978-0-89821-766-7
Library of Congress Control Number: 2009934706

For other Taste of Home books and products, visit shoptasteofhome.com.

For more Reader's Digest products and information,
visit rd.com (in the United States)
or see rd.ca (in Canada).

COVER PHOTOGRAPHY

Photographers	Rob Hagen, Grace Sheldon
Food Stylists	Dolores Jacq, Alynna Malson
Set Stylists	Sarah Thompson, Grace Sheldon

Pictured on front cover (from top left): Grilled Pound Cake with Berries (p. 241),
Barbecued Veggie Platter (p. 33), Grilled Steak and Portobello Stacks (p. 78),
Sausage Shrimp Kabobs (p. 194) and Sweet 'n' Smokey Kansas City Ribs (p. 187).

Pictured on the back cover: Grilled Chicken Veggie Dinner (p. 131),
Chipotle Chicken Fajitas (p. 153) and Santa Maria Roast Beef (p. 97).

Wood Grain photo: Chen Ping Hung/Shutterstock.com

Printed in China

1 3 5 7 9 10 8 6 4 2

TABLE of CONTENTS

BECOME THE
GRILL MASTER
OF YOUR DREAMS

IT'S EASY!

PARTICULARLY WHEN YOU HAVE THE RIGHT TRICKS UP YOUR SLEEVE. CONSIDER THESE COMMON QUESTIONS AND ANSWERS; THEN TURN THE PAGE AND GET GRILLING!

QUESTION:

How do the pros get diamond-shaped grill marks onto steaks?

ANSWER:

The trick is to sear the food just long enough to get good grill lines, then rotate the food 90 degrees without flipping it. Continue searing until you have the second set of lines.

Generally, only one side of the steak has grill marks since too much time over high heat will dry out the food. Once the steak is nicely marked, move it to a cooler area of the grill to finish cooking.

QUESTION:

Can marinade be added to uncooked meat and frozen for later use?

ANSWER:

Uncooked beef, chicken and pork can indeed be marinated and frozen. In fact, when you're ready to use it, the marinade will flavor the meat as it defrosts.

For the best (and safest) results, use only freshly purchased meat—nothing that was previously frozen or has been sitting in the fridge. Fill a resealable freezer bag with the meat and marinade. Carefully squeeze out any air before sealing the bag.

Keep in mind that marinated, uncooked meats have a shorter freezer storage life and should be used with 2 months. Always defrost the meat in the refrigerator, and drain and discard the marinade from the meat.

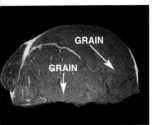

GRAIN

GRAIN

QUESTION:

What does it mean to slice a piece of meat "against the grain?"

ANSWER:

Bundles of long muscle fibers give meat texture; the "grain" refers to the direction these fibers run. Slicing in the opposite direction of the grain, or "against the grain," shortens the fibers, making the meat tender to chew.

Not all cuts of meat have fibers that run vertically or horizontally. Some fibers run diagonally, while others have multiple muscle sections. In this case, carve each section separately.

QUESTION:

What do medium-rare, medium and well-done steaks look like?

ANSWER:

A medium-rare steak has a slightly pinkish-red color in the center and is slightly brown on the exterior. When a steak is medium, it has a pink center and is brown toward the exterior. Well-done steaks are uniformly brown throughout.

Consider purchasing an instant-read thermometer to help assure accurate doneness. See the guide at right.

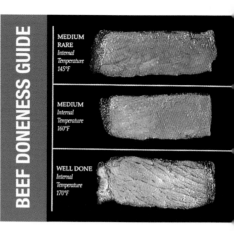

BEEF DONENESS GUIDE

MEDIUM RARE
Internal Temperature 145°F

MEDIUM
Internal Temperature 160°F

WELL DONE
Internal Temperature 170°F

QUESTION:

Why do hamburgers dry out on the grill?

ANSWER:

Juicy burgers start with 80-85% lean ground beef. Anything leaner has too little fat to stay moist while grilling. Anything fatter shrinks the patty, causing flare-ups that can dry out the burger.

If your recipe requires you to combine the beef with other ingredients, don't overmix it. Combine the ingredients gently, and lightly form the patties with your hands.

Grill burgers over medium-hot heat for 5 to 8 minutes, turning once. Resist the urge to press on the burgers with a spatula as they cook.

QUESTION:

Can a large variety of sausages be grilled at one time? If so, how long should the sausages be cooked?

ANSWER:

You can grill a variety of sausages at once, but they likely won't be done in unison. Always keep them well separated on the grill so you can best monitor their cooking times.

Be sure to cook any uncooked sausages, such as Italians or bratwurst, in water or beer before setting them on the grill grate. Grill these items over direct medium heat until they are nicely browned and reach an internal temperature of 165°.

Fully cooked smoked sausages, like hot dogs and kielbasa, should be grilled over direct medium heat, turning occasionally, until browned and heated through (7 to 10 minutes).

1
APPETIZERS & SNACKS

PG. **11** **CHICKEN SKEWERS** WITH COOL AVOCADO **SAUCE**

NOTHING FIRES UP A BACKYARD BARBECUE LIKE A SAVORY SPECIALTY GRILLED TO PERFECTION. GET YOUR EVENT OFF TO A TASTY START WITH ANY OF THESE MOUTHWATERING SENSATIONS. FROM BARBECUED CHICKEN WINGS TO CRISPY GARLIC BREAD, THIS ASSORTMENT OF SNACKS IS SURE TO BE THE LIFE OF THE PARTY.

GRILLED FETA QUESADILLAS

Here's a great appetizer, especially when having company over for a barbecue. I had something similar at a Memorial Day party, and I tried to re-create the flavor with lower-fat ingredients.
—Jacqui Correa, Landing, New Jersey

3	ounces fat-free cream cheese
1/2	cup shredded reduced-fat Mexican cheese blend
1/3	cup crumbled feta cheese
1/2	teaspoon dried oregano
4	flour tortillas (6 inches), warmed
1/4	cup chopped pitted ripe olives
2	tablespoons diced pimientos
1	green onion, chopped

In a small bowl, beat cheeses with oregano until blended. Spread 3 tablespoons of cheese mixture over half of each tortilla; top with olives, pimientos and onion. Fold tortillas over.

Coat grill rack with cooking spray before starting the grill. Grill quesadillas, uncovered, over medium heat for 1-2 minutes on each side or until golden brown. Cut each quesadilla into three wedges. Serve warm. **YIELD: 12 WEDGES.**

BACON GARLIC BREAD

1/3   **cup butter, softened**

1/3   **cup mayonnaise**

4   **bacon strips, cooked and crumbled**

5   **garlic cloves, minced**

1   **loaf (1 pound) French bread, halved lengthwise**

1   **cup (4 ounces) shredded Italian cheese blend**

In a small bowl, combine the butter, mayonnaise, bacon and garlic. Spread over cut sides of bread; reassemble loaf. Wrap in a large piece of heavy-duty foil (about 36 in. x 18 in.); seal tightly.

Grill, covered, over medium heat for 4-5 minutes on each side. Unwrap and separate bread halves. Sprinkle with cheese. Grill 5 minutes longer or until cheese is melted. **YIELD: 10-12 SERVINGS.**

Guests at your next backyard barbecue will request our home economists' recipe for this grilled garlic bread. Serve it as an appetizer or savory side dish.

—Taste of Home Test Kitchen

MARINATED PORK TENDERLOIN SANDWICHES

1/2   **cup soy sauce**

1/4   **cup packed brown sugar**

2   **tablespoons canola oil**

1   **teaspoon ground ginger**

1/2   **teaspoon ground mustard**

2   **garlic cloves, minced**

1   **pound pork tenderloin**

12   **dinner rolls, warmed**

In a large bowl, combine the soy sauce, brown sugar, oil, ginger, mustard and garlic. Pour 3/4 cup marinade into a large resealable plastic bag; add the pork. Seal bag and turn to coat; refrigerate for 12 hours or overnight, turning several times. Cover and refrigerate remaining marinade.

Drain and discard marinade. Coat grill rack with cooking spray before starting the grill. Grill pork, uncovered, over medium heat for 7-8 minutes on each side or until a meat thermometer reads 160°. Baste with remaining marinade during the last 7 minutes of cooking.

Let stand for 10 minutes; carve in thin slices and serve on rolls. **YIELD: 1 DOZEN.**

Every January, we host a large family get-together, and these tasty finger sandwiches scored big with everyone who tried them. I like to prepare the pork ahead of time and assemble the sandwiches shortly before they're needed.

—Alice Gregory
Overland Park, Kansas

GRILLED CORN DIP

- 6   medium ears sweet corn, husks removed
- 1   large onion, chopped
- 1   jalapeno pepper, finely chopped
- 2   tablespoons butter
- 2   garlic cloves, minced
- 1   cup mayonnaise
- 1/2   cup sour cream
- 1/2   teaspoon chili powder
- 2   cups (8 ounces) shredded Monterey Jack cheese
- 1   can (2-1/4 ounces) sliced ripe olives, drained
- 2   tablespoons sliced green onions

Tortilla chips

Grill corn, covered, over medium heat for 10-12 minutes or until tender, turning occasionally. Cut corn from cobs.

In a large skillet, saute the onion and jalapeno in butter for 2-3 minutes or until almost tender. Add corn and garlic; saute 1-2 minutes longer or until vegetables are tender. Remove from the heat.

In a large bowl, combine the mayonnaise, sour cream and chili powder. Stir in cheese and corn mixture. Transfer to a greased 2-qt. baking dish.

Bake, uncovered, at 400° for 25-30 minutes or until bubbly and golden brown. Sprinkle with olives and green onions; serve with chips. **YIELD: 5 CUPS.**

EDITOR'S NOTE: When cutting hot peppers, disposable gloves are recommended. Avoid touching your face.

Great for summer, this tasty appetizer is a must-have on weekend family gatherings at our cottage on Sandusky Bay. It's well worth the time it takes to grill the corn and cut from the cob.

—Cathy Myers
   Monroeville, Ohio

BEST BARBECUE WINGS

1/2	cup finely chopped onion
1/4	cup canola oil
3	teaspoons minced garlic
1-1/2	cups ketchup
3/4	cup cider vinegar, *divided*
1/3	cup packed brown sugar
1/3	cup Worcestershire sauce
2	teaspoons chili powder
1/2	teaspoon cayenne pepper
1/2	teaspoon ground cumin
1/8	teaspoon hot pepper sauce
1/4	cup olive oil
1/8	teaspoon salt
1/8	teaspoon pepper
30	frozen chicken wingettes, thawed

For barbecue sauce, in a large saucepan, saute onion in canola oil until tender. Add garlic; cook 1 minute longer. Stir in ketchup, 1/2 cup vinegar, brown sugar, Worcestershire sauce, chili powder, cayenne and cumin. Simmer, uncovered, for 8-10 minutes, stirring often. Remove from the heat; stir in pepper sauce. Set aside 2/3 cup for serving.

Coat grill rack with cooking spray before starting the grill. In a large resealable plastic bag, combine the remaining 1/4 cup vinegar, olive oil, salt and pepper; add chicken wings in batches and turn to coat.

Grill wings, covered, over medium heat for 12-16 minutes, turning occasionally. Brush with some of the remaining barbecue sauce.

Grill, uncovered, 8-10 minutes longer or until juices run clear, basting and turning several times. Serve with reserved barbecue sauce. **YIELD: 2-1/2 DOZEN.**

DISJOINTING CHICKEN WINGS

1. Place chicken wing on a cutting board. With a sharp knife, cut between the joint at the top of the tip end. Discard tips or use for preparing chicken broth.

2. Take remaining wing and cut between the joints. Proceed with recipe as directed.

CHEESE-STUFFED JALAPENOS

8	ounces Monterey Jack cheese, cut into 2-inch x 1/2-inch x 1/4-inch strips
15	jalapeno peppers, halved lengthwise and seeded
1/4	cup dry bread crumbs
1/4	cup real bacon bits

Place a cheese strip in each pepper half; sprinkle with bread crumbs and bacon. Grill peppers, covered, over medium-hot heat for 4-6 minutes or until peppers are tender and cheese is melted. Serve warm. **YIELD: 2-1/2 DOZEN.**

EDITOR'S NOTE: When cutting hot peppers, disposable gloves are recommended. Avoid touching your face.

We make these several times throughout the summer, and everyone loves them. With ooey-gooey cheese and salty bacon, these stuffed jalapenos are irresistible!
—Bruce Hahne, Acworth, Georgia

CHICKEN SKEWERS WITH COOL AVOCADO SAUCE

1	pound boneless skinless chicken breasts
1/2	cup lime juice
1	tablespoon balsamic vinegar
2	teaspoons minced chipotle pepper in adobo sauce
1/2	teaspoon salt

SAUCE:

1	medium ripe avocado, peeled and pitted
1/2	cup fat-free sour cream
2	tablespoons minced fresh cilantro
2	teaspoons lime juice
1	teaspoon grated lime peel
1/4	teaspoon salt

Flatten chicken to 1/4-in. thickness; cut lengthwise into sixteen 1-in.-wide strips. In a large resealable plastic bag, combine the lime juice, vinegar, chipotle pepper and salt; add the chicken. Seal bag and turn to coat; refrigerate for 30 minutes.

Meanwhile, for the sauce, place remaining ingredients in a food processor; cover and process until blended. Transfer sauce to a serving bowl; cover and refrigerate until serving.

Drain chicken and discard marinade. Thread onto 16 metal or soaked wooden skewers. Coat grill rack with cooking spray before starting the grill. Grill, covered, over medium heat for 4-6 minutes on each side or until no longer pink. Serve with sauce. **YIELD: 16 SKEWERS (3/4 CUP SAUCE).**

I'm always looking for lighter recipes to take on tailgate outings. This one is quick and easy to marinate and take along. It's also great tasting and a family favorite.
—Veronica Callagha Glastonbury, Connecticut

APPETIZER PIZZAS

    9   flour tortillas (6 inches)

    3   tablespoons olive oil

TRADITIONAL PIZZAS:

  1/3   cup chopped pepperoni

  3/4   cup shredded Colby-Monterey Jack cheese

    1   jar (14 ounces) pizza sauce

MEDITERRANEAN PIZZAS:

  1/2   cup chopped seeded tomato

  1/3   cup sliced ripe olives

  3/4   cup crumbled feta cheese

  1/4   cup thinly sliced green onions

    1   carton (7 ounces) hummus

MARGHERITA PIZZAS:

    9   thin slices tomato

    1   package (8 ounces) small fresh mozzarella cheese balls, sliced

    1   tablespoon minced fresh basil

    1   cup prepared pesto

To keep a summer kitchen cool, our home economists suggest preparing pizzas on the grill! A variety of ingredients tops flour tortillas for three terrific tastes.

—Taste of Home
    Test Kitchen

Brush one side of each tortilla with oil. Place oiled side down on grill rack. Grill, uncovered, over medium heat for 2-3 minutes or until puffed. Brush tortillas with oil; turn and top with pizza toppings.

FOR TRADITIONAL PIZZAS: Top three grilled tortillas with pepperoni and cheese. Cover and grill for 2-3 minutes or until cheese is melted. Cut into wedges; serve with pizza sauce.

FOR MEDITERRANEAN PIZZAS: Top three grilled tortillas with tomato, olives, feta cheese and onions. Cover and grill for 2-3 minutes or until cheese is heated through. Cut into wedges; serve with hummus.

FOR MARGHERITA PIZZAS: Top three grilled tortillas with tomato slices, mozzarella cheese and basil. Cover and grill for 2-3 minutes or until cheese is melted. Cut into wedges; serve with pesto. **YIELD: 9 PIZZAS.**

GRILLING TIP

GRILLED PIZZAS are a great way to mix up traditional party fare as well as dinnertime standbys. Instead of tortillas, try grilling packaged pizza shells, available from just about any supermarket.

GRILLED BACON-ONION APPETIZERS

- 2 large sweet onions
- 12 hickory-smoked bacon strips
- 1/2 cup packed brown sugar
- 1/2 cup balsamic vinegar
- 1/4 cup molasses
- 2 tablespoons barbecue sauce

Cut each onion into 12 wedges. Cut bacon strips in half widthwise; wrap a piece of bacon around each onion wedge and secure with toothpicks. Place in an ungreased 13-in. x 9-in. dish.

In a small bowl, combine the brown sugar, vinegar, molasses and barbecue sauce; pour 1/2 cup over onions. Cover and refrigerate for 1 hour, turning once. Cover and refrigerate remaining marinade for basting.

Drain and discard marinade. Grill onions, covered, over medium heat for 10-15 minutes, turning and basting frequently with reserved marinade. **YIELD: 2 DOZEN.**

I'm the father of three girls who loves cooking for the family for lots of different meals and occasions. All of us really love this savory treat whenever it's served.

—Dayton Hulst
Moorhead, Minnesota

SAGE SHRIMP SKEWERS

- 10 bacon strips
- 10 uncooked jumbo shrimp, peeled and deveined
- 1 tablespoon olive oil
- 10 fresh sage leaves

In a large skillet, cook bacon over medium heat until partially cooked but not crisp. Remove to paper towels to drain.

Coat grill rack with cooking spray before starting the grill. Sprinkle shrimp with oil. Place a sage leaf on each shrimp; wrap with a strip of bacon. Thread shrimp onto two metal or soaked wooden skewers.

Grill, covered, over medium heat for 2-3 minutes on each side or until shrimp turn pink. **YIELD: 10 APPETIZERS.**

This is such a simple and unique grill recipe. And with just four ingredients, it's very easy to change the amounts for a crowd.

—Lacey Kirsch, Vancouver, Washington

TACO-FLAVORED CHICKEN WINGS

- 1 **envelope taco seasoning**
- 3 **tablespoons canola oil**
- 2 **tablespoons red wine vinegar**
- 2 **teaspoons hot pepper sauce,** *divided*
- 34 **fresh** *or* **frozen chicken wingettes (about 4 pounds)**
- 1 **cup ranch salad dressing**

In a large resealable plastic bag, combine the taco seasoning, oil, vinegar and 1 teaspoon hot pepper sauce; add chicken. Seal bag and turn to coat.

Grill chicken, covered, over medium heat for 5 minutes. Grill 10-15 minutes longer or until juices run clear, turning occasionally.

In a small bowl, combine ranch dressing and remaining hot pepper sauce. Serve with chicken. **YIELD: ABOUT 2-1/2 DOZEN.**

I dress up chicken wings with grill marks and a lively marinade to create a fantastic summertime appetizer that's always a hit. I like these wings spicy, so I often add a little extra hot sauce.

—Deb Keslar, Utica, Nebraska

BASIL SHRIMP

My husband loves shrimp and agrees nothing beats this incredibly easy, seafood appetizer. You can double the recipe when entertaining.

—Natalie Corona, Maple Grove, Minnesota

- 1 **tablespoon minced fresh basil**
- 1 **tablespoon olive oil**
- 1 **tablespoon butter, melted**
- 1 **tablespoon Dijon mustard**
- 2 **teaspoons lemon juice**
- 1 **garlic clove, minced**

Dash salt and white pepper

- 8 **uncooked large shrimp, peeled and deveined**

In a small bowl, combine the basil, oil, butter, mustard, lemon juice, garlic, salt and pepper. Pour 3 tablespoons into a small resealable plastic bag; add shrimp. Seal bag and turn to coat; let stand at room temperature for 15-20 minutes. Set remaining marinade aside.

Drain and discard marinade. Thread shrimp onto two metal or soaked wooden skewers. Grill, covered, over medium heat for 2-3 minutes on each side or until shrimp turn pink, basting occasionally with reserved marinade. **YIELD: 2 SERVINGS.**

GRILLING TIP

WOODEN SKEWERS work best on the grill when they've been soaked in water for a few hours. Soaking helps prevent the wood from splintering while assembling and grilling the kabobs. In addition, skewers that have been soaked in water won't burn as quickly on the grill.

Consider wooden skewers when grilling delicate items such as shrimp or thin slices of vegetables. Thicker, steel skewers work best for hearty items such as large chunks of meat.

PROSCIUTTO CHICKEN KABOBS

3/4   cup five-cheese Italian salad dressing

1/4   cup lime juice

2   teaspoons white Worcestershire sauce for chicken

1/2   pound boneless skinless chicken breasts, cut into 3-inch x 1/2-inch strips

12   thin slices prosciutto

24   fresh basil leaves

AVOCADO DIP:

2   medium ripe avocados, peeled

1/4   cup minced fresh cilantro

2   green onions, chopped

2   tablespoons lime juice

2   tablespoons mayonnaise

1-1/2   teaspoons prepared horseradish

1   garlic clove, minced

1/4   teaspoon salt

Everyone will think you spent hours preparing these simple, clever grilled wraps, served with a guacamole-like dip. Basil gives the chicken a lovely fresh herb flavor.

—Elaine Sweet
Dallas, Texas

In a large resealable plastic bag, combine the salad dressing, lime juice and Worcestershire sauce; add chicken. Seal bag and turn to coat; refrigerate for 1 hour.

Drain and discard marinade. Fold prosciutto slices in half; top each with two basil leaves and a chicken strip. Roll up jelly-roll style, starting with a short side. Thread onto metal or soaked wooden skewers.

Grill, covered, over medium heat for 5 minutes on each side or until chicken is no longer pink.

Meanwhile, in a small bowl, mash the avocados. Stir in the cilantro, onions, lime juice, mayonnaise, horseradish, garlic and salt. Serve with kabobs. **YIELD: 12 KABOBS.**

2
ENTREE SALADS

PG. 24 | **FETA SALMON SALAD**

COMBINE THE THRILL OF THE GRILL WITH A CRISP SALAD, AND YOU'VE GOT A SENSATIONAL MEAL-IN-ONE. THIS CHAPTER FEATURES GRILLED GREATS SERVED OVER LETTUCE TO KEEP BACKYARD DINING LIGHT AND LIVELY. "BEEF KABOB SPINACH SALAD" AND "RASPBERRY-CHILI TUNA ON GREENS" ARE JUST SOME OF THE SPECIALTIES FOUND HERE.

MANDARIN PORK SALAD

Try something different for dinner! This interesting main-dish salad tosses together pork, mandarin oranges, beets and goat cheese. The flavors will burst in your mouth.

—Nanci Jenkins, Ann Arbor, Michigan

1	pork tenderloin (1/2 pound)
3	cups torn mixed salad greens
1	snack-size cup (4 ounces) mandarin oranges, drained
1/2	small red onion, thinly sliced
1/4	cup crumbled goat cheese
1/4	cup canned sliced beets, julienned
2	tablespoons minced fresh cilantro
1	teaspoon finely chopped seeded jalapeno pepper
2	tablespoons balsamic vinegar
2	teaspoons olive oil
1/2	teaspoon salt

Grill pork tenderoin, covered, over medium heat or broil 4 in. from heat for 8-10 minutes on each side or until a meat thermometer reads 160°.

Meanwhile, in a large bowl, combine the salad greens, oranges, onion, cheese, beets, cilantro and jalapeno. Transfer to a serving platter. Whisk the vinegar, oil and salt. Thinly slice pork; arrange over salad. Drizzle with dressing. **YIELD: 2 SERVINGS.**

EDITOR'S NOTE: When cutting hot peppers, disposable gloves are recommended. Avoid touching your face.

PIZZA SALAD

2   prebaked mini pizza crusts

1/2   cup Western, Catalina *or* French salad dressing

1   tablespoon minced fresh basil *or* oregano

1   package (10 ounces) torn romaine lettuce (8 cups)

1   cup sliced pepperoni *or* chopped Canadian bacon

1   cup (4 ounces) shredded part-skim mozzarella cheese *or* cheese blend

1   can (2-1/4 ounces) sliced ripe olives, drained

Grill pizza crusts over medium heat until desired crispness or bake at 400° for 8-10 minutes. When cool enough to handle, tear into bite-size pieces; set aside.

In a small bowl, combine salad dressing and basil; set aside. In a salad bowl, combine lettuce, pizza crust pieces, pepperoni, cheese and olives. Toss to mix ingredients. Drizzle each serving with dressing. **YIELD: 4 SERVINGS.**

If your family loves pizza, try this recipe. It has such a wonderful flavor and will become a favorite with your family.

—Taste of Home Test Kitchen

STEAK AND POTATO SALAD

1/2   cup red wine vinegar

1/4   cup olive oil

1/4   cup soy sauce

1   beef top sirloin steak (2 pounds)

6   cups cubed cooked potatoes

1   cup diced green pepper

1/3   cup chopped green onions

1/4   cup minced fresh parsley

1/2   cup creamy Caesar salad dressing

Lettuce leaves, optional

In a large resealable plastic bag, combine the vinegar, oil and soy sauce; add steak. Seal bag and turn to coat. Refrigerate for 1 hour or overnight.

Drain and discard marinade. Grill steak over medium heat or broil 3-4 in. from the heat for 8-10 minutes on each side or until meat reaches desired doneness (for medium-rare, a meat thermometer should read 145°; medium, 160°; well-done, 170°).

Slice into thin strips across the grain and place in a large bowl. Add the potatoes, green pepper, onions, parsley and dressing; toss to coat. Serve on lettuce if desired. **YIELD: 8-10 SERVINGS.**

I like to spend a lot of time with our family and friends on weekends. That's when this meat-and-potatoes recipe comes in handy. We marinate the meat in the fridge overnight, then grill it quickly for a fast and filling meal.

—Linda Emily Dow
  Princeton Junction,
  New Jersey

MEXICAN SHRIMP SALAD

1	small onion, halved and thinly sliced
1/4	cup minced fresh cilantro
1	jalapeno pepper, seeded and chopped
2	tablespoons canola oil
2	teaspoons chili powder
1/2	teaspoon ground cumin
1/2	teaspoon ground coriander
1/2	teaspoon pepper
1/4	teaspoon salt
1	pound uncooked medium shrimp, peeled and deveined
6	cups torn leaf lettuce
1/2	cup fat-free ranch salad dressing

The grilled shrimp are yummy in this salad, but you could also serve them with tortillas or with Mexican rice. Jalapeno and the chili powder lend just the right amount of heat and a wonderful aroma!

—Marie Bason
  Bend, Oregon

In a large resealable plastic bag, combine the first nine ingredients; add shrimp. Seal bag and turn to coat. Cover and refrigerate for 30 minutes.

If grilling the shrimp, coat grill rack with cooking spray before starting the grill. Thread shrimp onto four metal or soaked wooden skewers; discard onion mixture.

Grill, covered, over medium heat or broil 4 in. from the heat for 3-4 minutes on each side or until shrimp turn pink.

Divide lettuce among four plates; top with shrimp. Serve immediately with dressing. **YIELD: 4 SERVINGS.**

EDITOR'S NOTE: When cutting hot peppers, disposable gloves are recommended. Avoid touching your face.

GRILL-SIDE TURKEY SALAD

- **2** turkey breast tenderloins (1-1/2 pounds)
- **2** teaspoons dried tarragon, *divided*
- **1/2** cup thinly sliced celery
- **1/2** cup chopped green pepper
- **1/2** cup chopped red onion
- **2** tablespoons canola oil
- **1** tablespoon soy sauce
- **1** tablespoon lemon juice
- **1** tablespoon red wine vinegar
- **1/8** teaspoon pepper
- **1/4** teaspoon salt, optional

Lettuce leaves

Chopped salted peanuts, optional

Turkey salad gets a snappy update with soy sauce, red wine vinegar and dried tarragon with this recipe. Peanuts add a fantastic crunch you'll love.

—Barbara Young
Bethesda, Maryland

Sprinkle each tenderloin with 1/2 teaspoon tarragon. Grill, uncovered, over medium-hot heat for 8-10 minutes on each side or until a meat thermometer reads 170°. Cool.

Cut into cubes; place in a large bowl. Add the celery, green pepper and onion. In a small bowl, combine the oil, soy sauce, lemon juice, vinegar, pepper, salt if desired and remaining tarragon. Pour over turkey mixture; toss to coat. Refrigerate for at least 3 hours.

Serve on lettuce leaves; sprinkle with peanuts if desired. **YIELD: 4 SERVINGS.**

RASPBERRY-CHILI TUNA ON GREENS

I turn grilled tuna into something sensational with a zippy marinade featuring raspberry preserves and Thai chili sauce. Serve on romaine lettuce, garnish with fresh veggies and this entree is special enough for guests.

—Kathy Hawkins
  Ingleside, Illinois

6	tablespoons seedless raspberry preserves
1/4	cup balsamic vinegar
2	teaspoons Thai chili sauce
2	teaspoons minced fresh basil *or* 1/2 teaspoon dried basil
1/2	teaspoon salt
1/4	teaspoon pepper
4	tuna steaks (6 ounces *each*)
1	package (10 ounces) torn romaine
1/2	cup shredded carrot
1/2	cup thinly sliced cucumber

In a small bowl, combine the first six ingredients. Pour 1/4 cup marinade into a large resealable plastic bag; add tuna steaks. Seal bag and turn to coat; refrigerate for 30 minutes, turning occasionally. Cover and refrigerate remaining marinade for dressing.

If grilling the tuna, coat grill rack with cooking spray before starting the grill. Drain and discard marinade. Grill tuna, covered, over medium-hot heat or broil 4 in. from the heat for 3-4 minutes on each side for medium-rare or until slightly pink in the center.

In a large bowl, combine the romaine, carrot and cucumber; drizzle with reserved marinade and toss to coat. Divide among four plates. Top with grilled tuna. **YIELD: 4 SERVINGS.**

GRILLED SCALLOP SALAD

24	asparagus spears, trimmed	1/4	cup crumbled cooked bacon
2	tablespoons olive oil	1	cup chopped walnuts, toasted
1	teaspoon soy sauce	2	tablespoons grated Romano cheese
24	sea scallops	1/2	cup balsamic vinaigrette salad dressing
2	cups sliced fresh mushrooms		
2	cups torn red leaf lettuce		
2	cups torn Bibb lettuce *or* Boston lettuce		

In a large saucepan, bring 6 cups water to a boil. Add asparagus; cover and boil for 3 minutes. Drain and immediately place asparagus in ice water. Drain and pat dry; set aside. In a large resealable plastic bag, combine oil and soy sauce; add scallops. Seal bag and turn to coat. Let stand for 10 minutes.

Drain and discard marinade. Coat grill rack with cooking spray before starting the grill. Grill scallops, uncovered, over medium heat for 7-8 minutes on each side or until the scallops are firm and opaque.

Arrange mushrooms on a 9-in.-square piece of heavy-duty foil coated with cooking spray. Grill mushrooms on foil, uncovered, over medium heat for 10-15 minutes or until tender, stirring often.

Arrange the lettuce on four serving plates. Top with the asparagus, scallops, mushrooms, bacon, walnuts and cheese. Drizzle with dressing. **YIELD: 4 SERVINGS.**

I rely on scallops, asparagus, bacon and walnuts for this main course salad.

—Dennis Reed
Henry, Illinois

GRILLED CHICKEN SALAD

1	can (8 ounces) unsweetened sliced pineapple	4	boneless skinless chicken breast halves (1 pound)
3	tablespoons canola oil	1/2	to 1 teaspoon black pepper
2	tablespoons light soy sauce	5	cups torn salad greens
1	tablespoon white vinegar	1	small green pepper, julienned
1	tablespoon honey	1	small sweet red pepper, julienned
1/4	teaspoon ground ginger	1	cup sliced fresh mushrooms
1/4	teaspoon cayenne pepper	1	small onion, sliced into rings

Drain pineapple, reserving 2 tablespoons juice. In a small bowl, combine the juice, oil, soy sauce, vinegar, honey, ginger and cayenne. Brush some over pineapple slices; set aside.

Sprinkle both sides of chicken with pepper; grill or broil for 4-5 minutes on each side or until a meat thermometer reads 170°. Slice into strips.

Grill or broil pineapple, turning to brown both sides, for 2-3 minutes or until heated through. In a large bowl, toss the greens, peppers, mushrooms and onion. Top with chicken and pineapple; or arrange on four plates. Drizzle with remaining dressing. **YIELD: 4 SERVINGS.**

I frequently prepare this fabulous, filling salad for supper. What a delicious change-of-pace it is.

—Brenda
Eichelberger
Williamsport,
Maryland

BEEF KABOB SPINACH SALAD

1/4	cup packed brown sugar
4	teaspoons white vinegar
2	teaspoons chili powder
1	teaspoon salt
1	teaspoon canola oil
1/2	to 1 teaspoon hot pepper sauce
2	pounds boneless beef sirloin steak, cut into 1-inch cubes
1	cup (8 ounces) plain yogurt
1/3	cup chopped green onions
1	garlic clove, minced
1	package (10 ounces) fresh baby spinach

I found this easy recipe many years ago, and we never grow tired of it. I like to serve this zippy salad with roasted potatoes and warm rolls.

—Gail Reinford
Souderton,
Pennsylvania

In a large resealable storage bag, combine the brown sugar, vinegar, chili powder, salt, oil and hot pepper sauce. Add beef; seal bag and turn to coat. Refrigerate for 30 minutes. Meanwhile, in a small bowl, combine the yogurt, onions and garlic; cover and refrigerate until serving.

Drain and discard marinade. Thread the beef cubes onto eight metal or soaked wooden skewers. Grill, covered, over medium heat for 4-6 minutes on each side or until meat reaches desired doneness. Serve with spinach and yogurt sauce. **YIELD: 8 SERVINGS.**

STEAK AND MUSHROOM SALAD

6	tablespoons olive oil, *divided*
2	tablespoons Dijon mustard, *divided*
1/2	teaspoon salt
1/4	teaspoon pepper
1-1/2	pounds beef top sirloin steak (3/4 inch)
1	pound fresh mushrooms, sliced
1/4	cup red wine vinegar
1	medium bunch romaine, torn

In a small bowl, whisk 1 tablespoon oil, 1 tablespoon mustard, salt and pepper; set aside.

Grill steak, covered, over medium-hot heat for 4 minutes. Turn; spread with mustard mixture. Grill 4 minutes longer or until meat reaches desired doneness (for medium-rare, a meat thermometer should read 145°; medium, 160°; well-done, 170°).

Meanwhile, in a large skillet, cook mushrooms in 1 tablespoon oil until tender. Stir in the vinegar, remaining oil and mustard; mix well.

Thinly slice steak across the grain; add to mushroom mixture. Serve over romaine. **YIELD: 6 SERVINGS.**

My husband loves this supper, especially during summertime. He says he feels like he's eating a healthy salad and getting his steak, too! I always serve it with a loaf of homemade bread.

—Julie Cashion, Sanford, Florida

FETA SALMON SALAD

1/4	teaspoon salt
1/4	teaspoon garlic powder
1/4	teaspoon ground ginger
1/4	teaspoon dried parsley flakes
1/4	teaspoon pepper
4	salmon fillets (6 ounces *each*)
1	package (5 ounces) spring mix salad greens
1	large cucumber, chopped
1	large tomato, chopped
1/2	cup crumbled feta cheese
1/4	cup red wine vinaigrette

Coat grill rack with cooking spray before starting the grill. Combine the seasonings; sprinkle over salmon. Grill, covered, over medium heat or broil 4 in. from the heat for 8-12 minutes or until fish flakes easily with a fork.

In a large bowl, combine the salad greens, cucumber, tomato and feta cheese; divide among four plates. Top with salmon; drizzle with vinaigrette. **YIELD: 4 SERVINGS.**

My son always ordered a salmon sandwich at a local restaurant. In trying to replicate it, he came up with this salad. It's the only recipe he's ever made, and our entire family thinks it's great.

—Susan Griffiths
Mt. Pleasant, South Carolina

RAMEN-VEGGIE CHICKEN SALAD

1/4	cup sugar	1	tablespoon sesame seeds
1/4	cup canola oil	1	boneless skinless chicken breast half (6 ounces)
2	tablespoons cider vinegar		
1	tablespoon reduced-sodium soy sauce	4	cups shredded Chinese *or* napa cabbage
1	package (3 ounces) ramen noodles	1/2	large sweet red pepper, thinly sliced
1	tablespoon butter	3	green onions, thinly sliced
1/3	cup sliced almonds	1	medium carrot, julienned

In a small saucepan, combine the sugar, oil, vinegar and soy sauce. Bring to a boil; cook and stir for 1 minute or until sugar is dissolved. Set aside to cool.

Meanwhile, break noodles into small pieces (save seasoning packet for another use). In a small skillet, melt butter over medium heat. Add the noodles, almonds and sesame seeds; cook and stir for 1-2 minutes or until lightly toasted.

Grill chicken, covered, over medium heat for 4-7 minutes on each side or until a meat thermometer reads 170°.

Meanwhile, arrange the cabbage, red pepper, onions and carrot on two serving plates. Slice chicken; place on salad. Top with noodle mixture; drizzle with dressing. **YIELD: 2 SERVINGS.**

Like a salad with plenty of crunch? Then, this refreshing recipe is sure to please. Toasted noodles, almonds and sesame seeds provide a change-of-pace topping.

—Linda Gearhart
Greensboro,
North Carolina

ARTICHOKE STEAK SALAD

2	pounds boneless beef sirloin steaks
12	cherry tomatoes
1	medium red onion, sliced
1	jar (7-1/2 ounces) marinated artichoke hearts, drained and sliced
1	cup sliced fresh mushrooms
1/4	cup red wine vinegar
1/4	cup olive oil
1	teaspoon sugar
1	teaspoon salt
1/2	teaspoon dried oregano
1/2	teaspoon dried rosemary, crushed
1/2	teaspoon pepper
1/2	teaspoon minced garlic
6	cups torn fresh spinach

Loaded with veggies and laced with a tasty herb dressing, this satisfying steak salad boasts an easygoing elegance. Pair it with a crusty loaf of bread and red wine or iced tea for a patio dinner.

—Taste of Home
Test Kitchen

Grill steaks, covered, over medium heat or broil 4 in. from the heat for 5-7 minutes on each side or until meat reaches desired doneness (for medium-rare, a meat thermometer should read 145°; medium, 160°; well-done, 170°).

Meanwhile, in a large bowl, combine the tomatoes, onion, artichokes and mushrooms. In a small bowl, whisk the vinegar, oil, sugar, salt, oregano, rosemary, pepper and garlic. Pour over vegetable mixture; toss to coat.

Thinly slice steaks across the grain. Add beef and spinach to vegetable mixture; toss to coat. **YIELD: 6 SERVINGS.**

GRILLED THAI SALAD

- 1/2 **cup hot water**
- 2 **tablespoons lime juice**
- 3/4 **cup flaked coconut**
- 2 **teaspoons curry powder**
- 2 **teaspoons minced fresh gingerroot**
- 1 **teaspoon salt**
- 4 **boneless skinless chicken breast halves (4 ounces** *each***)**
- 4 **cups torn mixed salad greens**
- 1/2 **medium sweet red pepper, julienned**
- 1/2 **cup canned bean sprouts, rinsed and drained**
- 1/2 **cup fresh sugar snap peas**

DRESSING:
- 1/4 **cup reduced-sodium soy sauce**
- 2 **tablespoons lime juice**
- 2 **tablespoons coconut milk**
- 2 **tablespoons reduced-fat creamy peanut butter**
- 4 **teaspoons sugar**

In a blender, combine the first six ingredients; cover and process until blended. Pour into a large resealable plastic bag; add chicken. Seal bag and turn to coat; refrigerate for at least 1 hour.

If grilling the chicken, coat grill rack with cooking spray before starting the grill. Drain and discard marinade. Grill chicken, covered, over medium heat or broil 4 in. from the heat for 4-7 minutes on each side or a meat thermometer reads 170°.

In a large salad bowl, combine the greens, red pepper, bean sprouts and peas. In a small bowl, whisk the dressing ingredients until smooth. Pour over salad and toss to coat. Cut chicken into strips; arrange over salad. **YIELD: 4 SERVINGS.**

My husband and I love to eat Thai and Indian food, but notice that most of these cuisines do not offer fresh salads on their menus. We developed this recipe to savor all those ethnic flavors when we also want a light dinner.

—Grace Kunert
Salt Lake City, Utah

GRILLING TIP

COOKING SPRAY is a valuable tool for most backyard chefs. Before starting the grill, coat the rack with cooking spray when cooking foods that are naturally low in fat, such as chicken breasts, turkey tenderloin, fish and vegetables.

FLANK STEAK SALAD

- 1/4　cup olive oil
- 1/3　cup balsamic vinegar
- 1　tablespoon brown sugar
- 1　tablespoon Dijon mustard
- 1/2　teaspoon minced garlic
- 1/2　teaspoon pepper
- 1　beef flank steak (3/4 pound)
- 1　package (5 ounces) spring mix salad greens
- 1　plum tomato, cut into wedges
- 1/4　cup sliced radishes
- 1/4　cup chopped celery
- 2　green onions, cut into 1-inch strips

This is one of our favorite recipes! The marinade gives the meat such a wonderful flavor. It's a great meal-in-one that takes advantage of the grill.

—Mitzi Sentiff
　Annapolis, Maryland

In a small bowl, whisk the first six ingredients. Pour 1/3 cup into a large resealable plastic bag; add steak. Seal bag and turn to coat; refrigerate for 3 hours. Cover and refrigerate remaining marinade for dressing.

Drain and discard marinade from steak. Grill, covered, over indirect medium heat for 11-12 minutes on each side or until meat reaches desired doneness (for medium-rare, a meat thermometer should read 145°; medium, 160°; well-done, 170°). Cut across the grain into thin slices.

In a large serving bowl, combine the greens, tomato, radishes, celery, onions and beef. Drizzle with reserved marinade; toss to coat. **YIELD: 4 SERVINGS.**

MEDITERRANEAN LAMB AND BEAN SALAD

- 1　pound boneless leg of lamb
- 2　jars (6-1/2 ounces *each*) marinated artichoke hearts, drained
- 1　can (16 ounces) kidney beans, rinsed and drained
- 2　cups frozen cut green beans, thawed
- 1/2　cup julienned sweet red pepper
- 1/4　cup chopped red onion
- 1/2　cup fat-free Italian salad dressing
- 1/4　cup red wine vinegar
- 1/4　teaspoon pepper

Crumbled reduced-fat feta cheese, optional

This unique salad combines lamb, artichokes, beans and feta cheese with a tangy dressing...but it's also good with chicken or beef in place of the lamb.

—Lora Winckler
　Benton City, Washington

Grill lamb, covered, over medium heat for 10-20 minutes or until meat reaches desired doneness (for medium-rare, a meat thermometer should read 145°; medium, 160°; well-done, 170°). Cut into cubes.

In a large bowl, combine the lamb, artichokes, kidney beans, green beans, red pepper and onion. In a small bowl, whisk the salad dressing, vinegar and pepper; pour over salad and toss to coat. Cover and refrigerate for at least 4 hours. Serve with feta cheese if desired. **YIELD: 6 SERVINGS.**

3
SIDE DISHES

PG. 57 | **THREE-CHEESE POTATOES**

IT'S EASY TO ROUND OUT A MEAL WITH A COLORFUL VEGETABLE MEDLEY, CRISPY LOAF OF BREAD OR CREAMY PASTA SALAD. AND IF YOU ARE GRILLING THE MAIN COURSE, WHY NOT FIRE UP A NO-FUSS SIDE DISH, TOO? TURN TO THIS HANDY CHAPTER THE NEXT TIME YOU'RE LOOKING TO ADD A LITTLE SIZZLE TO YOUR SUMMER MENUS.

GRILLED GARDEN VEGGIES

Zucchini, yellow summer squash, mushrooms and more are seasoned with garlic and rosemary in my versatile side dish.

—Holly Wilhelm, Madison, South Dakota

2	tablespoons olive oil, *divided*
1	small onion, chopped
2	garlic cloves, minced
1	teaspoon dried rosemary, crushed, *divided*
2	small zucchini, sliced
2	small yellow summer squash, sliced
1/2	pound medium fresh mushrooms, quartered
1	large tomato, diced
3/4	teaspoon salt
1/4	teaspoon pepper

Drizzle 1 tablespoon oil over a double thickness of heavy-duty foil (about 24 in. x 12 in.). Combine the onion, garlic and 1/2 teaspoon rosemary; spoon over foil. Top with zucchini, yellow squash, mushrooms and tomato; drizzle with the remaining oil. Sprinkle with salt, pepper and remaining rosemary.

Fold foil around vegetables and seal tightly. Grill, covered, over medium heat for 15-20 minutes or until tender. Open foil carefully to allow steam to escape. **YIELD: 8 SERVINGS.**

GRILLED BROCCOLI

- **6 cups fresh broccoli spears**
- **2 tablespoons plus 1-1/2 teaspoons lemon juice**
- **2 tablespoons olive oil**
- **1/4 teaspoon salt**
- **1/4 teaspoon pepper**
- **3/4 cup grated Parmesan cheese**

Place broccoli in a large bowl. Combine the lemon juice, oil, salt and pepper; drizzle over broccoli and toss to coat. Let stand for 30 minutes.

Coat grill rack with cooking spray before starting the grill. Prepare grill for indirect heat. Toss broccoli, then drain marinade. Place cheese in a large resealable plastic bag. Add broccoli, a few pieces at a time, and shake to coat. Grill broccoli, covered, over indirect medium heat for 8-10 minutes on each side or until crisp-tender. **YIELD: 6 SERVINGS.**

I started using this recipe in 1987, when I began cooking light, and it's been a favorite side dish ever since. With its lemon and Parmesan flavors, it once took second-place in a cooking contest.

—Alice Null
  Woodstock, Illinois

Here's a tasty mushroom dish that is so filling, it's almost a meal in itself. The mushrooms can be served as a hearty side dish or alongside a small garden salad for an entree.

—Sarah Vasques, Milford, New Hampshire

PORTOBELLOS WITH MOZZARELLA SALAD

- **2 cups grape tomatoes, halved**
- **3 ounces fresh mozzarella cheese, cubed**
- **3 fresh basil leaves, thinly sliced**
- **2 teaspoons olive oil**
- **2 garlic cloves, minced**
- **1/4 teaspoon salt**
- **1/4 teaspoon pepper**
- **4 large portobello mushrooms (4 to 4-1/2 inches), stems removed**
- **Cooking spray**

In a small bowl, combine the first seven ingredients; cover and chill until serving.

Coat grill rack with cooking spray before starting the grill. Spritz mushrooms with cooking spray. Grill mushrooms, covered, over medium heat for 6-8 minutes on each side or until tender. Spoon 1/2 cup tomato mixture into each mushroom cap. **YIELD: 4 SERVINGS.**

VEGETABLE GRILLING CHART

There's no better way to bring out the naturally delicious taste of garden produce than by grilling them. Follow these guidelines. Grill vegetables until tender. Turn halfway through grilling time for even cooking.

TYPE	WEIGHT OR THICKNESS	HEAT	APPROXIMATE COOKING TIME (IN MINUTES)
ASPARAGUS	1/2 in. thick	medium/direct	6 to 8
SWEET PEPPERS	halved or quartered	medium/direct	8 to 10
CORN	in husk	medium/direct	25 to 30
	husk removed	medium/direct	10 to 12
EGGPLANT	1/2-in. slices	medium/direct	8 to 10
FENNEL	1/4-in. slices	medium/direct	10 to 12
MUSHROOMS	Button	medium/direct	8 to 10
	Portobello, whole	medium/direct	12 to 15
ONIONS	1/2-in. slices	medium/direct	8 to 12
POTATOES	whole	medium/indirect	45 to 60

ONIONS ON THE GRILL

It's almost hard to believe that such a satisfying side dish can be so easy to make. This recipe calls for just four basic ingredients.

—Pattie Ann Forssberg, Logan, Kansas

3	large onions, sliced
2	tablespoons honey
1/2	teaspoon salt
1/2	teaspoon ground mustard

In a large bowl, combine all of the ingredients; toss to coat. Place on a double thickness of heavy-duty foil (about 18 in. square). Fold foil around onion mixture and seal tightly.

Grill, covered, over medium heat for 20-25 minutes or until onions are tender, turning once. Open foil carefully to allow steam to escape. **YIELD: 6 SERVINGS.**

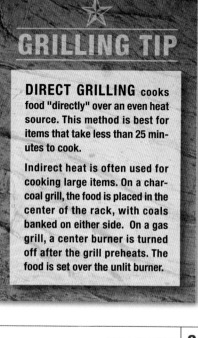

GRILLING TIP

DIRECT GRILLING cooks food "directly" over an even heat source. This method is best for items that take less than 25 minutes to cook.

Indirect heat is often used for cooking large items. On a charcoal grill, the food is placed in the center of the rack, with coals banked on either side. On a gas grill, a center burner is turned off after the grill preheats. The food is set over the unlit burner.

GRILLED SWEET ONIONS

4	large sweet onions
4	teaspoons beef bouillon granules
4	tablespoons butter
1/2	teaspoon dried thyme
1/4	teaspoon salt
1/4	teaspoon pepper
4	teaspoons white wine *or* beef broth, optional

With a knife, carefully remove a 1-in. core from the center of each onion. Cut each onion into four wedges to within 1/2 in. of root end.

Place each onion on a double thickness of heavy-duty foil (about 12 in. square). Place bouillon in the centers of onions; top with butter, thyme, salt and pepper. Drizzle with wine if desired. Fold foil around onions and seal tightly.

Prepare grill for indirect heat. Grill onions, covered, over indirect medium heat for 35-40 minutes or until tender. Open foil carefully to allow steam to escape. **YIELD: 4 SERVINGS.**

SALSA ZUCCHINI

I rely on three ingredients to create this tasty and super-easy side dish. It's great on the grill, but the best part is there's no mess.

—Terri Wolfson, Knoxville, Tennessee

2	small zucchini, cut into 1/2-inch slices
1	cup salsa
1/2	cup shredded Monterey Jack cheese

Place zucchini on a double thickness of heavy-duty foil (about 18 in. x 12 in.). Top with salsa. Fold foil around zucchini and seal tightly.

Grill, covered, over medium heat for 25-30 minutes or until zucchini is crisp-tender. Open foil carefully to allow steam to escape. Transfer zucchini to a serving bowl; sprinkle with cheese. **YIELD: 4 SERVINGS.**

BARBECUED VEGGIE PLATTER

1/4 cup olive oil

2 tablespoons honey

1 tablespoon plus 1/2 teaspoon balsamic vinegar, *divided*

1 teaspoon dried oregano

1/2 teaspoon garlic powder

1 pound fresh asparagus, trimmed

3 small carrots, cut in half lengthwise

1 large sweet red pepper, cut into 1-inch strips

1 medium yellow summer squash, cut into 1/2-inch slices

1 medium red onion, cut into four wedges

1/8 teaspoon pepper

Dash salt

In a small bowl, combine the oil, honey, 1 tablespoon vinegar, oregano and garlic powder. Pour 3 tablespoons marinade into a large resealable plastic bag; add the vegetables. Seal bag and turn to coat; refrigerate for 1-1/2 hours. Cover and refrigerate remaining marinade.

Place vegetables on a grilling grid. Transfer to grill rack. Grill, covered, over medium heat for 4-6 minutes on each side or until crisp-tender.

Transfer to a large serving platter. Combine reserved marinade and remaining vinegar; drizzle over vegetables. Sprinkle with pepper and salt. **YIELD: 6 SERVINGS.**

EDITOR'S NOTE: If you do not have a grilling grid, use a disposable foil pan. Poke holes in the bottom of the pan with a meat fork to allow liquid to drain.

Brightly colored and packed with flavor, these no-fuss veggies are perfect for entertaining or even as a light snack. Grilling brings out their natural sweetness while the seasoning kicks them up a notch.

—Heidi Hall
North St. Paul,
Minnesota

HAWAIIAN KABOBS

- 1 can (20 ounces) unsweetened pineapple chunks
- 2 large green peppers, cut into 1-inch pieces
- 1 large onion, quartered, optional
- 12 to 16 fresh mushrooms
- 16 to 18 cherry tomatoes
- 1/2 cup soy sauce
- 1/4 cup olive oil
- 1 tablespoon brown sugar
- 2 teaspoons ground ginger
- 1 teaspoon garlic powder
- 1 teaspoon ground mustard
- 1/4 teaspoon pepper

Drain pineapple, reserving 1/2 cup juice. Place pineapple chunks and vegetables in a large bowl; set aside.

In a small saucepan, combine reserved pineapple juice with the soy sauce, olive oil, brown sugar and seasonings; bring to a boil. Reduce heat and simmer, uncovered, for 5 minutes. Pour over vegetable mixture; cover and refrigerate for at least 1 hour, stirring occasionally.

Remove pineapple and vegetables from marinade and reserve marinade. On eight metal or soaked wooden skewers, alternately thread the pineapple, green pepper, onion if desired, mushrooms and tomatoes.

Grill kabobs for 20 minutes or until soft, turning and basting with marinade frequently. **YIELD: 8 SERVINGS.**

Fun and different, these kabobs are a treat exclusively from the grill! The pineapple gives ordinary summer vegetables a fresh, tropical taste. They're colorful and always a hit at summer get-togethers.

—Sharon Bickett
  Chester, South Carolina

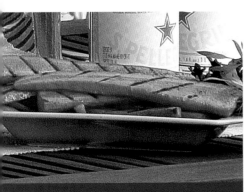

Family and friends are surprised when I tell them these carrots are prepared on the grill. The soy sauce and ginger flavors complement a variety of meaty entrees.
—Carol Gaus, Elk Grove Village, Illinois

CARROTS ON THE GRILL

- 1/4 cup soy sauce
- 1/4 cup canola oil
- 1 tablespoon minced fresh gingerroot
- 1 tablespoon cider vinegar
- 1 garlic clove, minced
- 1 pound large carrots, halved lengthwise

In a large bowl, combine the soy sauce, oil, ginger, vinegar and garlic. Add carrots; toss to coat.

With tongs, place carrots on grill rack. Grill, covered, over medium heat for 15-20 minutes or until tender, turning and basting frequently with soy sauce mixture. **YIELD: 4-6 SERVINGS.**

WARM POTATO SALAD WITH BALSAMIC DRESSING

6	medium red potatoes (about 1-1/2 pounds), quartered
2-1/4	teaspoons canola oil
3	cups fresh baby spinach
1	cup fresh *or* frozen corn, thawed
1/2	medium sweet red pepper, julienned
1/2	poblano pepper, seeded and julienned
1/2	medium red onion, thinly sliced
3	green onions, chopped
6	bacon strips, diced
3	garlic cloves, minced
2	shallots, minced
1/2	cup balsamic vinegar
2	tablespoons whole grain mustard
1	teaspoon pepper
2	hard-cooked eggs, coarsely chopped
1/4	cup sunflower kernels

Place potatoes in a large saucepan; cover with water. Bring to a boil. Reduce heat; cover and cook for 8-10 minutes or until crisp-tender. Drain; toss potatoes with oil.

Place potatoes in a grill wok or basket. Grill, covered, over medium heat for 8-12 minutes or golden brown, stirring frequently. Transfer to a large salad bowl; add the spinach, corn, peppers and onions. Set aside.

In a large skillet, cook bacon over medium heat until partially cooked but not crisp. Add garlic and shallots; cook for 1-2 minutes or until tender. Stir in the vinegar, mustard and pepper. Bring to a gentle boil; cook and stir for 2-3 minutes or until slightly thickened.

Drizzle over potato mixture and gently toss to coat. Sprinkle with eggs and sunflower kernels. Serve immediately. **YIELD: 12 SERVINGS.**

EDITOR'S NOTE: When cutting hot peppers, disposable gloves are recommended. Avoid touching your face.

A Texas-size family reunion requires a substantial salad like this one on the buffet table. Made with red potatoes, real bacon, tangy dressing and more, it's guaranteed to be gobbled up quickly.

—Elaine Sweet
Dallas, Texas

BASIL GARLIC BREAD

1/4	cup butter
2	tablespoons minced fresh parsley
1-1/2	teaspoons minced fresh basil *or* 1/2 teaspoon dried basil
1	garlic clove, minced
1/4	cup grated Parmesan cheese
1	loaf (8 ounces) French bread

In a microwave-safe bowl, combine the butter, parsley, basil and garlic. Cover and microwave until butter is melted. Stir in cheese.

Cut the bread in half lengthwise; place cut side down on an uncovered grill over medium heat for 2 minutes or until lightly toasted. Brush cut side with the butter mixture. Grill or broil 1-2 minutes longer. **YIELD: 4 SERVINGS.**

This is a must-have accompaniment in my home. It goes well with everything from an Italian dish to a simple salad.

—Stephanie Moon-Martin
Bremerton, Washington

GRILLED CAJUN GREEN BEANS

This is a perfect way to use up your garden's green beans. The cajun flavor makes it different from regular green bean recipes.

—Shannon Lewis, Andover, Minnesota

1	pound fresh green beans, trimmed
1/2	teaspoon Cajun seasoning
1	tablespoon butter

Place green beans on a double thickness of heavy-duty foil (about 18 in. square). Sprinkle with Cajun seasoning and dot with butter. Fold foil around beans and seal tightly.

Grill, covered, over medium heat for 10 minutes. Turn packet over; grill 8-12 minutes longer or until beans are tender. Carefully open foil to allow steam to escape. **YIELD: 4 SERVINGS.**

GRILLING TIP

FOIL PACKETS allow you to grill vegetables and even entire meals that suit a variety of tastes, with little to no cleanup.

To create the packets swiftly, center the food on a double thickness of heavy foil. Bring sides of foil together and double fold with 1-inch folds, making sure to leave enough room for heat and steam circulation at the top. Double fold the ends with 1-inch folds.

After the foil packets are grilled (according to the recipe instructions), open both ends to let the steam escape and then open the top of each packet. Serve food out of packets or spoon onto plates.

BACON-CORN STUFFED PEPPERS

Filled with corn, salsa, green onions, mozzarella cheese and bacon, these grilled pepper halves are sure to liven up your next cookout. They have a wonderful taste and give a fun twist to the usual corn on the cob.

—Mitzi Sentiff
  Annapolis, Maryland

2	cups frozen corn, thawed
1/3	cup salsa
6	green onions, chopped
1	medium green pepper, halved and seeded
1	medium sweet red pepper, halved and seeded
1/4	cup shredded part-skim mozzarella cheese
2	bacon strips, cooked and crumbled

Additional salsa, optional

In a large bowl, combine the corn, salsa and onions. Spoon into pepper halves. Place each stuffed pepper half on a piece of heavy-duty foil (about 18 in. x 12 in.). Fold foil around peppers and seal tightly.

Grill, covered, over medium heat for 25-30 minutes or until peppers are crisp-tender. Carefully open packets to allow steam to escape. Sprinkle with cheese and bacon. Return to the grill for 3-5 minutes or until cheese is melted. Serve with additional salsa if desired. **YIELD: 4 SERVINGS.**

VEGGIE KABOBS WITH GINGERED YOGURT

- 1 carton (8 ounces) reduced-fat plain yogurt
- 2 green onions, finely chopped
- 1 teaspoon grated fresh gingerroot
- 1 teaspoon honey
- 1/2 teaspoon ground mustard
- 1 garlic clove, minced
- 1/4 teaspoon salt
- 2 large sweet red peppers, cut into eight pieces
- 1 large zucchini, cut into eight slices
- 1 medium eggplant, peeled and cut into eight slices
- 1 large green pepper, cut into eight pieces
- 4 teaspoons canola oil

In a small bowl, combine the yogurt, onions, ginger, honey, mustard, garlic and salt. Cover and refrigerate until serving.

On four metal or soaked wooden skewers, alternately thread the red peppers, zucchini, eggplant and green pepper; brush with oil. Grill, covered, over medium heat for 15-18 minutes or until vegetables are tender, turning occasionally. Serve with yogurt sauce. **YIELD: 4 SERVINGS.**

This is a great way to serve vegetables during a colorful, summery meal. They're eye-appealing, tasty and oh-so easy to prepare.

—Marie Rizzio
Interlochen, Michigan

CURRIED CORN ON THE COB

- 6 medium ears sweet corn in husks
- 1/2 cup goat cheese
- 1 tablespoon sugar
- 2 teaspoons salt-free seasoning blend
- 1/2 teaspoon curry powder
- 1/4 teaspoon salt
- 1/4 teaspoon pepper

Carefully peel back corn husks to within 1 in. of bottoms; remove silk. Rewrap corn in husks and secure with kitchen string. Place in a large kettle; cover with cold water. Soak for 20 minutes; drain.

Grill corn, covered, over medium heat for 25-30 minutes or until tender, turning often. In a small bowl, combine the remaining ingredients; spread over warm corn. **YIELD: 6 SERVINGS.**

Here's a deliciously different way to enjoy corn on the cob. If goat cheese is not to your liking, try queso fresco or any other crumbly cheese such as feta. Parmesan is also good, and even though it won't spread well, you can easily sprinkle the mixture on.

—Laura Fall-Sutton, Buhl, Idaho

GRILLED ASPARAGUS WITH TANGERINE DRESSING

1/3	cup tangerine *or* orange juice	1	pound fresh asparagus, trimmed
2	teaspoons rice vinegar	1	teaspoon olive oil
1-1/2	teaspoons sesame oil	2	large tangerines *or* navel oranges, peeled and sectioned
1/2	teaspoon grated tangerine *or* orange peel		
1/2	teaspoon minced fresh gingerroot	3	tablespoons finely chopped dry roasted peanuts
1	garlic clove, minced	1	green onion, thinly sliced

My family's favorite way to eat asparagus is when it has been grilled. It gets such a tasty, smoky flavor.

—Tracy Woolbright
Lakewood, Ohio

For dressing, in a small bowl, whisk the first six ingredients; set aside. Toss asparagus with olive oil; place on a grilling grid. Transfer to grill rack.

Grill, covered, over medium heat for 3-4 minutes on each side or until crisp-tender. Place asparagus and tangerine sections on a serving platter; drizzle with dressing. Sprinkle with peanuts and onion. **YIELD: 4 SERVINGS.**

These zucchini boats taste great with the grilled chops on my favorite menu. I've served them with fish and with other grilled meats. I've also made them in the oven on occasion.

—Nancy Zimmerman
Cape May Court House,
New Jersey

STUFFED GRILLED ZUCCHINI

4	medium zucchini
5	teaspoons olive oil, *divided*
2	tablespoons finely chopped red onion
1/4	teaspoon minced garlic
1/2	cup dry bread crumbs
1/2	cup shredded part-skim mozzarella cheese
1	tablespoon minced fresh mint
1/2	teaspoon salt
3	tablespoons grated Parmesan cheese

Cut zucchini in half lengthwise; scoop out pulp, leaving 1/4-in. shells. Brush with 2 teaspoons oil; set aside. Chop pulp.

In a large skillet, saute pulp and onion in remaining oil. Add garlic; cook 1 minute longer. Add bread crumbs; cook and stir for 2 minutes or until golden brown.

Remove from the heat. Stir in the mozzarella cheese, mint and salt. Spoon into zucchini shells. Sprinkle with Parmesan cheese.

Grill, covered, over medium heat for 8-10 minutes or until zucchini is tender. **YIELD: 4 SERVINGS.**

CHEESE POTATO PACKET

- **2 medium potatoes, sliced**
- **3 tablespoons water**
- **2 bacon strips, diced**
- **1 small onion, thinly sliced**
- **4 ounces process cheese (Velveeta), cubed**
- **3 tablespoons butter, cubed**

Place potatoes and water in a microwave-safe bowl. Cover and microwave on high for 2-3 minutes or until almost tender. Meanwhile, in a small skillet, cook bacon over medium heat until partially cooked but not crisp. Remove bacon to paper towels to drain.

Drain potatoes. On a double thickness of greased heavy-duty foil (about 18 in. square), layer half of the potatoes, bacon, onion, cheese and butter. Repeat layers.

Fold foil around potato mixture and seal tightly. Grill, covered, over medium heat for 12-14 minutes or until potatoes are tender and cheese is melted. Carefully open foil to allow steam to escape. **YIELD: 2 SERVINGS.**

My dad has made these easy and delicious potatoes since I was little. The bacon adds to the smoky grilled taste.

—Shannon Talmage
    Alexandria, Indiana

POCKET VEGGIES

Whenever I make burgers on the grill, these vegetable packets are our usual accompaniment.

—Judi Garst
  Springfield, Illinois

1 *each* medium green, sweet red and yellow peppers, julienned
1 cup fresh baby carrots
1 cup fresh whole green beans
4 medium plum tomatoes, quartered
3 tablespoons white vinegar
3 tablespoons olive oil
2 teaspoons dried oregano
1/2 teaspoon pepper

Combine the peppers, carrots and beans; place on a double thickness of heavy-duty foil (about 24 in. x 12 in.). Top with tomatoes.

In a small bowl, whisk the vinegar, oil, oregano and pepper. Pour over vegetables. Fold foil around vegetables and seal tightly.

Grill, covered, over medium heat for 15-20 minutes or until tender. Open foil carefully to allow steam to escape. **YIELD: 6 SERVINGS.**

CURRIED BUTTERNUT SQUASH KABOBS

1	butternut squash (2 pounds), peeled, seeded and cut into 1-inch cubes
3	tablespoons butter, melted
1	teaspoon curry powder
1/4	teaspoon salt

Place squash in a greased 13-in. x 9-in. baking dish. Combine the butter, curry powder and salt; drizzle over squash and toss to coat.

Bake, uncovered, at 450° for 20-25 minutes or until tender and lightly browned, stirring twice. Cool on a wire rack.

On 12 metal or soaked wooden skewers, thread squash cubes. Grill, covered, over medium heat for 3-5 minutes on each side or until heated through. **YIELD: 12 SERVINGS.**

These baked squash cubes pick up a mouth-watering grilled taste along with a mild curry butter flavor. The pretty orange side dish adds a bit of interest to traditional summer entrees.
—Mary Relyea, Canastota, New York

GRILLED ONION

With just three ingredients, this recipe may be simple, but it always gets a terrific reaction, even from folks who don't usually care for onions.
—Stanley Pichon, Slidell, Louisiana

1	large onion, peeled
1	tablespoon butter
1	teaspoon beef bouillon granules

Hollow center of onion to a depth of 1 in.; chop removed onion. Place butter and bouillon in center of onion; top with the chopped onion. Wrap tightly in heavy-duty foil.

Grill, covered, over medium heat for 25-30 minutes or until tender. Open foil carefully to allow steam to escape. Cut into wedges. **YIELD: 4 SERVINGS.**

GRILLING TIP

GRILLED side dish recipes often call for everything from simple foil pouches to grill trays or woks and baskets.

Aluminum foil pouches allow vegetables of various sizes to cook together. Steam circulates inside the pouch, cooking the veggies to a tender consistency.

A grill tray is a flat platter with several holes in it. Set over the heat source, the tray allows you to cook small pieces of food without steaming them in a foil pouch.

Grill woks and baskets work the same, but they have far less surface areas, and the food may need to be stirred occasionally.

MAPLE VEGETABLE MEDLEY

Terrific for summer, this recipe calls for fresh vegetables brushed with a mild maple glaze and then grilled to perfection. They go well with any main course you serve.

—Lorraine Caland
   Thunder Bay, Ontario

1/3   cup balsamic vinegar

1/3   cup maple syrup

1   large red onion

1   pound fresh asparagus, trimmed

1   pound baby carrots

2   medium zucchini, cut lengthwise into thirds and seeded

1   medium sweet red pepper, cut into eight pieces

1   medium sweet yellow pepper, cut into eight pieces

2   tablespoons olive oil

1   tablespoon minced fresh thyme *or* 1 teaspoon dried thyme

1/2   teaspoon salt

1/2   teaspoon pepper

For glaze, in a small saucepan, bring vinegar and syrup to a boil. Reduce heat; cook and stir over medium heat for 6-8 minutes or until thickened. Remove from the heat; set aside.

Cut onion into eight wedges to 1/2 in. of the bottom. Place the onion, asparagus, carrots, zucchini and peppers in a large bowl. Drizzle with oil and sprinkle with seasonings; toss to coat.

Coat grill rack with cooking spray before starting the grill. Arrange vegetables on rack. Grill, covered, over medium heat for 10 minutes on each side. Brush with half of the glaze; grill 5-8 minutes longer or until crisp-tender. Before serving, brush with remaining glaze. **YIELD: 8 SERVINGS.**

JUST DELISH VEGGIE KABOBS

8	small red potatoes, halved
3	tablespoons unsweetened apple juice
3	tablespoons red wine vinegar
2	tablespoons minced fresh basil
1	tablespoon Dijon mustard
1	tablespoon honey
1	tablespoon reduced-sodium soy sauce
2	teaspoons olive oil
2	garlic cloves, minced
1/4	teaspoon pepper
12	medium fresh mushrooms
1	large sweet red pepper, cut into 1-inch pieces
1	medium zucchini, cut into 1/2-inch slices

Place potatoes in a steamer basket; place in a large saucepan over 1 in. of water. Bring to a boil; cover and steam for 7-9 minutes or just until tender. Cool.

In a large resealable plastic bag, combine the apple juice, vinegar, basil, mustard, honey, soy sauce, oil, garlic and pepper. Add the mushrooms, red pepper, zucchini and cooked potatoes. Seal bag and turn to coat; refrigerate for 2 hours.

Coat grill rack with cooking spray before starting the grill. Drain and reserve marinade. On four metal or soaked wooden skewers, alternately thread vegetables.

Grill, covered, over medium heat for 10-15 minutes, turning and basting occasionally with reserved marinade. **YIELD: 4 SERVINGS.**

JUDGING TEMPERATURE

IT'S EASY to tell how hot the coals in a charcoal grill are. Cautiously hold your hand 4 inches over the coals. Start counting the number of seconds you can hold your hand in place before the heat forces you to pull away. If you can hold your hand above the fire for no more than 2 seconds, the heat level is "hot," but if you can hold your hand above the coals for 3 seconds, the heat level is "medium-hot." If you can hold your hand above the coals for no more than 4 seconds, the heat level is "medium."

BAKED STUFFED TOMATOES

    6 medium tomatoes

STUFFING:

    1 cup garlic/cheese croutons, crushed

    2 tablespoons grated Parmesan cheese

    2 tablespoons grated American *or* cheddar cheese

    4 tablespoons butter, melted

    1/2 teaspoon salt

    1/4 teaspoon freshly ground pepper

Chopped fresh parsley for garnish

Cut a thin slice off the top of each tomato. Scoop out pulp, leaving a 1/2-in. shell. Invert onto paper towels to drain. Mix stuffing ingredients. Spoon into tomatoes; sprinkle with parsley.

Place tomatoes in a metal baking pan; cover tomatoes with aluminum foil to prevent over-browning of stuffing. Cook on grill or bake at 350° for 30 minutes. **YIELD: 6 SERVINGS.**

I make this side dish often—my family really likes it. Besides being flavorful, the tomatoes make a colorful, zesty addition to any summer meal.

—Edna Jackson, Kokomo, Indiana

Peppers add plenty of punch to this mouthwatering grilled sweet corn.

—Grace Camp
Owingsville, Kentucky

SWEET CORN 'N' PEPPERS

    1 medium sweet red pepper, julienned

    1 medium green pepper, julienned

    1 medium jalapeno pepper, seeded and julienned

    1 medium sweet onion, cut into thin wedges

    1/2 teaspoon salt

    1/2 teaspoon pepper

    1/8 teaspoon cayenne pepper

Dash paprika

    6 large ears sweet corn, husks removed and halved

In a small bowl, combine peppers and onion. Combine the salt, pepper, cayenne and paprika; sprinkle half over the vegetables and set aside. Sprinkle remaining seasoning mixture over corn.

Place the corn on a vegetable grilling rack coated with cooking spray or in a perforated disposable aluminum pan.

Grill, covered, over medium heat for 10 minutes. Add reserved vegetables. Grill, covered, 5-10 minutes longer or until vegetables are tender, stirring occasionally and rotating corn. **YIELD: 6 SERVINGS.**

EDITOR'S NOTE: When cutting hot peppers, disposable gloves are recommended. Avoid touching your face.

RED POTATO SKEWERS

       2   pounds red potatoes (about 6 medium), quartered
     1/2   cup water
     1/2   cup mayonnaise
     1/4   cup chicken broth
       2   teaspoons dried oregano
     1/2   teaspoon garlic salt
     1/2   teaspoon onion powder

Place the potatoes and water in an ungreased microwave-safe 2-qt. dish. Cover and microwave on high for 10-12 minutes or until almost tender, stirring once; drain. In a large bowl, combine the remaining ingredients; add potatoes. Cover and refrigerate for 1 hour.

Drain, reserving mayonnaise mixture. On six metal or soaked wooden skewers, thread potatoes.

Grill, uncovered, over medium heat for 4 minutes on each side, brushing occasionally with reserved mayonnaise mixture or until potatoes are tender and golden brown. **YIELD: 6 SERVINGS.**

EDITOR'S NOTE: This recipe was tested in a 1,100-watt microwave.

A seasoned mayonnaise mixture keeps these quartered red potatoes moist and heavenly. My mouth waters just thinking about how they'll taste.

—Dawn Finch
  Prosser, Washington

A friend and I came up with this corn recipe one evening when getting ready to grill. The buttery corn, with its sweet-spicy seasoning, won top honors over our steaks.

—Linda Landers, Kalispell, Montana

SMOKY GRILLED CORN

       2   tablespoons plus 1-1/2 teaspoons butter
     1/2   cup honey
       2   large garlic cloves, minced
       2   tablespoons hot pepper sauce
     1/2   teaspoon salt
     1/4   teaspoon pepper
     1/4   teaspoon paprika
       6   medium ears sweet corn, husks removed

In a small saucepan, melt butter. Stir in the honey, garlic, pepper sauce and seasonings until blended; heat through. Brush over corn.

Coat grill rack with cooking spray before starting the grill. Grill, covered, over medium heat for 10-12 minutes or until the corn is tender, turning and basting occasionally. Serve corn with remaining butter mixture. **YIELD: 6 SERVINGS.**

CASHEW TURKEY PASTA SALAD

2	bone-in turkey breast (5 to 6 pounds *each*)
3	cups uncooked tricolor spiral pasta
2	celery ribs, diced
6	green onions, chopped
1/2	cup diced green pepper
1-1/2	cups mayonnaise
3/4	cup packed brown sugar
1	tablespoon cider vinegar
1-1/2	teaspoons salt
1-1/2	teaspoons lemon juice
2	cups salted cashew halves

Grill turkey, covered, over medium heat for 25-30 minutes on each side or until a meat thermometer reads 170°. Cool slightly. Cover and refrigerate until cool. Meanwhile, cook pasta according to package directions; drain and rinse in cold water.

Remove skin from turkey; chop turkey and place in a large bowl. Add the pasta, celery, onions and green pepper. In a small bowl, combine the mayonnaise, brown sugar, vinegar, salt and lemon juice; pour over pasta mixture and toss to coat.

Cover and refrigerate for at least 2 hours. Just before serving, stir in cashews. **YIELD: 12 SERVINGS.**

Cashews add a nice crunch to this grilled turkey and spiral pasta combo. I first tasted it at a baby shower and asked the hostess for her recipe. Since then, I've served it for many parties.

—Karen Wyffels, Lino Lakes, Minnesota

GRILLED MUSHROOMS

Once reserved for Asian royalty and guarded by warriors, shiitake mushrooms are prized for their rich flavor and meaty texture. Seasoned with oil and herbs, they taste great hot off the grill.

—Steven Stumpf, Shiocton, Wisconsin

1/2	pound fresh shiitake mushrooms
1/4	cup olive oil
1	tablespoon *each* minced fresh thyme, sage, oregano and basil
	Salt and pepper to taste

Remove and discard stems from mushroom caps. Score caps lightly with a sharp knife. Brush both sides with oil. In a small bowl, combine herbs. Rub mushrooms with herbs and sprinkle with salt and pepper.

Grill, cap side down, over medium heat for 2-3 minutes on each side or until juices form in the caps and mushrooms are tender. Serve hot or at room temperature. **YIELD: 8-10 SERVINGS.**

★ GRILLING TIP

VEGGIES that have been grilled to perfection make excellent side dishes, but they also add plenty of smoky flavor to other items.

Want to jazz up a green salad or soup? Try grilling the vegetables before adding them to the recipe. You'll also find that flame-broiled vegetables enhance sandwiches, wraps, pizzas and even pasta creations.

PIT STOP POTATOES

2	large potatoes, thinly sliced
1/4	cup chopped onion
1/4	cup sliced baby portobello mushrooms
1/4	cup chopped green pepper
1/2	teaspoon salt
1/2	teaspoon pepper
1/2	teaspoon taco seasoning
2	tablespoons butter, cut into small cubes

In a greased disposable foil pan, layer the potatoes, onion, mushrooms and green pepper. Sprinkle with the salt, pepper and taco seasoning; dot with butter.

Cover with foil. Grill over medium-hot heat for 20-25 minutes or until potatoes are tender. Open foil carefully to allow steam to escape. **YIELD: 3 SERVINGS.**

We love fried potatoes and experimented with several recipes until we came up with this grilled version. Using a disposable foil pan means easy cleanup.
—Annette Frahmann
Shelton, Washington

GRILLING TIP

PREPARING POTATOES

Scrub potatoes with a vegetable brush under cold water, and remove any eyes. Before grilling whole potatoes, pierce with a fork. Peeled potato cubes should be placed in cold water to prevent discoloration.

GRILLED SWEET POTATOES

Sweet potato wedges are seasoned to please in this savory side. My husband and I love the sweet spuds any way they are cooked. This idea, from a friend, is not only different, it's delicious, too.
—Gay Nell Nicholas, Henderson, Texas

2	pounds sweet potatoes, peeled and cut into wedges
3	tablespoons reduced-sodium soy sauce
2	tablespoons sherry *or* apple juice
2	tablespoons honey
2	tablespoons water
1	garlic clove, minced
1	tablespoon sesame oil

Place sweet potatoes in a steamer basket; place in a saucepan over 1 in. of water. Bring to a boil; cover and steam for 5-7 minutes.

Place potatoes in a large bowl. In another bowl, combine the soy sauce, sherry or juice, honey, water and garlic; pour over potatoes and toss gently.

Drain sweet potatoes, reserving soy sauce mixture. Arrange sweet potatoes in a single layer in a grill basket coated with cooking spray. Brush potatoes with oil. Grill, covered, over medium heat for 8-10 minutes or until tender, basting with reserved soy sauce mixture and turning occasionally. **YIELD: 8 SERVINGS.**

GRILLED CABBAGE

I don't really like cabbage, but I fixed this dish and couldn't believe how good it was! We threw some burgers on the grill and our dinner was complete.

—Elizabeth Wheeler
Thornville, Ohio

1	medium head cabbage (about 1-1/2 pounds)
1/3	cup butter, softened
1/4	cup chopped onion
1/2	teaspoon garlic salt
1/4	teaspoon pepper

Cut cabbage into eight wedges; place on a double thickness of heavy-duty foil (about 24 in. x 12 in.). Spread cut sides with butter. Sprinkle with onion, garlic salt and pepper.

Fold foil around cabbage and seal tightly. Grill, covered, over medium heat for 20 minutes or until tender. Open foil carefully to allow steam to escape. **YIELD: 8 SERVINGS.**

DILLY VEGETABLE MEDLEY

1/4   **cup olive oil**

2   **tablespoons minced fresh basil**

2   **teaspoons dill weed**

1/2   **teaspoon salt**

1/2   **teaspoon pepper**

7   **small yellow summer squash, cut into 1/2-inch slices**

1   **pound Yukon Gold potatoes, cut into 1/2-inch cubes**

5   **small carrots, cut into 1/2-inch slices**

In a very large bowl, combine the first five ingredients. Add vegetables and toss to coat.

Place half of the vegetables on a double thickness of heavy-duty foil (about 18 in. square). Fold foil around vegetables and seal tightly. Repeat with remaining vegetables.

Grill, covered, over medium heat for 20-25 minutes or until potatoes are tender, turning once. Open foil carefully to allow steam to escape. **YIELD: 13 SERVINGS.**

I love to eat what I grow, and I have tried many combinations of the fresh vegetables from my garden. This one is really great! I never have leftovers when I make this tasty dinner accompaniment.

—Rebecca Barjonah, Coralville, Iowa

GREEK-STYLE SQUASH

2   **small yellow summer squash, thinly sliced**

2   **small zucchini, thinly sliced**

1   **medium tomato, seeded and chopped**

1/4   **cup pitted ripe olives**

2   **tablespoons chopped green onion**

2   **teaspoons olive oil**

1   **teaspoon lemon juice**

3/4   **teaspoon garlic salt**

1/4   **teaspoon dried oregano**

1/8   **teaspoon pepper**

2   **tablespoons grated Parmesan cheese**

Place the yellow squash, zucchini, tomato, olives and onion on a double thickness of heavy-duty foil (about 17 in. x 18 in.). Combine the oil, lemon juice, garlic salt, oregano and pepper; pour over vegetables. Fold foil around mixture and seal tightly.

Grill, covered, over medium heat for 30-35 minutes or until vegetables are tender. Open foil carefully to allow steam to escape. Transfer vegetables to a serving bowl. Sprinkle with cheese. **YIELD: 4 SERVINGS.**

What a great way to use up all that summer squash! You can almost taste the sunshine in this colorful and quick vegetable dish. And the foil packets make for carefree cleanup.

—Betty Washburn
Reno, Nevada

GRILLED CHERRY TOMATOES

2 pints cherry tomatoes, halved

2 garlic cloves, minced

1/2 teaspoon dried oregano

3 tablespoons butter

Place tomatoes on a double thickness of heavy-duty foil (about 24 in. x 12 in.). In a skillet, saute garlic and oregano in butter for 2 minutes. Pour over tomatoes. Fold foil around tomatoes and seal tightly.

Grill, covered, over medium heat for 4-5 minutes on each side or until tomatoes are heated through. Open foil carefully to allow steam to escape. **YIELD: 4-6 SERVINGS.**

Four ingredients and a grill are all it takes to set this change-of-pace side dish on the table.

—Lucy Meyring
Walden, Colorado

COUSCOUS WITH GRILLED VEGETABLES

2 small zucchini, quartered lengthwise

1/2 medium eggplant, sliced widthwise 1/2 inch thick

1 medium sweet red pepper, quartered

1 small onion, sliced 1/2 inch thick

Cooking spray

3/4 teaspoon salt, *divided*

1/2 teaspoon pepper, *divided*

2 cups reduced-sodium chicken *or* vegetable broth

1 package (10 ounces) couscous

1/2 cup chopped green onions

4-1/2 teaspoons lemon juice

2-1/4 teaspoons minced fresh thyme *or* 1/2 teaspoon dried thyme

Spritz vegetables with cooking spray; sprinkle with 1/4 teaspoon salt and 1/4 teaspoon pepper. Coat grill rack with cooking spray before preparing the grill for indirect heat. Arrange vegetables on grill over indirect heat.

Grill, covered, over medium indirect heat for 4-5 minutes on each side or until tender. Let stand until cool enough to handle.

In a saucepan, bring broth to a boil. Stir in couscous. Remove from heat; cover and let stand for 5 minutes or until liquid is absorbed.

Cut grilled vegetables into 1/2-in. pieces. Fluff couscous with a fork. Add the vegetables, green onions, lemon juice, thyme and remaining salt and pepper; toss until combined. **YIELD: 8 SERVINGS.**

This hearty specialty is almost a meal in itself. I grill several fresh vegetables, then add them to couscous.

—Kathy Herrala, Martinez, California

THREE-VEGETABLE SKILLET

1	medium onion, cut into small wedges
1	medium sweet red pepper, julienned
1-1/2	cups sliced fresh mushrooms
1	tablespoon olive oil
1	garlic clove, minced
1	tablespoon minced fresh basil
1/4	teaspoon salt
1/8	teaspoon pepper

These vegetables are great alongside many entrees. You can also prepare this dish in a cast-iron skillet.

—Taste of Home
   Test Kitchen

Coat grill-and-serve skillet with cooking spray; place on grill. Cook the onion, red pepper and mushrooms in oil over medium heat until crisp-tender, about 6-8 minutes. Add garlic; cook 1 minute longer. Remove skillet from grill. Stir in the basil, salt and pepper. **YIELD: 2 SERVINGS.**

STEAMED VEGGIE BUNDLES

- 1 medium yellow summer squash, halved and cut into 3/4-inch slices
- 1 medium zucchini, cut into 3/4-inch slices
- 6 large fresh mushrooms, quartered
- 2 large tomatoes, cut into wedges
- 1 medium sweet red pepper, julienned
- 1 medium green pepper, julienned
- 1/2 cup fresh baby carrots, quartered lengthwise
- 1/4 cup prepared ranch salad dressing
- 1/4 cup prepared Italian salad dressing

Divide vegetables between two pieces of double thickness heavy-duty foil (about 18 in. square). Fold foil around vegetables and seal tightly. Grill, covered, over medium heat for 10-13 minutes on each side or until vegetables are tender.

Open foil carefully to allow steam to escape. With a slotted spoon, remove vegetables to a serving dish. Combine the salad dressings; drizzle over vegetables and toss to coat. **YIELD: 6 SERVINGS.**

In late summer, when we have an abundance of garden produce, we enjoy this medley of fresh veggies. Usually, we pop the packets on the grill, alongside our main dish meat, fish or poultry.

—Terri Mule
Angola, New York

CORN ON THE COB WITH LEMON-PEPPER BUTTER

- 8 medium ears sweet corn
- 1 cup butter, softened
- 2 tablespoons lemon-pepper seasoning

Carefully peel back corn husks to within 1 in. of bottoms; remove silk. Rewrap corn in husks and secure with kitchen string. Place in a large kettle; cover with cold water. Soak for 20 minutes; drain.

Meanwhile, in a small bowl, combine butter and lemon-pepper; set aside. Grill corn, covered, over medium heat for 25-30 minutes or until tender, turning often. Serve with butter mixture. **YIELD: 8 SERVINGS.**

Roasting corn this way is as old as the Ozark hills in which I was raised. My grandpa always salted and peppered his butter on the edge of his plate before spreading it on his corn, and I did the same as a kid. Roast plenty—this corn is a favorite!

—Allene Bary-Cooper, Wichita Falls, Texas

ASIAN GREEN BEANS

1	tablespoon brown sugar
1	tablespoon sesame oil
1	tablespoon reduced-sodium soy sauce
2	garlic cloves, minced
1/2	teaspoon crushed red pepper flakes
1-1/2	pounds fresh green beans, trimmed
1	medium red onion, halved and thinly sliced
6	medium fresh mushrooms, quartered

In a large bowl, combine the first five ingredients. Add the beans, onion and mushrooms; toss to coat.

Place half of the vegetables on a double thickness of heavy-duty foil (about 18 in. square); fold foil around vegetables and seal tightly. Repeat with remaining vegetables.

Grill, covered, over medium heat for 18-22 minutes or until beans are tender, turning packets over once. Open foil carefully to allow steam to escape. **YIELD: 8 SERVINGS.**

You'll love the great flavor and easy preparation of my fresh side dish. I simply toss bright green beans in a sweet sauce that offers a subtle kick.

—Trisha Kruse, Eagle, Idaho

GRILLED PATTYPANS

Just a few minutes and a handful of ingredients are all you'll need for this scrumptious side dish. Hoisin sauce and rice vinegar give grilled pattypans terrific Asian flair.

—Taste of Home Test Kitchen

6	cups pattypan squash (about 1-1/2 pounds)
1/4	cup apricot spreadable fruit
2	teaspoons hoisin sauce
1	teaspoon rice vinegar
1/2	teaspoon sesame oil
1/4	teaspoon salt
1/8	teaspoon ground ginger

Place squash in a grill wok or basket coated with cooking spray. Grill, covered, over medium heat for 4 minutes on each side or until tender.

Meanwhile, in a small bowl, combine the remaining ingredients. Transfer squash to a serving bowl; add sauce and toss gently. **YIELD: 6 SERVINGS.**

EDITOR'S NOTE: If you do not have a grill wok or basket, use a disposable foil pan. Poke holes in the bottom of the pan with a meat fork to allow liquid to drain.

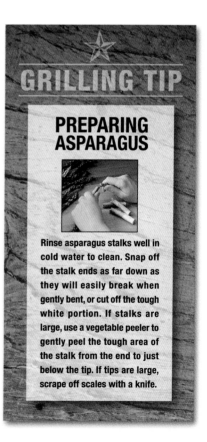

GRILLING TIP

PREPARING ASPARAGUS

Rinse asparagus stalks well in cold water to clean. Snap off the stalk ends as far down as they will easily break when gently bent, or cut off the tough white portion. If stalks are large, use a vegetable peeler to gently peel the tough area of the stalk from the end to just below the tip. If tips are large, scrape off scales with a knife.

ASPARAGUS WITH MUSTARD VINAIGRETTE

This is a great item to serve at a bridge luncheon with a chicken dish or salad. It gives some color to the meal, and it is very tasty.

—Jo Durlam, Ames, Iowa

1   **pound fresh asparagus, trimmed**
3   **tablespoons unsweetened pineapple juice**
1   **tablespoon balsamic vinegar**
1   **teaspoon Dijon mustard**
1   **teaspoon olive oil**
1/2   **teaspoon minced garlic**

In a large skillet, bring 1/2 in. of water to a boil. Add asparagus; cover and boil for 3 minutes; drain. When cool enough to handle, pat dry. Thread several spears onto two parallel metal or soaked wooden skewers. Repeat with remaining asparagus.

Grill, uncovered, over medium heat for 2 minutes on each side or until crisp-tender.

For vinaigrette, combine the remaining ingredients in a small bowl. Remove asparagus from skewers; drizzle with vinaigrette. **YIELD: 3 SERVINGS.**

BUNDLE OF VEGGIES

1/2   **pound medium fresh mushrooms**
1/2   **pound cherry tomatoes**
1   **cup sliced zucchini**
1   **tablespoon olive oil**
1   **tablespoon butter, melted**
1/2   **teaspoon salt**
1/2   **teaspoon onion powder**
1/2   **teaspoon Italian seasoning**
1/8   **teaspoon garlic powder**
Dash pepper

Place mushrooms, tomatoes and zucchini on a double thickness of heavy-duty foil (about 18 in. square). Combine the remaining ingredients; drizzle over vegetables. Fold the foil around vegetables and seal tightly.

Grill, covered, over medium heat for 20-25 minutes or until tender. Carefully open foil to allow steam to escape. **YIELD: 6 SERVINGS.**

This grilled vegetable medley is a big hit at home and while camping. The bundles are cooked in a foil packet, so cleanup is easy.

—Sheila Dedman, New Dundee, Ontario

BACON-WRAPPED ASPARAGUS

10	fresh asparagus spears, trimmed
1/8	teaspoon pepper
5	bacon strips, halved lengthwise

Place asparagus on a sheet of waxed paper; coat with cooking spray. Sprinkle with pepper; turn to coat. Wrap a bacon piece around each asparagus spear; secure ends with toothpicks.

Grill, uncovered, over medium heat for 4-6 minutes on each side or until bacon is crisp. Discard toothpicks. **YIELD: 2-3 SERVINGS.**

My husband and I grill dinner almost every night, and I love grilling asparagus. I serve this three-ingredient side dish with grilled meat and sliced fresh tomatoes for a wonderful meal.

—Patricia Kitts
 Dickinson, Texas

THREE-CHEESE POTATOES

- 3 large potatoes, peeled and cut into 1-inch cubes
- 1 medium onion, chopped
- 3 tablespoons grated Parmesan cheese
- 1 tablespoon minced chives
- 1/2 teaspoon seasoned salt
- 1/4 teaspoon pepper
- 2 tablespoons butter
- 1/2 cup crumbled cooked bacon
- 1/2 cup shredded part-skim mozzarella cheese
- 1/2 cup shredded cheddar cheese

In a large bowl, combine the first six ingredients. Transfer to a double thickness of greased heavy-duty foil (about 18 in. square). Dot with butter.

Fold foil around potato mixture and seal tightly. Grill, covered, over medium heat for 15-18 minutes on each side or until potatoes are tender.

Carefully open foil. Sprinkle the bacon and cheeses over potato mixture. Rewrap; grill 3-5 minutes longer or until cheese is melted. Open foil carefully to allow steam to escape. **YIELD: 4-6 SERVINGS.**

With its bacon and cheese flair, this side dish makes a welcome addition to barbecues. My husband and I love potatoes made this way.
—Cheryl Hille, Askum, Illinois

Take vegetables from the garden to the grill and to the table in minutes with this simple idea. The colorful combination of yellow summer squash, carrot, onion and zucchini makes a great addition to any menu...regardless of the main course.
—Kathleen Ruggio
Oswego, New York

GRILLED SQUASH MEDLEY

- 1 small zucchini, julienned
- 1 small yellow summer squash, julienned
- 1 medium carrot, julienned
- 1 small onion, chopped
- 2 tablespoons butter

Salt, pepper and garlic powder to taste

- 2 tablespoons grated Parmesan cheese
- 2 tablespoons shredded part-skim mozzarella cheese

Place vegetables on a double thickness of heavy-duty foil (about 18 in. x 12 in.). Dot with butter; season with salt, pepper and garlic powder. Fold foil around vegetables and seal tightly.

Grill, covered, over medium heat for 15-20 minutes or until vegetables are tender, turning once. Open foil carefully to allow steam to escape. Sprinkle with cheeses. **YIELD: 4 SERVINGS.**

4
BURGERS, BRATS & MORE

PG. **78** GRILLED STEAK
AND PORTOBELLO
STACKS

WHEN IT COMES TO FLAME-BROILED FAVORITES, HAMBURGERS ARE A NO-BRAINER. TOSS A FEW HOT DOGS ON THE GRILL, AND YOU'RE SET FOR A TASTY GET-TOGETHER. TURN TO THIS CHAPTER WHEN YOU WANT TO KICK THINGS UP A NOTCH. STUFFED BURGERS, BEEFY WRAPS AND CHICKEN SANDWICHES ARE SOME OF THE HANDHELD GREATS YOU'LL FIND HERE!

GRILLED SEASONED BRATWURST

For a savory take on a summer classic, our home economists came up with a brat that's sure to please. Great summer eating doesn't get much easier than this.

—Taste of Home Test Kitchen

2	uncooked bratwurst links
1	can (12 ounces) beer *or* nonalcoholic beer
1	small onion, halved and sliced
1-1/2	teaspoons fennel seed
2	brat buns, split and toasted

Place bratwurst in a large saucepan; add the beer, onion and fennel. Bring to a boil. Reduce heat; cover and simmer for 8-10 minutes or until meat is no longer pink. Drain and discard beer mixture.

Grill bratwurst, covered, over indirect medium heat for 7-8 minutes or until browned. Serve on buns. **YIELD: 2 SERVINGS.**

GRILLING TIP

FLARE UPS are pretty common when grilling foods that are high in fat, such as sausages. To prevent your brats and burgers from burning due to such flare ups, make sure to keep a spray bottle of water nearby. A simple squirt or two is usually enough to do the trick.

TUSCAN PORK WRAPS

1/2	teaspoon garlic powder	1/2	cup balsamic vinegar
1/2	teaspoon dried oregano	1	tablespoon brown sugar
1/2	teaspoon ground coriander	2	flour tortillas (8 inches)
1/2	teaspoon pepper, *divided*	4	teaspoons Dijon mustard
1/4	teaspoon salt	2	romaine leaves
1/2	pound pork tenderloin	1	small red onion, sliced

In a small bowl, combine the garlic powder, oregano, coriander, 1/4 teaspoon pepper and salt; rub over pork. Grill pork, covered, over medium heat for 8-10 minutes on each side or until a meat thermometer reads 160°.

Meanwhile, in a small saucepan, combine the vinegar, brown sugar and remaining pepper. Bring to a boil; cook until liquid is reduced by half. Brush 2 tablespoons sauce mixture over pork; cut into thin strips.

Spread tortillas with mustard. Layer with the lettuce, pork and onion. Drizzle with remaining sauce. Fold in edges of tortilla and roll up. **YIELD: 2 SERVINGS.**

Though these great roll-ups have an easy summer feel, you'll think you're dining in a fancy corner bistro.

—Robyn Cavallaro, Easton, Pennsylvania

TURKEY BRATS WITH SLAW

4	cups beer *or* nonalcoholic beer	6	cups broccoli coleslaw mix
3	teaspoons celery salt, *divided*	2/3	cup chopped red onion
		4	teaspoons canola oil
2	teaspoons minced garlic	2/3	cup dried cranberries
2	packages (19-1/2 ounces *each*) turkey bratwurst links	1/4	cup red wine vinegar
		2	tablespoons honey
		10	brat buns, split

In a Dutch oven, bring the beer, 2 teaspoons celery salt and garlic to a boil. Add bratwurst. Reduce heat; simmer, uncovered, for 20-25 minutes or until firm and cooked through.

Meanwhile, in a large skillet, saute coleslaw mix and onion in oil for 7-9 minutes or until tender. Stir in the cranberries, vinegar, honey and remaining celery salt; heat through. Set aside.

Drain bratwurst. Grill, covered, over medium heat or broil 4 in. from the heat for 2 to 2-1/2 minutes on each side or until browned. Serve on buns with coleslaw mixture. **YIELD: 10 SERVINGS.**

The cooked slaw-and-cranberry topping on these beer-boiled brats can be served either warm or cold. It makes a tasty and colorful change from kraut or conventional condiments.

—Christy Hinrichs Parkville, Missouri

PEPPER STEAK QUESADILLAS

I came up with this savory snack when my family needed a quick lunch before running off in several directions. I threw together what I had in the fridge, and it was a big hit!

—Barbara Moore
    Farmington, New Mexico

1/2	pound beef top sirloin steak
1/2	*each* medium green, sweet red and yellow pepper, julienned
1	tablespoon chopped red onion
1	garlic clove, minced
1	tablespoon minced fresh cilantro
1/4	teaspoon dried rosemary, crushed
4	flour tortillas (6 inches)
6	cherry tomatoes, halved
1/4	cup sliced fresh mushrooms
1	cup (4 ounces) shredded part-skim mozzarella cheese

Coat grill rack with cooking spray before starting the grill. Grill steak, covered, over medium heat or broil 4 in. from the heat for 4-6 minutes on each side or until meat reaches desired doneness (for medium-rare, a meat thermometer should read 145°; medium, 160°; well-done, 170°). Let stand for 10 minutes.

Meanwhile, in a large skillet coated with cooking spray, saute peppers and onion for 5-6 minutes or until tender. Add garlic; cook 1 minute longer. Sprinkle with cilantro and rosemary.

Place two tortillas on a baking sheet coated with cooking spray. Cut steak into thin strips; place on tortillas. Using a slotted spoon, place pepper mixture over steak. Top with tomatoes, mushrooms, cheese and remaining tortillas; lightly spray top of tortillas with cooking spray.

Bake at 425° for 5-10 minutes or until golden brown and cheese is melted. Cut each quesadilla into four wedges. **YIELD: 4 SERVINGS.**

GRILLED PEPPER JACK CHICKEN

- **2 boneless skinless chicken breast halves (4 ounces *each*)**
- **1 teaspoon poultry seasoning**
- **2 center-cut bacon strips, cooked and halved**
- **2 slices (1/2 ounce *each*) pepper Jack cheese**
- **2 hamburger buns, split**
- **2 lettuce leaves**
- **1 slice onion, separated into rings**
- **2 slices tomato**
- **Dill pickle slices, optional**

Sprinkle chicken with poultry seasoning. Coat grill rack with cooking spray before starting the grill. Grill chicken, covered, over medium heat for 4-7 minutes on each side or until juices run clear. Top with bacon and cheese; cover and grill 1-2 minutes longer or until cheese is melted.

Serve on buns with lettuce, onion, tomato and pickles if desired. **YIELD: 2 SERVINGS.**

This is a great meal for summer days. Basic, yet packed with flavor, this sandwich gets a kick from zesty cheese and strips of savory bacon.

—Linda Foreman
Locust Grove,
Oklahoma

GLAZED CORNED BEEF SANDWICHES

1 **corned beef brisket with spice packet (3 to 4 pounds)**

12 **peppercorns**

4 **bay leaves**

3 **garlic cloves, minced**

2 **cinnamon sticks (3 inches), broken**

1 **tablespoon crushed red pepper flakes**

Sandwich buns

GLAZE:

1/2 **cup packed brown sugar**

1/2 **teaspoon ground cloves**

1/2 **teaspoon ground ginger**

1/2 **teaspoon ground mustard**

1/4 **teaspoon celery salt**

1/4 **teaspoon caraway seeds**

Place corned beef with seasoning packet in a Dutch oven; cover with water. Add seasonings and bring to a boil. Reduce heat; cover and simmer for 4 to 4-1/4 hours or until meat is tender. Drain, discarding juices; blot brisket dry.

In a small bowl, combine glaze ingredients. Rub onto top of warm meat. Grill for 5-10 minutes on each side until glazed. Slice meat and serve warm or chilled on buns. **YIELD: 12-16 SERVINGS.**

Fans of good food will cheer when you bring out these full-flavored, hearty sandwiches! Made of tender corned beef and a special sweet and spicy seasoning, they're a hit no matter when you serve them.

—Rita Reifenstein, Evans City, Pennsylvania

Looking for a twist on the usual grilled tailgate fare? With French dressing and Monterey Jack cheese, these brats kick things up a notch! Instead of brats, you can also try this recipe with fully-cooked Italian sausage links.

—Laura McDowell
Lake Villa, Illinois

GAME DAY BRATS

6 **fully cooked bratwurst links (1 to 1-1/4 pounds)**

3/4 **cup sauerkraut, rinsed and well drained**

6 **tablespoons French salad dressing**

6 **tablespoons shredded Monterey Jack cheese**

6 **brat buns, split**

Make a lengthwise slit three-fourths of the way through each bratwurst to within 1/2 in. of each end. Fill with sauerkraut; top with dressing and cheese.

Place bratwurst in buns; wrap individually in a double thickness of heavy-duty foil (about 12 in. x 10 in.). Grill, covered, over medium-hot heat for 10-15 minutes or until heated through and cheese is melted. **YIELD: 6 SERVINGS.**

ITALIAN SAUSAGE BRATS

6 Italian sausage links (4 ounces *each*)	2 teaspoons minced garlic
1 bottle (14.9 ounces) dark beer *or* nonalcoholic beer	1/2 cup chopped fresh tomato
	3/4 teaspoon salt
2 cups julienned green peppers	1/2 teaspoon pepper
	6 brat buns, split
1 cup sliced onion	6 slices provolone cheese, halved
2 tablespoons olive oil	

Place sausages in a large saucepan; add beer. Bring to a boil. Reduce heat; cover and simmer for 8-10 minutes or until meat is no longer pink.

Meanwhile, in a large skillet, saute green peppers and onion in oil until tender. Add garlic, cook 1 minute longer. Add the tomato, salt and pepper; heat through.

Drain and discard beer. Grill sausages, covered, over direct medium heat for 4-5 minutes or until browned, turning occasionally. Serve on buns with green pepper mixture and cheese. **YIELD: 6 SERVINGS.**

Need a different type of sandwich? Try this recipe, and everyone will be complimenting your grilling know-how.

—Taste of Home Test Kitchen

SUPREME PIZZA BURGERS

1/3 cup *each* chopped fresh mushrooms, onion and green pepper	1/3 cup seasoned bread crumbs
	1 pound lean ground beef
1/3 cup chopped ripe olives	4 whole wheat hamburger buns, split
10 slices turkey pepperoni	
2 tablespoons tomato paste	4 slices provolone cheese
2 teaspoons Italian seasoning	4 tablespoons pizza sauce
	OPTIONAL TOPPINGS:
1/4 teaspoon garlic powder	Sliced ripe olives, fresh
1/4 teaspoon salt	mushrooms *and/or* green pepper
1/4 teaspoon pepper	rings

In a food processor, combine the vegetables, olives, pepperoni, tomato paste and seasonings; cover and pulse just until blended. Transfer to a large bowl; stir in bread crumbs. Crumble beef over mixture and mix well. Shape into four patties.

Coat grill rack with cooking spray before starting the grill. Grill burgers, covered, over medium heat for 5-7 minutes on each side or until a meat thermometer reads 160° and juices run clear. Serve on buns with cheese and pizza sauce. Add toppings if desired. **YIELD: 4 SERVINGS.**

One night I couldn't decide what I wanted more, pizza or hamburgers, so I combined the two. Now my young daughter cheers every time we have these pizza burgers.

—Anna Rhyne Anderson, South Carolina

ROASTED PEPPER CHICKEN SANDWICHES

- 1 tablespoon lemon juice
- 1 tablespoon Dijon mustard
- 2 teaspoons olive oil
- 1 garlic clove, minced
- 1/4 teaspoon dried thyme
- 1/4 teaspoon dried marjoram
- 4 boneless skinless chicken breast halves (4 ounces *each*)

PEPPER MIXTURE:

- 1 large onion, thinly sliced
- 1 teaspoon sugar
- 3/4 teaspoon fennel seed, crushed
- 1/4 teaspoon crushed red pepper flakes
- 1/8 teaspoon salt
- 1/8 teaspoon pepper
- 4 garlic cloves, minced
- 1 jar (7 ounces) roasted sweet red peppers, drained and sliced
- 1 tablespoon red wine vinegar

SANDWICHES:

- 1 loaf (8 ounces) focaccia bread
- 4 teaspoons fat-free mayonnaise
- 4 slices reduced-fat Swiss cheese

In a large resealable plastic bag, combine the first six ingredients; add chicken. Seal bag and turn to coat; refrigerate for 1 hour.

In a large nonstick skillet coated with cooking spray, cook and stir the onion, sugar and seasonings over medium heat until tender. Add garlic; cook for 1 minute. Stir in roasted peppers and vinegar; cook 2 minutes longer. Remove from the heat; keep warm.

Coat grill rack with cooking spray before starting the grill. Drain chicken if necessary, discarding any excess marinade. Grill chicken, covered, over medium heat for 4-7 minutes on each side or until a meat thermometer reads 170°. Cut into 1/2-in. strips.

Cut focaccia bread in half lengthwise; spread mayonnaise over cut side of bread bottom. Layer with cheese, chicken strips and pepper mixture. Replace bread top; lightly press down. Grill, covered, for 2-3 minutes or until cheese is melted. Cut into four sandwiches. **YIELD: 4 SERVINGS.**

MEDITERRANEAN SALAD SANDWICHES

2	tablespoons olive oil, *divided*
1	garlic clove, minced
1/4	teaspoon salt
4	large portobello mushrooms, stems removed
2	cups spring mix salad greens
1	medium tomato, chopped
1/2	cup chopped roasted sweet red peppers
1/4	cup crumbled feta cheese
2	tablespoons chopped pitted Greek olives
1	tablespoon red wine vinegar
1/2	teaspoon dried oregano
4	slices sourdough bread, toasted and halved

These meatless, fresh-flavored sandwiches taste like a summer salad on a bun. Add iced tea, a side of sorbet and call it an easy supper.

—Candice Garcia
  Winter Haven, Florida

In a small bowl, combine 1 tablespoon oil, garlic and salt; brush over mushrooms.

Coat grill rack with cooking spray before starting the grill. Grill mushrooms, covered, over medium heat for 6-8 minutes on each side or until tender.

In a large bowl, combine the salad greens, tomato, peppers, cheese and olives. In a small bowl, whisk the vinegar, oregano and remaining oil. Pour over salad mixture; toss to coat. Layer each of four half slices of toast with a mushroom and 3/4 cup salad mixture; top with remaining toast. **YIELD: 4 SERVINGS.**

HOT DOGS WITH THE WORKS

What screams summer more than grilled hot dogs? I place hot dogs in buns before topping them with a zesty cheese sauce and grilling them in a double layer of foil.

—Maria Regakis
Somerville,
Massachusetts

1-1/2 cups (6 ounces) shredded pepper Jack cheese
3/4 cup chopped seeded tomato
3 tablespoons chopped onion
2 tablespoons sweet pickle relish
8 hot dogs
8 hot dog buns

In a small bowl, combine the cheese, tomato, onion and relish. Place hot dogs in buns; top with cheese mixture.

Wrap each hot dog in a double thickness of heavy-duty foil (about 12 in. x 10 in.). Grill, covered, over medium-hot heat for 8-10 minutes or until heated through. Open foil carefully to allow steam to escape. **YIELD: 8 SERVINGS.**

DRESSED-UP BACON BURGERS

3/4 cup mayonnaise
3 tablespoons sweet pickle relish
3 tablespoons ketchup
1 tablespoon sugar
1 tablespoon dried minced onion
1 tablespoon Worcestershire sauce
1/2 teaspoon salt
1/4 teaspoon garlic powder
1/4 teaspoon pepper
2 pounds ground beef
8 bacon strips
8 slices cheddar cheese
8 hamburger buns, split and toasted
Lettuce leaves

In a small bowl, whisk the mayonnaise, pickle relish, ketchup, sugar and onion until well blended. Cover and refrigerate. In a large bowl, combine the Worcestershire sauce, salt, garlic powder and pepper. Crumble beef over mixture; mix well. Shape into eight patties.

Place bacon on a piece of heavy-duty foil on one side of the grill. Place the patties on the other side of the grill. Grill, covered, over medium-hot heat for 8-10 minutes on each side or until a meat thermometer reads 160° and juices run clear and until bacon is crisp. Drain bacon on paper towels.

Place a cheese slice on each patty; cover and grill until cheese is melted. Layer bottom half of each bun with the lettuce, patty, bacon and mayonnaise mixture. Replace bun tops. **YIELD: 8 SERVINGS.**

The tangy homemade sauce that tops these mouthwatering burgers helps them stand out from the rest. This recipe is a cinch to throw together. Because the bacon cooks on the grill alongside the burgers, cleanup is a breeze, too.

—Carol Mizell, Ruston, Louisiana

GRILLED TOMATO SANDWICHES

8 slices tomato
(3/4 inch thick)

1/2 teaspoon salt, *divided*

6 tablespoons mayonnaise

1 teaspoon lemon juice

1 round cheese focaccia
bread *or* focaccia
bread of your choice
(12 inches), halved
lengthwise

1 garlic clove, minced

1 tablespoon balsamic
vinegar

1/4 teaspoon pepper

1 cup chopped water-
packed artichoke hearts,
rinsed and drained

3 cups torn romaine
or spinach

Grilling a loaf of store-bought focaccia puts a fun but no-fuss twist on traditional sandwiches. Best of all, the tomato slices and artichoke hearts are a nice change-of-pace from deli-meat standbys.

—Wendy Stenman
Germantown,
Wisconsin

Sprinkle one side of tomato slices with 1/8 teaspoon salt. Place salt side down on paper towels for 10 minutes. Repeat with second side. In a small bowl, combine the mayonnaise, lemon juice and garlic; set aside.

Coat grill rack with cooking spray before starting the grill. Place bread cut side down on grill. Grill, covered, over medium heat for 2 minutes or until bread is golden brown.

Sprinkle tomatoes with the vinegar, pepper and remaining salt. Spread mayonnaise mixture over bread. On the bottom half, layer tomatoes, artichokes and romaine; replace bread top. Cut into wedges; serve immediately. **YIELD: 4 SERVINGS.**

VEGGIE SANDWICHES

1 small zucchini

1 small yellow
summer squash

1 small eggplant

Cooking spray

1 medium onion,
sliced

1 large sweet red
pepper, cut into
rings

4 whole wheat
hamburger buns,
split

3 ounces fat-free
cream cheese

1/4 cup crumbled goat
cheese

1 garlic clove, minced

1/8 teaspoon salt

1/8 teaspoon pepper

Coat grill rack with cooking spray before starting the grill. Cut the zucchini, squash and eggplant into 1/4-in.-thick strips; spritz with cooking spray. Spritz onion and red pepper with cooking spray.

Grill vegetables, covered, over medium heat for 4-5 minutes on each side or until crisp-tender. Remove and keep warm.

Grill buns, cut side down, over medium heat for 30-60 seconds or until toasted.

In a small bowl, combine the cheeses, garlic, salt and pepper; spread over bun bottoms. Top with vegetables. Replace bun tops. **YIELD: 4 SERVINGS.**

Get a grip on lunch! Here's a fun recipe for using up those summer garden veggies. Meat-eaters won't even miss the meat in these fresh-tasting specialties.

—Melissa Wilbanks, Memphis, Tennessee

FLAVORFUL TURKEY WRAPS

These tangy wraps blend grilled turkey with hoisin sauce, gingerroot, sesame oil and other Asian ingredients. Everyone always asks for seconds.

—Josephine Piro
 Easton, Pennsylvania

1/4	cup hoisin sauce
2	tablespoons orange juice
2	tablespoons reduced-sodium soy sauce
1	tablespoon honey
2	teaspoons grated fresh gingerroot
1	garlic clove, minced
4	turkey breast tenderloins (4 ounces *each*)
3	cups shredded lettuce
3/4	cup shredded carrots
3/4	cup chopped green onions
1	tablespoon rice vinegar
1	tablespoon sesame oil
2	tablespoons sesame seeds, toasted
6	flour tortillas (8 inches), warmed

In a large resealable plastic bag, combine the first six ingredients; add turkey. Seal bag and turn to coat; refrigerate for 6 hours or overnight.

Coat grill rack with cooking spray before starting the grill. Drain and discard marinade. Grill turkey, uncovered, over medium heat for 6-8 minutes on each side or until a meat thermometer reads 170°.

In a large bowl, combine the lettuce, carrots and onions. In a small bowl, whisk vinegar and oil; stir in sesame seeds. Drizzle over lettuce mixture and toss to coat.

Cut turkey into 1/2-in. strips; place down the center of each tortilla. Top with lettuce mixture and roll up; secure with toothpicks. **YIELD: 6 SERVINGS.**

OPEN-FACED SWORDFISH SANDWICHES

1	cup canned bean sprouts, rinsed and drained
3/4	cup julienned carrots
1/4	cup thinly sliced red onion
1	tablespoon lime juice
1	teaspoon sugar
1/2	teaspoon minced fresh gingerroot
4	swordfish steaks (5 ounces *each*)
1	tablespoon olive oil
1/2	teaspoon salt
1/8	teaspoon cayenne pepper
4	slices sourdough bread (1/2 inch thick), toasted
8	teaspoons fat-free blue cheese salad dressing

Topped with mellow blue cheese salad dressing and a festive combination of carrots, red onion and lime juice, these warm sandwiches are a special way to welcome dinnertime at your home.

—Alicia Montalvo Pagan
New Bedford,
Massachusetts

In a small bowl, combine the bean sprouts, carrots and onion. Combine the lime juice, sugar and ginger; stir into vegetable mixture. Cover and refrigerate for 30 minutes.

Brush both sides of swordfish steaks with oil; sprinkle with salt and cayenne. Coat grill rack with cooking spray before starting the grill. Grill fish, uncovered, over medium-hot heat or broil 4-6 in. from the heat for 4-6 minutes on each side or until fish just turns opaque.

Place a swordfish steak on each piece of toast; top with 2 teaspoons blue cheese dressing and about 1/2 cup bean sprout mixture. **YIELD: 4 SERVINGS.**

ALL-AMERICAN LOADED BURGERS

- 1   cup dry bread crumbs
- 1/2   cup finely chopped onion
- 1/2   cup Italian salad dressing
- 2   eggs, lightly beaten
- 2   pounds ground beef
- 6   kaiser rolls, split

Leaf lettuce, Colby cheese slices, tomato slices, ketchup, prepared mustard and french-fried onions, optional

In a large bowl, combine the bread crumbs, onion, salad dressing and eggs. Crumble beef over mixture and mix well. Shape into six patties.

Grill burgers, covered, over medium heat or broil 4 in. from heat for 5-7 minutes on each side or until a meat thermometer reads 160° and juices run clear. Serve on rolls with lettuce, cheese, tomato, ketchup, mustard and french-fried onions if desired. **YIELD: 6 SERVINGS.**

I found this recipe almost 8 years ago and tried it for my daughter's first birthday party. I got so many compliments and requests for the recipe, I don't make burgers any other way now!

—Marsha Urso
Pittsburgh,
Pennsylvania

GRILLED CHICKEN PESTO SANDWICHES

- 8   boneless skinless chicken breast halves (6 ounces *each*)
- 1/2   cup plus 2 tablespoons lemon juice, *divided*
- 1/4   cup plus 1 tablespoon olive oil, *divided*
- 2-1/4   teaspoons salt, *divided*
- 2-1/4   teaspoons pepper, *divided*
- 1-1/4   cups loosely packed basil leaves
- 1/4   cup shredded Parmesan cheese
- 1   garlic clove, peeled
- 1/4   cup pine nuts, toasted
- 8   hamburger buns, split
- 1/2   cup mayonnaise
- 8   slices provolone cheese
- 1-1/2   cups julienned roasted sweet red peppers

Flatten chicken to 1/4-in. thickness. In a large resealable plastic bag, combine 1/2 cup lemon juice, 1/4 cup oil, 2 teaspoons salt and 2 teaspoons pepper; add chicken. Seal bag and turn to coat. Refrigerate for 1 hour.

For pesto, place the basil, Parmesan cheese and garlic in a small food processor; cover and pulse until chopped. Add the pine nuts and remaining lemon juice, salt and pepper; cover and process until blended. While processing, gradually add remaining oil in a steady stream. Set aside.

Drain and discard marinade. Grill chicken, covered, over medium heat for 4-6 minutes on each side or until meat is no longer pink. Grill buns, covered, for 2-3 minutes or until golden brown.

Spread 1 tablespoon mayonnaise over cut side of bun bottoms. Layer with chicken, provolone cheese and roasted red peppers. Spread pesto over cut side of bun tops; place over sandwiches. **YIELD: 8 SERVINGS.**

Pesto and sweet red peppers really jazz up chicken sandwiches with this idea. Everyone loves them.

—Lisa Sneed
Bayfield, Colorado

BARBECUED CHICKEN SALAD SANDWICHES

1-1/2	pounds boneless skinless chicken breast	1/4	teaspoon salt
		1/4	teaspoon crushed red pepper flakes
1/2	cup barbecue sauce	8	kaiser rolls, split
1	cup mayonnaise	8	tomato slices
1/2	cup finely chopped onion	8	lettuce leaves
1/2	cup chopped celery		

Place the chicken in a large resealable plastic bag; add barbecue sauce. Seal the bag and turn to coat. Refrigerate overnight.

Grill chicken, covered, over medium-hot heat for 6-8 minutes on each side or until a meat thermometer reads 170°. Cool; cover and refrigerate chicken until chilled.

Chop chicken; place in a large bowl. Stir in the mayonnaise, onion, celery, salt and pepper flakes. Serve on rolls with tomato and lettuce. **YIELD: 8 SERVINGS.**

An impromptu picnic inspired me to put together this dressed-up chicken salad sandwich. The sauce even gives leftover poultry a scrumptious punch. An instant summertime favorite, these sandwiches have become a mainstay at our house.

—Linda Orme, Battleground, Washington

MOLASSES STEAK SANDWICHES

1/4	cup molasses
2	tablespoons brown sugar
1	tablespoon olive oil
1	tablespoon Dijon mustard
4	beef tenderloin steaks (4 ounces *each*)
2	large portobello mushrooms, stems removed
4	kaiser rolls, split
4	slices Swiss cheese

In a large resealable plastic bag, combine the molasses, brown sugar, oil and mustard; add steaks. Seal bag and turn to coat; refrigerate for up to 2 hours.

Drain and discard marinade. Grill steaks, covered, over medium heat for 4-6 minutes on each side or until meat reaches desired doneness (for medium-rare, a meat thermometer should read 145°; medium, 160°; well-done, 170°).

Grill mushrooms for 3-4 minutes or until lightly browned, turning every minute. Place buns, cut sides down, on grill for 2-3 minutes or until golden brown. Cut mushrooms into 1/4-in. slices.

Place the steaks, cheese and mushrooms on bun bottoms; replace tops. Serve immediately. **YIELD: 4 SERVINGS.**

Molasses adds a twist to this sandwich that will make it special enough to serve at any get-together.

—Taste of Home Test Kitchen

TERRIFIC TERIYAKI BURGERS

1/4	cup ketchup	
2	tablespoons reduced-sodium soy sauce	
1	tablespoon brown sugar	
1	tablespoon unsweetened crushed pineapple	
1-1/2	teaspoons minced fresh gingerroot	
1	garlic clove, minced	
1/2	teaspoon sesame oil	

BURGERS:

1	egg white, lightly beaten

1/3	cup dry bread crumbs	
3	green onions, chopped	
2	tablespoons unsweetened crushed pineapple	
3/4	pound ground beef	
3/4	pound lean ground turkey	
6	slices unsweetened pineapple	
6	hamburger buns, split and toasted	
6	lettuce leaves	
6	slices tomato	

Golden flecks of pineapple give my burgers a touch of sweetness, while the gingerroot adds a little spice. Ground chicken works well in this recipe, too.

—Margaret Wilson
Sun City, California

In a small bowl, combine the ketchup, soy sauce, brown sugar, pineapple, ginger, garlic and sesame oil; set aside.

In a large bowl, combine the egg white, bread crumbs, onions, crushed pineapple and 3 tablespoons reserved ketchup mixture. Crumble beef and turkey over mixture and mix well. Shape into six burgers.

Coat grill rack with cooking spray before starting the grill. Grill burgers, covered, over medium heat for 5-7 minutes on each side or until a meat thermometer reads 165° and juices run clear, brushing occasionally with remaining ketchup mixture.

Grill pineapple slices for 2-3 minutes on each side or until heated through. Serve burgers and pineapple on buns with lettuce and tomato. **YIELD: 6 SERVINGS.**

FLANK STEAK SANDWICHES

- 1 **cup chopped onion**
- 1 **cup dry red wine** *or* **beef broth**
- 3/4 **cup soy sauce**
- 1/2 **cup olive oil,** *divided*
- 4-1/2 **teaspoons minced garlic,** *divided*
- 1-1/2 **teaspoons ground mustard**
- 1-1/2 **teaspoons ground ginger**
- 1 **beef flank steak (1-1/2 pounds)**
- 1 **medium sweet red pepper, cut into 1-inch strips**
- 1 **medium sweet yellow pepper, cut into 1-inch strips**
- 1 **medium red onion, thickly sliced**
- 1/4 **teaspoon pepper**
- 6 **French rolls, split**

In a small bowl, combine the onion, wine or broth, soy sauce, 1/4 cup olive oil, 2-1/2 teaspoons garlic, mustard and ginger. Pour 1-3/4 cups into a large resealable plastic bag; add steak. Pour remaining marinade into another resealable plastic bag; add the peppers and onion. Seal bags and turn to coat; refrigerate for 3 hours or overnight, turning occasionally.

Drain and discard marinade from steak. Grill, covered, over medium heat for 6-7 minutes on each side or until meat reaches desired doneness (for medium-rare, a meat thermometer should read 145°; medium, 160°; well-done, 170°).

Drain and discard marinade from vegetables. Place in a grill basket or disposable foil pan with slits cut in the bottom. Grill, uncovered, over medium-hot heat for 9-11 minutes or until tender, stirring frequently.

In a small bowl, combine the pepper, and remaining oil and garlic; brush over cut sides of rolls. Place cut side down on grill for 2-3 minutes or until golden brown.

Thinly slice steak across the grain; place on bun bottoms. Top with vegetables and bun tops. Serve immediately. **YIELD: 6 SERVINGS.**

My sister and I found this recipe over 15 years ago, changed a few ingredients and made it our own. Now, when family and friends hear we're making these sandwiches, they come running! It's a quick, healthy crowd-pleaser that's perfect for casual summer meals.

—Elizabeth Hiner
    Chico, California

HAM & CHEESE SANDWICH LOAF

- 1 **loaf sourdough bread (1 pound)**
- 1 **cup sliced fresh mushrooms**
- 1 **medium green pepper, cut into strips**
- 1 **medium sweet red pepper, cut into strips**
- 1 **celery rib, sliced**
- 3 **green onions, sliced**
- 2 **tablespoons olive oil**
- 1/2 **cup mayonnaise**
- 2 **teaspoons Italian seasoning**
- 1/2 **teaspoon pepper**
- 1 **pound shaved deli ham**
- 1 **cup (4 ounces) shredded Colby cheese**
- 1/2 **cup shredded part-skim mozzarella cheese**

Cut bread in half horizontally. Hollow out top and bottom halves, leaving 1/2-in. shells. (Discard removed bread or save for another use.)

In a large skillet, saute the mushrooms, peppers, celery and onions in oil until tender. Remove from the heat; set aside.

Combine the mayonnaise, Italian seasoning and pepper; spread over bread. On the bread bottom, layer half of the ham, vegetable mixture and cheeses. Repeat layers, gently pressing down if needed. Replace bread top.

Wrap tightly in heavy-duty foil. Grill, covered, over medium heat for 30-35 minutes or until heated through. Cut into wedges with a serrated knife. **YIELD: 8 SERVINGS.**

This grilled stacked sandwich is loaded with great flavor. The crusty bread is filled with melted cheese, crisp vegetables and tender ham. It's sure to be a party favorite!
—Pat Stevens, Granbury, Texas

At our house, we enjoy these sandwiches as a change from plain hamburgers or hot dogs.
—June Burkert
Evans City,
Pennsylvania

SMOKED LINKBURGERS

- 1 **tablespoon brown sugar**
- 1 **tablespoon lemon juice**
- 1 **tablespoon finely chopped onion**
- 1/2 **teaspoon salt**

Dash pepper

- 1-1/2 **pounds ground beef**
- 1 **package (14 ounces) smoked sausage links**
- 8 **hot dog *or* hoagie buns, split**

In a large bowl, combine the first five ingredients. Crumble beef over mixture and mix well. Divide into eight portions and shape each portion around a sausage link.

Grill or broil until a meat thermometer reads 160° and juices run clear, turning frequently. Serve on buns. **YIELD: 8 SERVINGS.**

MEXICAN-INSPIRED TURKEY BURGERS

1/2	cup salsa, *divided*	1/4	teaspoon salt
1/4	cup shredded reduced-fat cheddar cheese	1/4	teaspoon cayenne pepper
3	teaspoons paprika	1	pound extra-lean ground turkey
1	teaspoon dried oregano	1/4	cup reduced-fat sour cream
1	teaspoon ground cumin		
3/4	teaspoon sugar	4	hamburger buns, split
3/4	teaspoon garlic powder	1/2	cup torn curly endive
1/2	teaspoon dried thyme	1	medium tomato, chopped

In a large bowl, combine 1/4 cup salsa, cheese, paprika, oregano, cumin, sugar, garlic powder, thyme, salt and cayenne. Crumble turkey over mixture and mix well. Shape into four burgers.

Coat grill rack with cooking spray before starting the grill. Grill, covered, over medium heat or broil 4 in. from the heat for 5-7 minutes on each side or until a meat thermometer reads 165° and juices run clear.

In a small bowl, combine sour cream and remaining salsa. Place burgers on buns; top with endive, tomato and sour cream mixture. **YIELD: 4 SERVINGS.**

We love burgers, but turkey burgers can be bland. That's why I used a spice combination from a taco recipe and tinkered with cheeses and different toppings for these patties.

—Heather Byers
Pittsburgh,
Pennsylvania

PAUL BUNYAN BURGERS

6	bacon strips, diced	1/2	teaspoon salt
1	cup sliced fresh mushrooms	1/2	teaspoon pepper
3	thin onion slices	1/2	teaspoon prepared horseradish
1	egg, lightly beaten	1	pound ground beef
1	tablespoon Worcestershire sauce	3	slices process American cheese
1/2	teaspoon seasoned salt	3	hamburger buns, split

In a large skillet, cook bacon until crisp. Remove with a slotted spoon to paper towels. In the drippings, saute mushrooms and onion until tender. Transfer to a large bowl with a slotted spoon; add bacon.

In another bowl, combine the egg, Worcestershire sauce, seasoned salt, salt, pepper and horseradish; sprinkle beef over mixture and mix well. Shape into six 1/4-in.-thick patties.

Divide bacon mixture among three patties. Top with a cheese slice; fold in corners of cheese. Top with remaining patties; seal edges.

Grill, uncovered, over medium-hot heat for 5-6 minutes on each side or until a thermometer reads 160° and meat juices run clear. Serve on buns. **YIELD: 3 SERVINGS.**

This is one of my favorite grilling recipes. To prepare the stuffed burgers faster, substitute bacon bits and canned mushrooms.

—Jo Reed, Craig, Colorado

CHIPOTLE BBQ PORK SANDWICHES

1/2   **cup barbecue sauce**

1   **tablespoon honey**

2   **chipotle peppers in adobo sauce, chopped**

1   **pork tenderloin (1 pound)**

1-1/2   **cups coleslaw mix**

2   **tablespoons reduced-fat sour cream**

2   **tablespoons Miracle Whip Light**

1   **tablespoon Dijon mustard**

4   **hamburger buns, split**

In a small bowl, combine the barbecue sauce, honey and peppers. Set aside 1/4 cup until serving.

Coat grill rack with cooking spray before starting the grill. Prepare grill for indirect heat. Grill pork, covered, over indirect medium-hot heat for 20-25 minutes or until a meat thermometer reads 160°, basting occasionally with remaining barbecue sauce. Let stand for 5 minutes before slicing.

Meanwhile, combine the coleslaw mix, sour cream, Miracle Whip Light and mustard. Brush cut sides of buns with reserved barbecue sauce. Cut pork into 1/4-in. slices; place on bun bottoms. Top with coleslaw and bun tops. **YIELD: 4 SERVINGS.**

I first made these for a summer barbecue with guests who enjoy traditional pulled pork sandwiches but wanted something lighter. They loved these and didn't miss the extra calories one bit. Crunchy coleslaw tames the heat!

—Priscilla Yee
  Concord, California

GRILLED STEAK AND PORTOBELLO STACKS

- 2 tablespoons plus 1/4 cup olive oil, *divided*
- 1 tablespoon herbes de Provence
- 1 beef tenderloin roast (1-1/4 pounds)
- 4 large portobello mushrooms
- 2 tablespoons balsamic vinegar

BALSAMIC ONION:

- 1 large onion, halved and thinly sliced
- 4-1/2 teaspoons sugar
- 1/2 teaspoon salt
- 1/2 teaspoon pepper
- 1 tablespoon olive oil
- 2 tablespoons balsamic vinegar

HORSERADISH SAUCE:

- 1/2 cup sour cream
- 1-1/2 teaspoons prepared horseradish
- 1/4 teaspoon Worcestershire sauce

SANDWICHES:

- 12 slices white bread
- 1/4 cup butter, melted
- 4 cups spring mix salad greens
- 2 tablespoons red wine vinaigrette
- 3/4 cup julienned roasted sweet red peppers

You don't need a special panini maker for these grilled bistro-style sandwiches. They may take a little bit of time to prepare, but they're well worth it!

—Judy Murphy
Coeur d' Alene, Idaho

In a small bowl, combine 2 tablespoons oil and herbes de Provence. Rub over tenderloin; cover and refrigerate for 2 hours. Place mushrooms in a small bowl; toss with vinegar and remaining oil. Cover and refrigerate until grilling.

In a large skillet, cook the onion, sugar, salt and pepper in oil over medium heat for 15-20 minutes or until golden brown, stirring frequently. Remove from the heat; stir in vinegar. Set aside.

In a small bowl, combine the sauce ingredients. Cover and refrigerate until serving.

Grill tenderloin and mushrooms, covered, over medium heat for 8-10 minutes on each side or until meat reaches desired doneness (for medium-rare, a meat thermometer should read 145°; medium, 160°; well-done, 170°) and mushrooms are tender. Let tenderloin stand for 10 minutes.

Meanwhile, brush both sides of bread with butter. Grill over medium heat for 1 minute on each side or until browned. Toss salad greens with vinaigrette. Cut tenderloin and mushrooms into thin slices.

Divide mushrooms among four slices of bread. Layer with roasted peppers, greens and another slice of bread. Top each with onion mixture and beef. Spread sauce over remaining slices of bread; place over beef. Cut each sandwich diagonally in half. **YIELD: 4-8 SERVINGS.**

EDITOR'S NOTE: Look for herbes de Provence in the spice aisle. It is also available from Penzeys Spices. Visit www.penzeys.com or call 1-800/741-7787.

GRILLED VEGGIE WRAPS

2	tablespoons balsamic vinegar	1	medium red onion, cut into 1/2-inch slices
1-1/2	teaspoons minced fresh basil	4	ounces whole fresh mushrooms, cut into 1/2-inch pieces
1-1/2	teaspoons olive oil	4	ounces fresh sugar snap peas
1-1/2	teaspoons molasses	1/2	cup crumbled feta cheese
3/4	teaspoon minced fresh thyme	3	tablespoons reduced-fat cream cheese
1/8	teaspoon salt		
1/8	teaspoon pepper	2	tablespoons grated Parmesan cheese
1	medium zucchini, cut lengthwise into 1/4-inch slices	1	tablespoon reduced-fat mayonnaise
1	medium sweet red pepper, cut into 1-inch pieces	4	flour tortillas (8 inches)
		4	romaine leaves

In a large resealable plastic bag, combine the first seven ingredients; add vegetables. Seal bag and turn to coat; refrigerate for 2 hours, turning once.

Drain and reserve marinade. In a small bowl, combine cheeses and mayonnaise; set aside. Place vegetables in a grill basket or disposable foil pan with slits cut in the bottom. Grill, uncovered, over medium-high heat for 5 minutes.

Set aside 1 teaspoon marinade. Turn vegetables; baste with remaining marinade. Grill 5-8 minutes longer or until tender. Brush one side of each tortilla with reserved marinade. Place tortillas, marinade side down, on grill for 1-3 minutes or until lightly toasted.

Spread 3 tablespoons of cheese mixture over ungrilled side of each tortilla. Top with romaine and 1 cup grilled vegetables; roll up. **YIELD: 4 SERVINGS.**

I first sampled these moist patties at an "Eating Right" class at our local library. And they can hold their own against any veggie burger you could buy at the supermarket. They're wonderful!

—Marguerite Shaeffer
 Sewell, New Jersey

BEAN PATTIES

1	large onion, finely chopped
1	tablespoon olive oil
4	garlic cloves, minced
1	medium carrot, shredded
1	to 2 teaspoons chili powder
1	teaspoon ground cumin
1	can (15 ounces) pinto beans, rinsed and drained
1	can (15 ounces) black beans, rinsed and drained
1-1/2	cups quick-cooking oats
2	tablespoons Dijon mustard
2	tablespoons reduced-sodium soy sauce
1	tablespoon ketchup
1/4	teaspoon pepper
8	whole wheat hamburger buns, split
8	lettuce leaves
8	tablespoons salsa

In a large nonstick skillet coated with cooking spray, saute onion in oil for 2 minutes. Add garlic; cook for 1 minute. Stir in the carrot, chili powder and cumin; cook 2 minutes longer or until carrot is tender. Remove from the heat; set aside.

In a large bowl, mash the pinto beans and black beans. Stir in oats. Add the mustard, soy sauce, ketchup, pepper and carrot mixture; mix well. Shape into eight 3-1/2-in. patties.

Coat grill rack with cooking spray before starting the grill. Grill patties, covered, over medium heat for 4-5 minutes on each side or until heated through. Serve on buns with lettuce and salsa. **YIELD: 8 SERVINGS.**

EDITOR'S NOTE: Our recipes sometimes give a range on certain herbs and spices to accommodate different tastes. If you like the heat of chili powder, use 2 teaspoons in your Bean Patties; for a milder version, use 1 teaspoon.

THE HEAT'S ON MEDIUM

MEDIUM HEAT is the way to go when cooking most burgers and sausages. If the heat is too high, the food is likely to quickly burn on the outside yet remain uncooked on the inside.

CHEESE-STUFFED BURGERS

1	tablespoon finely chopped onion
1	tablespoon ketchup
1	teaspoon prepared mustard
1/4	teaspoon salt
1/8	teaspoon pepper
1/2	pound lean ground beef)
1/4	cup finely shredded cheddar cheese
2	hamburger buns, split

Lettuce leaves and tomato slices, optional

In a small bowl, combine the first five ingredients. Crumble beef over mixture and mix well. Shape into four thin patties. Sprinkle cheese over two patties; top with remaining patties and press edges firmly to seal.

Grill, covered, over medium heat for 6 minutes on each side or until a meat thermometer reads 160° and juices run clear. Serve on buns with lettuce and tomato if desired. **YIELD: 2 SERVINGS.**

Here's a sandwich that does traditional burgers one better—with a pocket of cheddar! We enjoy the melted cheese center.

—Janet Wood
  Windham,
  New Hampshire

PITA BURGERS

1	small onion, chopped
1	garlic clove, minced
1	teaspoon dried oregano
3/4	teaspoon salt
1/2	teaspoon dried basil
1/4	teaspoon dried rosemary, crushed
1-1/2	pounds lean ground beef
2	cups shredded lettuce
1	medium cucumber, seeded and chopped
1	cup (8 ounces) reduced-fat plain yogurt
1	tablespoon sesame seeds, toasted
6	whole pita breads, halved

In a small bowl, combine the onion, garlic and seasonings; crumble beef over mixture and mix well. Shape into six patties.

Grill or broil for 5-7 minutes on each side or until a meat thermometer reads 160° and juices run clear.

Meanwhile, in a small bowl, combine the lettuce, cucumber, yogurt and sesame seeds. Top each burger with lettuce mixture; serve on pitas. **YIELD: 6 SERVINGS.**

I serve this tasty variation on the traditional hamburger at backyard get-togethers. Similar to Greek gyros, the herbed ground beef patties are stuffed in pita bread with a yummy cucumber-lettuce mixture.

—Dorothy Wiedeman, Eaton, Colorado

CORN 'N' SQUASH QUESADILLAS

2	medium ears sweet corn, husks removed
2	medium yellow summer squash, halved lengthwise
1/2	small sweet onion, cut into 1/4-inch slices
1	to 2 jalapeno peppers
1	tablespoon minced fresh basil
1-1/2	teaspoons minced fresh oregano
1	garlic clove, minced
1/4	teaspoon salt
1/4	teaspoon ground cumin
6	flour tortillas (8 inches), warmed
1	cup (4 ounces) shredded Monterey Jack cheese
1	tablespoon canola oil

Grilled vegetables give these quesadillas their distinctive flair, while cumin and jalapeno peppers add a little zip.

—Mildred Sherrer
  Fort Worth, Texas

Grill corn, covered, over medium heat for 10 minutes; turn. Place the squash, onion and jalapenos on grill; cover and cook for 5-6 minutes on each side. When vegetables are cool enough to handle, remove corn from the cobs, chop the squash and onion, and seed and chop the jalapenos. Place in a large bowl.

Stir in the basil, oregano, garlic, salt and cumin. Place 1/2 cup filling on one side of each tortilla; sprinkle with cheese. Fold tortillas over filling. On a griddle or large skillet, cook quesadillas in oil over medium heat for 1-2 minutes on each side or until heated through. Cut into wedges. **YIELD: 6 SERVINGS.**

EDITOR'S NOTE: When cutting hot peppers, disposable gloves are recommended. Avoid touching your face.

EGGPLANT-PORTOBELLO SANDWICH LOAF

- 1 loaf (1 pound) Italian bread
- 1/2 cup olive oil
- 2 teaspoons minced garlic
- 1 teaspoon Italian seasoning
- 1/2 teaspoon salt
- 1/4 teaspoon pepper
- 1 large eggplant (1 pound), cut into 1/2-inch slices
- 1 package (6 ounces) sliced portobello mushrooms
- 1 cup marinara sauce
- 2 tablespoons minced fresh basil
- 4 ounces smoked fresh mozzarella cheese, cut into 1/4-inch slices

Cut bread lengthwise in half. Carefully hollow out top and bottom, leaving a 1/2-in. shell; set aside. In a small bowl, combine the oil, garlic, Italian seasoning, salt and pepper. Brush over eggplant and mushrooms.

Grill, covered, over medium heat for 3-5 minutes on each side or until vegetables are tender.

Spread half of the marinara sauce over bottom of bread. Top with eggplant and mushrooms. Spread with remaining sauce; top with basil and cheese. Replace bread top.

Wrap loaf in a large piece of heavy-duty foil (about 28 in. x 18 in.); seal tightly. Grill, covered, over medium heat for 4-5 minutes on each side. **YIELD: 4 SERVINGS.**

This sandwich uses fresh eggplant and tasty marinara to make a hearty dinner for four. If you can't find smoked mozzarella, regular works just fine.

—Taste of Home Test Kitchen

GLORIFIED HOT DOGS

My parents always made hot dogs when they barbecued. They were not only a family favorite, but guests liked them, too. They're good hot or cold.

—Cheryl Gillpatrick
Loveland, Colorado

- 1 large whole dill pickle (5 inches)
- 1 block (4 ounces) cheddar *or* Colby cheese
- 8 hot dogs
- 4 teaspoons prepared mustard
- 8 bacon strips
- 8 hot dog buns

Cut pickle lengthwise into eight thin slices. Cut cheese into eight 5-in. x 1/2-in. x 1/4-in. sticks. Cut hot dogs in half lengthwise; spread cut surfaces with mustard. On eight hot dog halves, layer a pickle slice and a cheese stick; top with remaining hot dog halves.

Place one end of a bacon strip at the end of each hot dog; push a toothpick through the bacon and both hot dog pieces. Firmly wrap bacon around each hot dog and secure at the other end with a toothpick.

Grill, uncovered, over medium heat for 8-10 minutes or until bacon is completely cooked, turning occasionally. Discard toothpicks. Serve in buns. **YIELD: 8 SERVINGS.**

PORTOBELLO BURGERS WITH PEAR-WALNUT MAYONNAISE

- 1/4 **cup olive oil**
- 1/4 **cup balsamic vinegar**
- 3 **garlic cloves, minced**
- 1 **tablespoon minced fresh thyme** *or* **1 teaspoon dried thyme**
- 4 **large portobello mushrooms**
- 1 **medium pear, peeled and chopped**
- 1 **tablespoon olive oil**
- 1 **tablespoon lemon juice**
- 2 **tablespoons mayonnaise**
- 4-1/2 **teaspoons chopped walnuts**
- 4 **slices onion**
- 6 **ounces Gorgonzola cheese, thinly sliced**
- 4 **whole wheat hamburger buns, split**
- 2 **cups fresh arugula**

I found that a big, juicy grilled mushroom with a nutty pear mayonnaise and creamy blue cheese makes for a simply outstanding veggie burger.

—Lindsay Sprunk
Brentwood, Tennessee

In a large resealable plastic bag, combine the oil, vinegar, garlic and thyme; add mushrooms. Seal bag and turn to coat; refrigerate for up to 2 hours.

In a small skillet, saute pear in oil and lemon juice until tender; cool slightly. Place in a small food processor; cover and process until blended. Stir in mayonnaise and walnuts. Cover and refrigerate until serving.

Drain and discard marinade. Grill mushrooms, covered, over medium heat for 3-4 minutes on each side or until tender. Top with onion and cheese slices. Grill 2-3 minutes longer or until cheese is melted. Serve on buns with arugula and mayonnaise mixture. **YIELD: 4 SERVINGS.**

GREASING UP THE GRILL

KEEP foods from sticking by spraying the grate with cooking spray before igniting the heat. Grease a hot grate with a pad of paper towels held with tongs. Dip the pad in vegetable oil and rub over the grate.

GRILLED PORK TENDERLOIN SANDWICHES

2	tablespoons canola oil
2	tablespoons reduced-sodium soy sauce
2	tablespoons steak sauce
2	garlic cloves, minced
1-1/2	teaspoons brown sugar
1/2	teaspoon ground mustard
1/2	teaspoon minced fresh gingerroot
2	pork tenderloins (1 pound *each*)

MUSTARD HORSERADISH SAUCE:

1/4	cup fat-free mayonnaise
1/4	cup reduced-fat sour cream
1-1/2	teaspoons lemon juice
1	teaspoon sugar
1/2	teaspoon ground mustard
1/2	teaspoon Dijon mustard
1/2	teaspoon prepared horseradish
6	kaiser rolls, split
6	lettuce leaves

In a large resealable plastic bag, combine the first seven ingredients; add pork. Seal bag and turn to coat; refrigerate for 8 hours or overnight.

Coat grill rack with cooking spray before starting the grill. Prepare grill for indirect heat. Drain and discard marinade. Grill pork, covered, over indirect medium-hot heat for 25-40 minutes or until a meat thermometer reads 160°. Let stand for 5 minutes before slicing.

In a small bowl, combine the mayonnaise, sour cream, lemon juice, sugar, ground mustard, Dijon mustard and horseradish. Serve pork on rolls with lettuce and mustard horseradish sauce. **YIELD: 6 SERVINGS.**

I got the recipe for these quick-fixing pork sandwiches from a friend at work years ago. I'm always asked for it when I serve it.

*—Geri Bierschbach
Weidman, Michigan*

ITALIAN SAUSAGE SANDWICHES

2	jars (26 ounces *each*) meatless spaghetti sauce
2	medium green peppers, cut into strips
2	medium onions, thinly sliced
1/2	teaspoon garlic powder
1/2	teaspoon fennel seed, crushed
2	packages (20 ounces *each*) Italian turkey sausage links
10	sandwich buns, split

In a 3-qt. slow cooker, combine the spaghetti sauce, green peppers, onions, garlic powder and fennel seed. Cover and cook on low for 4 hours or until vegetables are tender.

Grill sausages according to package directions. Serve on buns with sauce. **YIELD: 10 SERVINGS.**

Need a different type of sandwich for a party? Try this recipe, and everyone will be complimenting your skill at the grill.

*—Taste of Home
Test Kitchen*

These are my family's favorite! My kids will eat anything we roll up in wraps. The original recipe called for all white flour and a lot of salt. I added whole wheat flour to make it healthier and cut back on the salt.

—Fay Strait, Waukee, Iowa

GRILLING TIP

IF YOU ENJOY the flavor of flame-broiled sandwiches but don't usually fire up the grill in cooler weather, you may want to invest in an electric or stovetop griddle. Both will allow you to grill four to six sandwiches at a time indoors.

Similarly, a George Foreman indoor grill or a panini sandwich maker often lend grilled flavor to sandwiches that are made in the kitchen.

Marinating meat that you plan to cook in an oven for sandwiches? Consider adding a dash of Liquid Smoke to the marinade for extra appeal.

SUPER FLATBREAD WRAPS

1/2	teaspoon active dry yeast
1/2	cup warm water (110° to 115°)
1	teaspoon olive oil
1/2	teaspoon salt
1/3	cup whole wheat flour
1	cup all-purpose flour

FILLING:

1	beef flank steak (1 pound)
1/2	teaspoon salt
1/4	teaspoon pepper
1	cup shredded lettuce
1/4	cup sliced ripe olives
2	tablespoons crumbled feta cheese

In a small bowl, dissolve yeast in warm water. Add the oil, salt, whole wheat flour and 3/4 cup all-purpose flour; beat on medium speed for 3 minutes. Stir in enough remaining flour to form a firm dough.

Turn onto a lightly floured surface; knead until smooth and elastic, about 6-8 minutes. Place in a large bowl coated with cooking spray, turning once to coat the top. Cover and let rise in a warm place until doubled, about 45 minutes.

Punch dough down. Turn onto a lightly floured surface; divide into four portions. Roll each into an 8-in. circle.

Heat a large nonstick skillet coated with cooking spray over medium heat; add a portion of dough. Cook for 30-60 seconds or until bubbles form on top. Turn and cook until the second side is golden brown. Remove and keep warm. Repeat with remaining dough, adding cooking spray as needed.

Coat grill rack with cooking spray before starting the grill. Sprinkle steak with salt and pepper. Grill, covered, over medium-high heat for 6-8 minutes on each side or until meat reaches desired doneness (for medium-rare, a meat thermometer should read 145°; medium, 160°; well-done, 170°).

Let stand for 5 minutes before cutting steak thinly across the grain. Serve on warm flatbreads with lettuce, olives and cheese. **YIELD: 4 SERVINGS.**

CRANBERRY TURKEY BURGERS

These turkey burgers are so good that you might give up traditional beef hamburgers altogether. The thick grilled patties are topped with prepared cranberry sauce and served on toasted English muffins for a nice change of pace.

—Barbara Lindauer
New Athens, Illinois

1	small tart apple, peeled and finely chopped
1	celery rib, chopped
1	small onion, chopped
1	teaspoon poultry seasoning
3/4	teaspoon salt
1/4	teaspoon pepper
1-1/4	pounds ground turkey
1/2	cup mayonnaise
6	English muffins, split and toasted
6	lettuce leaves
1	cup whole-berry cranberry sauce

In a large bowl, combine the first six ingredients. Crumble turkey over mixture and mix well. Shape into six patties.

Coat grill rack with cooking spray before starting the grill. Grill patties, covered, over medium heat for 10 minutes on each side or until a meat thermometer reads 165° and juices run clear.

Spread mayonnaise over muffin halves. Place the lettuce, turkey burgers and cranberry sauce on muffin bottoms; replace tops. **YIELD: 6 SERVINGS.**

TUSCAN STEAK FLATBREADS

SUN-DRIED TOMATO PESTO:

1/3	cup packed fresh parsley sprigs
2	tablespoons fresh basil leaves
1	garlic clove, quartered
2	tablespoons grated Parmesan cheese
2	tablespoons oil-packed sun-dried tomatoes, patted dry
2	tablespoons sherry
1/4	teaspoon salt
Dash pepper	
1/4	cup olive oil

STEAK FLATBREADS:

1	beef top sirloin steak (3/4 inch thick and 1-1/4 pounds)
1/4	teaspoon salt
1/4	teaspoon pepper
4	flatbreads *or* whole gyro-style pitas (6 inches)
2	tablespoons olive oil
1	cup (4 ounces) shredded fontina cheese
1/4	cup fresh basil leaves, thinly sliced

Take flatbreads grilled in pesto, wrap them around steak and top with cheese. You have an instant party! Guests will love the fun presentation and the mouthwatering taste.

—Michael Cohen
Los Angeles,
California

For pesto, place the parsley, basil and garlic in a food processor; cover and pulse until chopped. Add the Parmesan cheese, tomatoes, sherry, salt and pepper; cover and process until blended. While processing, gradually add the oil in a steady stream. Set aside.

Sprinkle steak with salt and pepper. Grill, covered, over medium heat for 6-10 minutes on each side or until meat reaches desired doneness (for medium-rare, a meat thermometer should read 145°; medium, 160°; well-done, 170°). Remove and keep warm.

Brush one side of each flatbread with oil; place oiled side down on grill rack. Grill, covered, over medium heat for 1-2 minutes or until heated through.

Spread pesto over grilled side of flatbreads. Cut steak into thin strips; place over pesto. Top with fontina cheese and basil. **YIELD: 4 SERVINGS.**

TANGY CHICKEN SANDWICHES

3/4   cup Louisiana-style hot sauce

1/3   cup packed brown sugar

3   tablespoons butter

4-1/2   teaspoons cider vinegar

3/4   teaspoon taco seasoning

2   boneless skinless chicken breast halves (5 ounces *each*)

2   tablespoons crumbled blue cheese

2   tablespoons buttermilk

2   tablespoons mayonnaise

1-1/2   teaspoons shredded Parmesan cheese

1-1/2   teaspoons minced chives

3/4   teaspoon lemon juice

1/4   teaspoon balsamic vinegar

1/8   teaspoon minced garlic

1/8   teaspoon pepper

2   onion rolls, split and toasted

2   cooked bacon strips

2   slices Colby cheese (3/4 ounce *each*)

2   lettuce leaves

2   slices tomato

2   slices red onion

I put a "Joe-style" twist on my chicken sandwiches with a spicy-sweet marinade and a homemade blue cheese dressing.
—Joe Slate, Port St Joe, Florida

In a small saucepan over medium heat, bring the first five ingredients to a boil; boil, uncovered, for 1 minute. Cool for 10 minutes; set aside 1/4 cup for basting. Flatten chicken to 1/2-in. thickness. Pour remaining marinade into a large resealable plastic bag; add chicken. Seal bag and turn to coat; refrigerate for at least 2 hours.

Drain and discard marinade from chicken. Grill chicken, covered, over medium heat or broil 4 in. from heat for 5-6 minutes on each side or until no longer pink, basting occasionally with reserved marinade.

In a small bowl, combine the blue cheese, buttermilk, mayonnaise, Parmesan cheese, chives, lemon juice, vinegar, garlic and pepper. Spread over roll bottoms; top with the chicken, bacon, cheese, lettuce, tomato and onion. Replace roll tops. **YIELD: 2 SERVINGS.**

5
BEEF

PG. **95** | **STEAK**
WITH CHIPOTLE-LIME
CHIMICHURRI

BEEF IS THE ONLY REASON MOST FOLKS NEED TO FIRE UP THEIR GRILLS. WHETHER JUICY BURGERS ARE ON THE MENU OR FLAME-BROILED T-BONE STEAKS, COOKS FROM COAST TO COAST CAN'T WAIT TO SINK THEIR TEETH INTO BEEF SPECIALTIES, HOT OFF THE COALS. HERE, YOU'LL FIND EVERYING FROM SIRLOIN STEAKS TO TENDERLOIN AND MORE!

BEEFSTRO BRUSCHETTA BURGERS

My mom always ate her hamburger on top of salads. I thought it was quite unusual as a child, but I adjusted the concept to make it a tasty meal for the whole family!

—Devon Delaney, Princeton, New Jersey

3	tablespoons Dijon mustard
3	tablespoons apricot preserves
1	tablespoon prepared horseradish
2	thin slices prosciutto *or* deli ham, chopped
1	pound lean ground beef
3/4	teaspoon lemon-pepper seasoning
8	slices French bread (1/2 inch thick)
1	cup fresh arugula *or* baby spinach
2	ounces Brie cheese, cut into eight thin slices
1/4	cup julienned roasted sweet red peppers

In a small bowl, combine the mustard, preserves and horseradish. In a small skillet coated with cooking spray, cook and stir prosciutto over medium heat until lightly browned. Set aside.

In a large bowl, combine ground beef and lemon-pepper. Shape into eight patties. Coat grill rack with cooking spray before starting the grill. Grill burgers, covered, over medium heat or broil 4 in. from heat for 3-4 minutes on each side or until a meat thermometer reads 160° and juices run clear. Remove and keep warm.

Grill bread for 1-2 minutes on each side or until toasted. Spread each slice of toast with 1-1/4 teaspoons reserved mustard sauce. Layer each with arugula, a burger, a cheese slice and 1-1/4 teaspoons additional sauce. Garnish with peppers and prosciutto. Serve immediately. **YIELD: 4 SERVINGS.**

GLAZED BEEF TOURNEDOS

3 **tablespoons steak sauce**

2 **tablespoons ketchup**

2 **tablespoons orange marmalade**

1 **tablespoon lemon juice**

1 **tablespoon finely chopped onion**

1 **garlic clove, minced**

4 **beef tenderloin steaks (6 ounces *each*)**

In a small bowl, combine the steak sauce, ketchup, marmalade, lemon juice, onion and garlic. Set aside 1/4 cup for serving.

Coat grill rack with cooking spray before starting the grill. Grill steaks, uncovered, over medium heat or broil 4-6 in. from the heat for 5-7 minutes on each side or until meat reaches desired doneness (for medium-rare, a meat thermometer should read 145°; medium, 160°; well-done, 170°), basting frequently with remaining sauce. Just before serving, brush steaks with reserved sauce. **YIELD: 4 SERVINGS.**

I found this wonderful grilled recipe in a book years ago. It's been a favorite for special occasions ever since! I like to serve it with twice-baked potatoes and a spinach salad.

—Janet Singleton, Bellevue, Ohio

GRILLED FAJITAS WITH PICO DE GALLO

3 **tablespoons lime juice, *divided***

2 **tablespoons canola oil**

2 **garlic cloves, minced**

1 **boneless beef sirloin steak (3/4 inch thick and 1 pound)**

3/4 **cup diced zucchini**

3/4 **cup chopped tomato**

1/3 **cup picante sauce**

8 **flour tortillas (8 inches), warmed**

In a large resealable plastic bag, combine 2 tablespoons lime juice, oil and garlic; add steak. Seal bag and turn to coat; refrigerate for 30 minutes.

For pico de gallo, in a small bowl, combine the zucchini, tomato, picante sauce and remaining lime juice; set aside.

Drain and discard marinade. Grill steak, covered, over medium heat for 6-8 minutes on each side or until meat reaches desired doneness (for medium-rare, a meat thermometer should read 145°; medium, 160°; well-done, 170°).

Thinly slice steak across the grain; place on tortillas. Top with pico de gallo; roll up and serve immediately. **YIELD: 4 SERVINGS.**

This is a good recipe when you're pressed for time. The beef doesn't need to marinate very long before grilling, and the accompanying vegetable relish is easy to stir up with just a few ingredients. It makes a delicious meal.

—Christine Yost
    Copeland, Kansas

BEEF FILLETS WITH GRILLED VEGETABLES

4   beef tenderloin fillets (1-1/2 inches thick and 4 ounces *each*)

3   teaspoons pepper, *divided*

1/2 cup creamy Caesar salad dressing

8   to 12 romaine leaves

2   medium tomatoes, cut into 1-inch slices

1   medium onion, sliced

3   tablespoons olive oil

2   tablespoons butter, melted

1/2 teaspoon salt

Here's a special, quick and easy, end-of-summer grilled entree...with no pots or pans to clean! Romaine lettuce leaves are a must for this recipe because they stand up to grilling. Basting with butter seals in the meat's juices and adds extra flavor.

—Cindie Haras
  Boca Raton, Florida

Rub fillets with 2 teaspoons pepper; place in a large resealable plastic bag. Add salad dressing; seal bag and turn to coat. Refrigerate for 10 minutes.

Meanwhile, brush romaine, tomatoes and onion with oil. Grill tomatoes and onion, uncovered, over medium heat for 4-5 minutes on each side or until onion is crisp-tender. Grill romaine for 30 seconds on each side or until heated through. Wrap vegetables in foil and set aside.

Drain and discard marinade. Grill fillets, covered, over medium heat for 7-8 minutes on each side or until meat reaches desired doneness (for medium-rare, a meat thermometer should read 145°; medium, 160°; well-done, 170°), basting occasionally with butter.

Serve with the grilled vegetables. Sprinkle with the salt and remaining pepper. **YIELD: 4 SERVINGS.**

STUFFED BURGERS ON PORTOBELLOS

1	teaspoon Worcestershire sauce
1/2	teaspoon salt
1/2	teaspoon pepper
1-1/3	pounds ground beef
1/2	cup shredded cheddar cheese
5	bacon strips, cooked and crumbled
4	portobello mushroom caps (about 4 inch diameter)
1	tablespoon olive oil
4	lettuce leaves
4	tomato slices

In a large bowl, combine the Worcestershire sauce, salt and pepper. Crumble beef over mixture; mix well. Shape into eight thin patties. Combine cheese and bacon. Spoon into center of four patties. Top with remaining patties; press edges firmly to seal.

Grill, covered, over medium heat for 6 minutes on each side or until a meat thermometer reads 160° and juices run clear.

Meanwhile, remove mushroom stems if necessary; brush with oil. Grill, covered, over medium heat for 3-4 minutes on each side or until tender. Place mushrooms, rounded side down, on serving plates. Top each with tomato, lettuce and a burger. **YIELD: 4 SERVINGS.**

Here' a low-carb treat that allows my husband and me to still enjoy burgers without compromising any of the taste. It's actually a combination of several recipes pulled together into one...and no one misses the bun.

—Debbie Driggers
Greenville, Texas

Our home economists treat these tender steaks to a buttery topping that's mixed with garlic, parsley and cumin. Delicious!

—Taste of Home Test Kitchen

GRILLED SIRLOIN STEAKS

2	tablespoons prepared mustard
1/4	teaspoon pepper
4	boneless beef petite sirloin steaks (5 ounces *each*)
1/4	cup butter, softened
3	tablespoons minced fresh parsley
1	teaspoon minced garlic
1/2	teaspoon ground cumin

Combine mustard and pepper; rub over both sides of steaks. Grill, covered, over medium heat or broil 4 in. from the heat for 4-5 minutes on each side or until meat reaches desired doneness (for medium-rare, a meat thermometer should read 145°; medium, 160°; well-done, 170°).

In a small bowl, combine the butter, parsley, garlic and cumin. Serve with steaks. **YIELD: 4 SERVINGS**.

STEAK WITH CHIPOTLE-LIME CHIMICHURRI

- 2 cups chopped fresh parsley
- 1-1/2 cups chopped fresh cilantro
- 1 small red onion, quartered
- 5 garlic cloves, quartered
- 2 chipotle peppers in adobo sauce
- 1/2 cup plus 5 tablespoons olive oil, *divided*
- 1/4 cup white wine vinegar
- 1/4 cup lime juice
- 1 tablespoon dried oregano
- 1 teaspoon grated lime peel
- 1-1/4 teaspoons salt, *divided*
- 3/4 teaspoon pepper, *divided*
- 2 beef flat iron steaks *or* top sirloin steaks (1 pound *each*)

For chimichurri, place the parsley, cilantro, onion, garlic and chipotle peppers in a food processor; cover and pulse until minced. Add 1/2 cup oil, vinegar, lime juice, oregano, lime peel, 1/2 teaspoon salt and 1/4 teaspoon pepper; cover and process until blended. Cover and refrigerate until serving.

Drizzle steaks with remaining oil; sprinkle with remaining salt and pepper. Grill, covered, over medium heat for 8-10 minutes on each side or until meat reaches desired doneness (for medium-rare, a meat thermometer should read 145°; medium, 160°; well-done, 170°). Thinly slice steaks across the grain; serve with the chimichurri. **YIELD: 8 SERVINGS.**

Steak gets a flavor kick from chimichurri. This piquant all-purpose herb sauce is so versatile, it complements most any grilled meat, poultry or fish.

—Laureen Pittman, Riverside, California

CAMPFIRE TACO SALAD

- 6 snack-size bags (1-1/2 ounces *each*) corn chips
- 1 can (15 ounces) chili without beans
- 3 cups (12 ounces) shredded cheddar cheese
- 3/4 cup sour cream
- 1 jar (8 ounces) mild salsa
- 1/2 medium head iceberg lettuce, shredded

Served in a corn chip bag, this easy outdoor meal is flavorful and fun. My neighbor entertained Girl Scouts with this clever recipe.

—Jean Komlos
Plymouth, Michigan

Cut the top off each bag of chips; set aside. Place chili in a saucepan; cook on a grill over medium heat for 10 minutes or until heated through, stirring occasionally. Spoon about 2 tablespoons of chili into each bag of chips. Top with cheese, sour cream, salsa and lettuce. **YIELD: 6 SERVINGS.**

BEEF GRILLING CHART

When cooking beef, a meat thermometer should read 145° for medium-rare, 160° for medium and 170° for well-done. Ground beef should be 160°. For direct grilling, turn meat halfway through grilling time. The cooking times given below are a guideline and are for medium-rare to medium doneness. Check for doneness with a meat thermometer or other appropriate doneness test.

CUT	WEIGHT OR THICKNESS	HEAT	APPROXIMATE COOKING TIME
RIBEYE STEAK	1 in.	medium/direct	11 to 14 minutes
	1-1/2 in.	medium/direct	17 to 22 minutes
T-BONE, PORTERHOUSE OR BONELESS TOP LOIN (STRIP)	3/4 in.	medium/direct	10 to 12 minutes
	1 in.	medium/direct	15 to 18 minutes
	1-1/2 in.	medium/direct	19 to 23 minutes
TENDERLOIN STEAK	1 in.	medium/direct	13 to 15 minutes
	1-1/2 in.	medium/direct	14 to 16 minutes
TOP SIRLOIN STEAK	1 in.	medium/direct	17 to 21 minutes
	1-1/2 in.	medium/direct	22 to 26 minutes
	2 in.	medium/direct	28 to 33 minutes
FLANK STEAK*	1-1/2 to 2 lbs.	medium/direct	12 to 15 minutes
SKIRT STEAK	1/4 to 1/2 in.	high/direct	6 to 8 minutes
TOP ROUND STEAK*	1 in.	medium/direct	16 to 18 minutes
CHUCK SHOULDER STEAK*	1 in.	medium/direct	16 to 20 minutes
TENDERLOIN ROAST	2 to 3 lbs.	medium-hot/indirect	45 to 60 minutes
	4 to 5 lbs.	medium-hot/indirect	1 to 1-1/4 hours
TRI-TIP ROAST	1-3/4 to 2 lbs.	medium/indirect	35 to 45 minutes
GROUND BEEF OR VEAL PATTY	4 oz. and 1/2 in.	medium/indirect	11 to 14 minutes

*These cuts of meat are best when marinated before grilling.

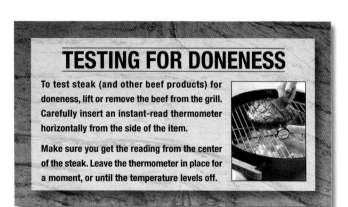

SANTA MARIA ROAST BEEF

4	tablespoons paprika
3	tablespoons brown sugar
2	tablespoons chili powder
1	tablespoon garlic powder
1	tablespoon white pepper
1	tablespoon celery salt
1	tablespoon ground cumin
1	tablespoon dried oregano
1	tablespoon pepper
2	teaspoons cayenne pepper
1	teaspoon ground mustard
1	beef tri-tip roast *or* beef sirloin tip roast (2 to 3 pounds)
2	cups soaked hickory wood chips *or* chunks
2	tablespoons canola oil

Combine the first 11 ingredients; rub desired amount over roast. Wrap in plastic wrap and refrigerate overnight. Store leftover dry rub in an airtight container for up to 6 months.

Remove roast from the refrigerator 1 hour before grilling. Prepare grill for indirect heat, using a drip pan. Add wood chips according to manufacturer's directions.

Unwrap roast and brush with oil; place over drip pan. Grill, covered, over medium-low indirect heat for 1 to 1-1/2 hours or until meat reaches desired doneness (for medium-rare, a meat thermometer should read 145°; medium, 160°; well-done, 170°). Let stand for 10-15 minutes before slicing. **YIELD: 6 SERVINGS.**

TESTING FOR DONENESS

To test steak (and other beef products) for doneness, lift or remove the beef from the grill. Carefully insert an instant-read thermometer horizontally from the side of the item.

Make sure you get the reading from the center of the steak. Leave the thermometer in place for a moment, or until the temperature levels off.

BEEF KABOBS WITH CHUTNEY SAUCE

1/2	cup plain yogurt
3	tablespoons mango chutney
1	teaspoon lemon juice
1/2	teaspoon curry powder
1/4	teaspoon ground cumin
1/8	teaspoon cayenne pepper

MARINATED BEEF:

1/4	cup mango chutney
1	tablespoon cider vinegar
1	tablespoon water
1	teaspoon curry powder
1/4	teaspoon cayenne pepper
1	pound beef top sirloin steak, cut into 1/4-inch strips

For sauce, in a small bowl, combine the first six ingredients. Cover and refrigerate until serving.

For marinade, in a large resealable plastic bag, combine the chutney, vinegar, water, curry and cayenne; add beef. Seal bag and turn to coat; refrigerate overnight.

Coat grill rack with cooking spray before starting the grill. Drain and discard marinade. Thread beef onto eight metal or soaked wooden skewers.

Grill kabobs, covered, over medium heat for 4-6 minutes or until meat reaches desired doneness, turning occasionally. Serve with dipping sauce. **YIELD: 8 KABOBS (ABOUT 1/2 CUP SAUCE).**

I created this speedy grilled entree for our daughter, a fan of Indian food. The mango chutney and subtle curry give the beef a delightful sweet and spicy flavor.

—Judy Thompson
Ankeny, Iowa

INDIVIDUAL CAMPFIRE STEW

1	egg, lightly beaten
1/4	cup ketchup
1	tablespoon Worcestershire sauce
3/4	cup dry bread crumbs
1	teaspoon seasoned salt
1	pound lean ground beef
2	cups frozen shredded hash brown potatoes, thawed
1	cup diced carrots
1	cup condensed cream of chicken soup, undiluted
1/4	cup milk

These pretty parcels are perfect for grilling or whipping up over a campfire. I can get several outdoor chores done while they're cooking outside.

—Margaret Rile
Tallahassee, Florida

Prepare grill for indirect heat. In a large bowl, combine the first five ingredients. Crumble beef over mixture and mix well. Shape into four patties. Place each patty on a greased double thickness of heavy-duty foil (about 12 in. square); sprinkle each with potatoes and carrots.

Combine soup and milk; spoon over meat and vegetables. Fold foil around mixture and seal tightly. Grill, covered, over indirect medium heat for 25-30 minutes or until a meat thermometer reads 160° and juices run clear. Open foil carefully to allow steam to escape. **YIELD: 4 SERVINGS.**

FILLETS WITH MUSHROOM SAUCE

4	beef tenderloin fillets (4 ounces *each*)
1	large onion, cut into 1/2-inch slices
1/2	pound fresh mushrooms, thickly sliced
2	tablespoons butter
1	can (14-1/2 ounces) diced tomatoes, undrained
1/4	cup water
1/2	teaspoon dried basil
1/2	teaspoon beef bouillon granules
1/8	teaspoon pepper

Grill steaks, covered, over medium heat for 6-9 minutes on each side or until meat reaches desired doneness (for medium-rare, a meat thermometer should read 145°; medium, 160°; well-done, 170°).

Meanwhile, in a large skillet, saute onion and mushrooms in butter until tender. Stir in the tomatoes, water, basil, bouillon and pepper. Bring to a boil; cook and stir over medium heat for 5 minutes or until thickened. Serve with beef. **YIELD: 4 SERVINGS.**

Grilled tenderloin steaks get an extra special treatment with the onion, mushroom and tomato sauce in this recipe. The sauce can be thrown together while the meat is on the grill for a special and quick main dish.

—Carolyn Brinkmeyer, Aurora, Colorado

MARINATED CHUCK STEAK

- 1/2   cup red wine vinegar
- 1/2   cup soy sauce
- 2   tablespoons lemon juice
- 1   tablespoon brown sugar
- 1   tablespoon Worcestershire sauce
- 2   garlic cloves, minced
- 1/4   teaspoon onion powder
- 2   pounds boneless chuck steak

In a large resealable plastic bag, combine the first seven ingredients. Add the beef; seal bag and turn to coat. Refrigerate for 8 hours or overnight.

Drain and discard marinade. Grill steak, covered, over medium heat for 8-10 minutes on each side or until meat reaches desired doneness (for medium-rare, a meat thermometer should read 145°; medium, 160°; well-done, 170°). Let stand for 10 minutes before slicing. **YIELD: 6 SERVINGS.**

You can turn an inexpensive cut of beef into a real treat with this easy marinade. It tenderizes and really boosts the flavor.

—Karen Haen
Sturgeon Bay,
Wisconsin

By using ingredients such as beef tenderloin, crabmeat and fresh asparagus, I easily grill up an elegant entree. Asparagus Steak Oscar is a fine recipe combining the delicious taste of asparagus with the finest of steaks.

—Cindy Dorsett, Lubbock, Texas

ASPARAGUS STEAK OSCAR

- 1   envelope bearnaise sauce
- 1   pound fresh asparagus, trimmed
- 1/4   pound fresh crabmeat
- 2   tablespoons butter
- 1/2   teaspoon minced garlic
- 1   tablespoon lemon juice
- 4   beef tenderloin steaks (1 inch thick and 3 ounces *each*)
- 1/8   teaspoon paprika

Prepare bearnaise sauce according to package directions. Meanwhile, place asparagus in a steamer basket; place in a large saucepan over 1 in. of water. Bring to a boil; cover and steam for 8-10 minutes or until crisp-tender.

In a large skillet, saute crab in butter for 3-4 minutes or until heated through. Add garlic; cook 1 minute longer. Stir in lemon juice; keep warm.

Grill steaks, covered, over medium heat or broil 4 in. from the heat for 6-8 minutes on each side or until meat reaches desired doneness (for medium-rare, a meat thermometer should read 145°; medium, 160°; well-done, 170°). Top with crab mixture, asparagus and bearnaise sauce. Sprinkle with paprika. **YIELD: 4 SERVINGS.**

STEAKS WITH MUSHROOM SAUCE FOR 2

2	beef top sirloin steaks (6 ounces *each*)
1/8	teaspoon salt
1/8	teaspoon pepper

SAUCE:

1/2	cup jarred sliced mushrooms
1/2	teaspoon canola oil
1/2	teaspoon minced garlic
1/4	cup French onion dip
1	tablespoon half-and-half cream
1/4	teaspoon minced chives
1/8	teaspoon pepper

Sprinkle steaks with salt and pepper. Grill steaks, covered, over medium heat or broil 4 in. from heat for 5-7 minutes on each side or until meat reaches desired doneness (for medium-rare, a meat thermometer should read 145°; medium, 160°; well-done, 170°).

In a small skillet, saute mushrooms in oil for 3 minutes. Add garlic; cook 1 minute longer. Stir in the onion dip, cream, chives and pepper. Bring to a gentle boil. Reduce heat; simmer, uncovered, for 2-3 minutes or until heated through. Serve with steaks. **YIELD: 2 SERVINGS.**

A versatile sauce tops these sirloin steaks and enhances their beefy flavor. It would also taste great over grilled chicken or pork.

—LaDonna Reed, Ponca City, Oklahoma

Be prepared for guests to ask for the recipe for this spicy steak. I've handed copies to many friends.

—Lorna Byrd
Colorado Springs,
Colorado

TAOS STEAK

1-1/2	teaspoons paprika
1	teaspoon fennel seeds
1/2	teaspoon whole peppercorns
1/4	teaspoon white pepper
1/8	teaspoon cayenne pepper
1	beef top sirloin steak (1 inch thick and 1-1/2 pounds)
6	slices Havarti cheese
1/3	cup green chili salsa

In a spice grinder or with a mortar and pestle, combine the first five ingredients; grind until mixture becomes a fine powder. Rub over both sides of steak.

Grill, covered, over medium heat for 8-11 minutes on each side or until meat reaches desired doneness (for medium-rare, a meat thermometer should read 145°; medium, 160°; well-done, 170°).

Top with cheese; cover and grill for 1-2 minutes or until cheese is melted. Let stand for 5 minutes before slicing. Top with salsa. **YIELD: 6 SERVINGS.**

GRILLED BURGERS

1	egg, lightly beaten
1/2	cup 4% cottage cheese
1	cup cooked long grain rice
1	small onion, finely chopped
1/2	cup shredded cheddar cheese
2	tablespoons plus 1-1/2 teaspoons gluten-free onion soup mix
2	tablespoons gluten-free all-purpose baking flour
2	tablespoons grated Parmesan cheese
1-1/2	teaspoons gluten-free Worcestershire sauce
3	garlic cloves, minced
1/2	teaspoon salt
1/4	teaspoon pepper
1-1/2	pounds ground beef

Sliced tomatoes, lettuce leaves and sliced onions, optional

In a large bowl, combine the first 12 ingredients. Crumble beef over mixture and mix well. Shape into 10 patties.

Grill, uncovered, over medium-hot heat for 5-6 minutes on each side or until a meat thermometer reads 160° and juices run clear. Serve with the tomatoes, lettuce and onions if desired. **YIELD: 10 SERVINGS.**

EDITOR'S NOTE: Ingredient formulas and production facilities vary among brands. If you're concerned that your brand may contain gluten, contact the company.

No way did I want to give up juicy, delicious hamburgers when I learned that I needed to start to eat gluten-free. I made a few adjustments to my recipe to meet the requirements—and the family has also given these wonderful burgers their hearty approval.

—Peggy Gwillim
Strasbourg,
Saskatchewan

BARBECUED CHUCK ROAST

- 1/4   cup red wine vinegar
- 1/4   cup ketchup
- 2   tablespoons reduced-sodium soy sauce
- 1   tablespoon Worcestershire sauce
- 2   teaspoons canola oil
- 1   teaspoon brown sugar
- 1   teaspoon prepared mustard
- 1/4   teaspoon garlic salt
- 1/4   teaspoon pepper
- 1   boneless beef chuck roast (1-1/2 pounds), trimmed

I won first place in a local recipe contest with this tasty roast. It's great for just the two of us or for company. I usually serve it with baked potatoes and corn on the cob.

—Bette Roman
Brookfield, Illinois

In a small bowl, combine the first nine ingredients. Pour 1/4 cup into a large re-sealable plastic bag; add roast. Seal bag and turn to coat; refrigerate for 2-3 hours, turning several times. Cover and refrigerate remaining marinade for basting.

Prepare grill for indirect heat, using a drip pan. Coat grill rack with cooking spray before starting the grill. Drain and discard marinade.

Grill beef, covered, over indirect medium heat for 1-1/2 to 1-3/4 hours or until tender, turning and basting occasionally with reserved marinade. Cut into thin slices. **YIELD: 5 SERVINGS.**

SIZZLING BEEF KABOBS

- 1/3   cup canola oil
- 1/4   cup soy sauce
- 2   tablespoons red wine vinegar
- 2   teaspoons garlic powder
- 2   pounds beef top sirloin steak, cut into 1-inch pieces
- 2   medium yellow summer squash, cut into 1/2-inch slices
- 1   large onion, cut into 1-inch chunks
- 1   large green pepper, cut into 1-inch pieces
- 1   large sweet red pepper, cut into 1-inch pieces

In a large resealable plastic bag, combine the oil, soy sauce, vinegar and garlic powder; add beef. Seal bag and turn to coat; refrigerate for at least 1 hour.

Drain and discard marinade. On eight metal or soaked wooden skewers, alternately thread beef and vegetables. Grill, covered, over medium-hot heat or broil 4-6 in. from the heat for 8-10 minutes or until meat reaches desired doneness, turning occasionally. **YIELD: 8 SERVINGS.**

With colorful chunks of yellow squash and sweet red and green peppers, these tender beef and veggie kabobs are perfect party fare. A mild soy sauce marinade lends an appealing flavor.

—Kathy Spang, Manheim, Pennsylvania

SAVORY GRILLED T-BONES

- 1/4 **cup chopped onion**
- 1/4 **cup olive oil**
-   2 **tablespoons lemon juice**
-   2 **tablespoons soy sauce**
-   1 **tablespoon sugar**
-   1 **tablespoon cider vinegar**
-   1 **tablespoon honey**
-   2 **teaspoons minced garlic**
-   2 **teaspoons Worcestershire sauce**
-   1 **teaspoon salt**
- 1/2 **teaspoon pepper**
-   6 **beef T-bone steaks (1 inch thick and 12 ounces *each*)**

Marinated and grilled to perfection, these must-try steaks are melt-in-your-mouth delicious. Don't let summer go by without grilling them up.

—Anna Davis, Half Way, Missouri

In a large resealable plastic bag, combine the first 11 ingredients; add steaks. Seal bag and turn to coat; refrigerate for 2-4 hours.

Drain and discard marinade. Grill steaks, covered, over medium heat for 6-10 minutes on each side or until meat reaches desired doneness (for medium-rare, a meat thermometer should read 145°; medium, 160°; well-done, 170°). **YIELD: 6 SERVINGS.**

SUCCULENT BEEF SKEWERS

-   2 **teaspoons Dijon mustard**
-   2 **teaspoons balsamic vinegar**
-   1 **teaspoon packed brown sugar**
-   1 **teaspoon olive oil**
-   1 **teaspoon minced fresh rosemary *or* 1/4 teaspoon dried rosemary, crushed**
- 1/2 **teaspoon minced fresh thyme *or* dash dried thyme**
-   1 **garlic clove, minced**
- 1/8 **teaspoon salt**
- 1/8 **teaspoon pepper**
- 1/2 **pound beef top sirloin steak, cut into 1-1/2-inch cubes**

In a large resealable plastic bag, combine the first nine ingredients. Add the beef; seal bag and turn to coat. Refrigerate for at least 2 hours or overnight, turning occasionally. Drain and discard marinade.

Coat grill rack with cooking spray before starting the grill. Thread beef onto metal or soaked wooden skewers. Grill, covered, over medium-hot heat for 8-10 minutes or until beef reaches desired doneness, turning occasionally. **YIELD: 6 SKEWERS.**

These are no ordinary beef kabobs! They're herb-infused and need to marinate a few hours or overnight for the best flavor. If you feel like splurging, this recipe's also fantastic with beef tenderloin.

—Agnes Ward
  Stratford, Ontario

MAPLE & BLUE CHEESE STEAK

6	tablespoons balsamic vinegar
6	tablespoons maple syrup, *divided*
2	tablespoons plus 1-1/2 teaspoons Dijon mustard
1	tablespoon minced fresh thyme *or* 1/4 teaspoon dried thyme
1/2	pound beef top sirloin steak
2	tablespoons chopped pecans
1-1/2	teaspoons olive oil
1/8	teaspoon salt
1/8	teaspoon pepper
1/4	cup crumbled blue cheese

Here's a wonderful, cheesy recipe that melts in your mouth. I love this traditional Canadian meal. It certainly has a special feel; the sauce is a fantastic complement to steak.

—Susan Jerrott
  Bedford, Nova Scotia

In a small bowl, combine the vinegar, 5 tablespoons maple syrup, mustard and thyme. Pour 2/3 cup marinade into a large resealable plastic bag; add the steak. Seal bag and turn to coat; refrigerate for up to 3 hours. Cover and refrigerate remaining marinade.

Meanwhile, in a small skillet, saute pecans in oil until toasted. Stir in remaining maple syrup. Bring to a boil; cook for 1 minute, stirring constantly. Remove from skillet and spread onto waxed paper to cool completely.

Drain and discard marinade. Sprinkle steak with salt and pepper. Grill, over medium heat, for 4-6 minutes on each side or until meat reaches desired doneness (for medium-rare, a meat thermometer should read 145°; medium, 160°; well-done, 170°). Let stand for 5 minutes before slicing.

Place reserved marinade in small saucepan. Bring to a boil; cook until liquid is reduced to 1/4 cup, about 2 minutes. Divide steak slices between two plates. Drizzle with sauce; sprinkle with blue cheese and pecans. **YIELD: 2 SERVINGS.**

GRILLED RED CHILI STEAK

3	tablespoons chili powder
2	teaspoons brown sugar
2	teaspoons pepper
2	garlic cloves, minced
1/2	teaspoon salt
1/2	teaspoon dried oregano
1/4	teaspoon ground cumin
1	pound beef top sirloin steak

Salsa

Combine the first seven ingredients; rub over steak.

Grill steak, covered, over medium heat for 5-7 minutes on each side or until meat reaches desired doneness (for medium-rare, a meat thermometer should read 145°; medium, 160°; well-done, 170°). Let stand for 10 minutes before slicing. Serve with salsa. **YIELD: 4 SERVINGS.**

This super-simple recipe turns regular steak into a mouthwatering entree. I like it best with ground chili powder and a little cumin.

—Mary Relyea
  Canastota, New York

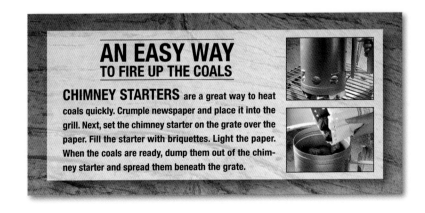

AN EASY WAY
TO FIRE UP THE COALS

CHIMNEY STARTERS are a great way to heat coals quickly. Crumple newspaper and place it into the grill. Next, set the chimney starter on the grate over the paper. Fill the starter with briquettes. Light the paper. When the coals are ready, dump them out of the chimney starter and spread them beneath the grate.

GRILLED BBQ MEATBALL PIZZAS

- 2 cups all-purpose flour
- 1 package (1/4 ounce) quick-rise yeast
- 1/2 teaspoon sugar
- 1/2 teaspoon salt
- 3/4 cup warm water (120° to 130°)
- 1 tablespoon olive oil
- 20 frozen cooked Italian meatballs (1/2 ounce *each*)
- 1/2 cup barbecue sauce
- 1/4 cup apricot preserves
- 2 cups (8 ounces) shredded Colby-Monterey Jack cheese
- 1/4 cup thinly sliced green onions

In a large bowl, combine the flour, yeast, sugar and salt. Add water and oil; mix until a soft dough forms. Turn onto a floured surface; knead until smooth and elastic, about 6-8 minutes. Cover and let stand for 15 minutes.

Meanwhile, cook meatballs according to package directions. Cut each meatball in half. In a large bowl, combine barbecue sauce and preserves. Add meatball halves; stir to coat.

Divide dough into fourths. Roll each portion into a 6-in. circle. Coat grill rack with cooking spray before starting the grill.

Grill dough, covered, over medium heat for 1-2 minutes or until the crust is lightly browned. Remove from grill.

Layer the grilled side of each pizza with meatball mixture, cheese and onions. Return pizzas to grill. Cover and cook for 4-5 minutes or until crust is lightly browned and cheese is melted. **YIELD: 4 PIZZAS.**

Be the hit of the party with these tasty treats featuring the ever-popular frozen meatball. You won't believe how much great grill flavor comes through.

—Willie DeWaard, Coralville, Iowa

SPINACH-MUSHROOM BEEF PATTIES

- 1 package (10 ounces) frozen chopped spinach, thawed and squeezed dry
- 1 cup (4 ounces) shredded part-skim mozzarella cheese
- 1 cup chopped fresh mushrooms
- 1 envelope onion mushroom soup mix
- 2 pounds ground beef

Whether grilled or broiled, these hearty patties that are flecked with spinach and cheese are always a yummy summertime favorite.

—Jan Komarek
Friendswood, Texas

In a large bowl, combine the spinach, cheese, mushrooms and soup mix. Crumble beef over mixture and mix well. Shape into eight patties.

Grill, covered, over medium-hot heat for 5-7 minutes on each side or until a meat thermometer reads 160° and juices run clear. **YIELD: 8 SERVINGS.**

FIESTA RIBEYE STEAKS

- 8 flour tortillas (6 inches)
- 8 beef ribeye steaks (3/4 inch thick and 8 ounces *each*)
- 1/4 cup lime juice
- 1 cup (4 ounces) shredded Colby-Monterey Jack cheese
- 2 cups salsa

Place tortillas on a sheet of heavy-duty foil (about 18 in. x 12 in.). Fold foil around tortillas and seal tightly; set aside.

Drizzle both sides of steaks with the lime juice. Grill, covered, over medium-hot heat for 7-9 minutes on each side or until the meat reaches desired doneness (for medium-rare, a meat thermometer should read 145°; medium, 160°; well-done, 170°).

Place tortillas on outer edge of grill; heat for 5-6 minutes, turning once. Sprinkle cheese over steaks; serve with salsa and warmed tortillas. **YIELD: 8 SERVINGS.**

This is a great recipe for grilling out or for camping trips. Adapt it for indoors by cooking the steaks in a skillet and heating the tortillas in a warm oven.

—Jodee Harding
Granville, Ohio

SIRLOIN WITH BLUE CHEESE BUTTER

- 1/2 cup crumbled blue cheese
- 1/4 cup butter, softened
- 1/4 cup chopped walnuts, toasted
- 2 tablespoons minced fresh parsley
- 1-3/4 teaspoons minced fresh rosemary, *divided*
- 6 large garlic cloves, peeled
- 1/4 teaspoon salt
- 1/4 teaspoon pepper
- 2 boneless beef sirloin steaks (6 ounces *each*)

In a small bowl, combine the blue cheese, butter, walnuts, parsley and 3/4 teaspoon rosemary. Shape into a 5-in. log; wrap in plastic wrap. Refrigerate for 30 minutes or until firm.

In a small food processor, combine the garlic cloves, salt, pepper and remaining rosemary. Cover and process until blended. Rub over both sides of steaks.

Grill steaks, covered, over medium heat or broil 4-6 in. from the heat for 5-6 minutes on each side or until meat reaches desired doneness (for medium-rare, a meat thermometer should read 145°; medium, 160°; well-done, 170°).

Unwrap blue cheese butter; cut two 1/2-in. slices from log. Place one slice on each steak. Rewrap remaining butter; refrigerate for 1 week or freeze for up to 3 months. **YIELD: 2 SERVINGS.**

Few meats are as juicy as a perfectly grilled steak. And when you top a tender sirloin with a savory blue cheese and walnut butter, it's even more memorable.

—Sharon Johnson
Minneapolis, Minnesota

CAESAR NEW YORK STRIPS

4 tablespoons creamy Caesar salad dressing, *divided*
2 teaspoons garlic powder
1 teaspoon salt
1 teaspoon coarsely ground pepper
2 boneless beef top loin steaks (12 ounces *each*)

In a small bowl, combine 2 tablespoons salad dressing, garlic powder, salt and pepper. Spoon over both sides of steaks.

Grill, covered, over medium heat or broil 4 in. from the heat for 7-9 minutes on each side or until meat reaches desired doneness (for medium-rare, a meat thermometer should read 145°; medium, 160°; well-done, 170°), basting occasionally with remaining salad dressing. Cut steaks in half to serve. **YIELD: 4 SERVINGS.**

EDITOR'S NOTE: Top loin steak may be labeled as strip steak, Kansas City steak, New York strip steak, ambassador steak or boneless club steak in your region.

I season New York strip steaks with a Caesar dressing mixture, then grill them for a tasty entree that's ready in minutes. For a side dish, serve baked potatoes topped with chunky salsa and sour cream.

—Melissa Morton
   Philadelphia, Pennsylvania

Kids usually love anything with the word "pizza" attached to it, so I came up with this top-your-own pizza burger recipe. Because the burgers are made on the grill, they add variety to pizza night at our house and go over well with us big kids, too.

—Robin Kornegay
   Seffner, Florida

PIZZA BURGERS

1 package (11-1/4 ounces) frozen garlic Texas toast
1-3/4 pounds ground beef
1 cup pizza sauce, *divided*
18 slices pepperoni
12 sliced part-skim mozzarella cheese, *divided*
6 teaspoons grated Parmesan cheese
1 cup sliced fresh mushrooms
2 teaspoons butter
Sliced green pepper and ripe olives, optional

Prepare six Texas toast slices according to package directions. Save remaining Texas toast for another use. Meanwhile, shape beef into 12 thin patties.

Top six patties with 1 tablespoon pizza sauce, three slices of pepperoni, and one slice of mozzarella cheese. Top with remaining patties; press edges firmly to seal.

Grill, covered, over medium heat for 8 minutes on each side or until a meat thermometer reads 160° and juices run clear. Meanwhile, in a small skillet, saute mushrooms in butter.

Top each burger with a rounded tablespoonful pizza sauce and one mozzarella cheese slice. Cover and cook 3 minutes longer or until cheese is melted. Top prepared Texas toast with green pepper slices if desired, burgers, sauteed mushrooms, olives and Parmesan cheese. **YIELD: 6 SERVINGS.**

BEEF FAJITAS WITH CILANTRO SAUCE

4	tablespoons lime juice, *divided*
3	tablespoons olive oil, *divided*
2	tablespoons minced fresh thyme
1	tablespoon hot pepper sauce
1	beef top sirloin steak (1-1/2 pounds)
1-1/2	cups fat-free plain yogurt
1/2	cup fresh cilantro leaves
1	jalapeno pepper, seeded
2	large green peppers, halved
2	large onions, thickly sliced
8	flour tortillas (6 inches), warmed

Shredded lettuce, tomato wedges and sliced ripe olives, optional

In a large resealable plastic bag, combine 3 tablespoons lime juice, 2 tablespoons oil, thyme and hot pepper sauce. Add the beef; seal bag and turn to coat. Refrigerate for at least 2 hours.

For sauce, place the yogurt, cilantro, jalapeno and remaining lime juice in a blender; cover and process until smooth. Transfer to a small bowl; refrigerate until serving. Brush green peppers and onions with remaining oil; set aside.

Drain and discard marinade. Grill beef, uncovered, over medium-hot heat for 6-7 minutes on each side or until meat reaches desired doneness (for medium-rare, a meat thermometer should read 145°; medium, 160°; well-done, 170°). Let stand for 10 minutes before slicing.

Meanwhile, grill green peppers and onions, uncovered, over medium-hot heat for 5 minutes on each side or until crisp-tender. Cut into strips; spoon onto tortillas. Top with sliced beef. Serve with cilantro sauce. Garnish with lettuce, tomatoes and olives if desired. Fold in sides. **YIELD: 8 SERVINGS.**

EDITOR'S NOTE: When cutting hot peppers, disposable gloves are recommended. Avoid touching your face.

I found this recipe in the local newspaper and made some variations. The jalapeno pepper gives just the slightest bit of zing to the otherwise cool, refreshing sauce.

—Rebecca Sodergren
Wichita Falls, Texas

MARDI GRAS BEEF

- 1 medium onion, chopped
- 1 small green pepper, cut into strips
- 1 teaspoon dried thyme
- 2 teaspoons garlic powder, *divided*
- 2 tablespoons canola oil
- 1 to 1-1/2 pounds sirloin steak (1 inch thick)
- 1 can (14-1/2 ounces) stewed tomatoes, juice drained and reserved
- 2 teaspoons cornstarch

Salt and pepper to taste

In a large skillet, saute onion, green pepper, thyme and 1/2 teaspoon garlic powder in oil until vegetables are crisp-tender. Meanwhile, sprinkle steak with remaining garlic powder.

Grill or broil steak 5 in. from the heat for 3-4 minutes (for medium-rare), on each side, or until desired doneness is reached.

Add tomatoes to skillet. Combine reserved tomato juice and cornstarch; add to vegetable mixture. Cook and stir for 2 minutes or until thickened. Season to taste with salt and pepper. Thinly slice meat; serve with vegetables. **YIELD: 4 SERVINGS.**

My beef recipe tastes great straight from the grill, which also speeds cleanup. The seasoning and vegetables give the beef a wonderful summertime twist.

—Lucy Meryring
Walden, Colorado

GRILLED STUFFED MEAT LOAF

2 cups sliced fresh mushrooms

1 medium onion, thinly sliced

1 tablespoon butter

1 egg, lightly beaten

1/3 cup milk

1/2 cup old-fashioned oats

1/2 teaspoon salt

1/4 teaspoon pepper

1-1/2 pounds ground beef

SAUCE:

1/2 cup ketchup

2 tablespoons brown sugar

2 teaspoons prepared mustard

A twist on traditional meat loaf, this dish lets you get out of the kitchen to enjoy the summer sun. My husband loves this dinner served with grilled corn on the cob.

—Melissa Maseda
Dixon, California

In a large skillet, saute mushrooms and onion in butter until tender; set aside.

In a large bowl, combine the egg, milk, oats, salt and pepper. Crumble beef over mixture and mix well. On a large piece of heavy-duty foil, pat beef mixture into a 12-in. x 8-in. rectangle; spoon mushroom mixture to within 1 in. of edges. Roll up jelly-roll style, starting with a short side and peeling foil away while rolling. Seal seam and ends. Discard foil.

Prepare grill for indirect heat, using a drip pan. Form a double thickness of heavy-duty foil (about 14 in. square); cut three slits in foil. Place meat loaf on foil; place on the grill rack over drip pan.

Grill, covered, over indirect medium heat for 35 minutes. Combine sauce ingredients; brush over loaf. Grill 15-20 minutes longer or until meat is no longer pink and a meat thermometer reads 160°. Let stand for 15 minutes before slicing. **YIELD: 8 SERVINGS.**

COLOSSAL CORNBURGER

1	egg, lightly beaten
1	cup cooked whole kernel corn
1/2	cup coarsely crushed cheese crackers
1/4	cup sliced green onions
1/4	cup chopped fresh parsley
1	teaspoon Worcestershire sauce
2	pounds ground beef
1	teaspoon salt
1/2	teaspoon pepper
1/2	teaspoon rubbed sage

In a medium bowl, combine the egg, corn, crackers, green onions, parsley and Worcestershire sauce; set aside. In a large bowl, combine the ground beef and the seasonings.

On sheets of waxed paper, pat half of the beef mixture at a time into an 8-1/2-in. circle. Spoon corn mixture onto one circle of meat to within 1 in. of the edge. Top with second circle of meat; remove top sheet of waxed paper and seal edges. Invert onto a well-greased wire grill basket; peel off waxed paper.

Grill, covered, over medium heat for 12-15 minutes on each side or until a meat thermometer reads 160° and juices run clear. For oven method, place burger on a baking pan. Bake at 350° for 40-45 minutes or until a meat thermometer reads 160° and juices run clear. Cut into wedges to serve. **YIELD: 6 SERVINGS.**

It's been such a long time since I added this incredible recipe to my file that I don't even remember where it came from!

—Louise Schmid
    Marshall, Minnesota

GRILLED SIRLOIN ROAST

3	tablespoons all-purpose flour		1/4	teaspoon pepper
3/4	cup ketchup		1	beef sirloin tip roast (3 pounds)
4-1/2	teaspoons Worcestershire sauce		1	pound fresh baby carrots
1	tablespoon brown sugar		2	medium tomatoes, quartered
1	tablespoon cider vinegar		1	medium onion, quartered
1-1/4	teaspoons salt, *divided*			
1/2	teaspoon prepared mustard			

In a small bowl, combine the flour, ketchup, Worcestershire sauce, brown sugar, vinegar, 1 teaspoon salt and mustard until smooth; set aside. Sprinkle pepper and remaining salt over roast.

Grill roast over medium heat for 5-10 minutes or until browned on all sides. Transfer to a heavy-duty 13-in. x 9-in. disposable foil pan. Pour reserved sauce over roast. Top with the carrots, tomatoes and onion. Cover pan with foil.

Grill over indirect medium heat for 3 to 3-1/2 hours or until meat is tender. **YIELD: 6-8 SERVINGS**.

My grandmother passed this recipe down to my mom, and it's a gem. The tasty sauce makes the beef and carrots so tender, and it's made with many ingredients you'll already have on hand. You won't want to eat pot roast any other way!

—Krista Smith Kliebenstei
    Westminster, Colorado

CAJUN BEEF TENDERLOIN

1	beef tenderloin roast (3 pounds)
4	teaspoons salt
1	tablespoon paprika
2-1/4	teaspoons onion powder
1-1/2	teaspoons garlic powder
1-1/2	teaspoons white pepper
1-1/2	teaspoons pepper
1	to 3 teaspoons cayenne pepper
1	teaspoon dried basil
1/2	teaspoon chili powder
1/8	teaspoon dried thyme
1/8	teaspoon ground mustard

Dash ground cloves

This spicy entree really warms up New Year's Eve, but it's fabulous any time of the year. The dry rub keeps the tenderloin nice and moist.

—Sue Dannahower
Parker, Colorado

Tie tenderloin at 2-in. intervals with kitchen string. Combine the seasonings; rub over beef roasts.

If grilling, prepare grill for indirect heat. Coat grill rack with cooking spray before starting the grill. Grill tenderloin, covered, over indirect medium heat for 50-60 minutes, turning occasionally, or until meat reaches desired doneness (for medium-rare, a meat thermometer should read 145°; medium, 160°; well-done, 170°). Let stand for 10 minutes before slicing.

To roast the tenderloin, bake on a rack in a shallow roasting pan at 425° for 45-60 minutes or until meat reaches desired doneness. **YIELD: 12 SERVINGS.**

FILET MIGNON WITH RED WINE SAUCE

1	medium onion, thinly sliced
3	tablespoons butter, *divided*
2	garlic cloves, minced
3/4	teaspoon salt, *divided*
1/2	teaspoon dried oregano
2	tablespoons tomato paste
1-1/4	cups dry red wine *or* beef broth
1/2	teaspoon pepper, *divided*
6	beef tenderloin steaks (4 to 6 ounces *each*)
3	tablespoons olive oil

In a large saucepan, saute onion in 1 tablespoon butter until tender. Add garlic, 1/4 teaspoon salt and oregano; cook and stir 1 minute. Add tomato paste; cook and stir 2 minutes longer.

Gradually whisk in wine. Bring to a boil. Reduce heat; simmer until reduced by half. Strain sauce and return to pan. Gradually stir in remaining butter until melted. Add 1/4 teaspoon pepper. Remove from the heat; keep warm.

Sprinkle steaks with remaining salt and pepper. Drizzle with oil. Grill, covered, over medium heat or broil 4 in. from the heat for 6-8 minutes on each side or until meat reaches desired doneness (for medium-rare, a meat thermometer should read 145°; medium, 160°; well-done, 170°). Cover and let stand for 3-5 minutes. Serve with wine sauce. **YIELD: 6 SERVINGS.**

If you need a company-pleasing entree, but have no time to fuss…let them eat steak! A savory wine sauce dresses up beef for any special occasion.

—Tarah Pessel, Clarkston, Michigan

ASIAN BEEF RIBBONS

A fellow nurse who also happens to be a fabulous cook shared this recipe with me. We like it served with steamed rice and stir-fried vegetables.

—Dianne Livingston
  Palo Cedro, California

1-1/2	pounds beef flank steak	1/4	teaspoon crushed red pepper flakes
1/4	cup teriyaki sauce	1	teaspoon sesame seeds, toasted
1	tablespoon canola oil		
2	garlic cloves, minced		
2	teaspoons minced fresh gingerroot		

Slice meat across the grain into 1/4-in. strips. In a large resealable plastic bag, combine the teriyaki sauce, oil, garlic, ginger and red pepper flakes; add meat. Seal bag and turn to coat; refrigerate for 8 hours or overnight, turning several times.

Coat grill rack with cooking spray before starting the grill. Drain and discard marinade. Thread meat onto metal or soaked wooden skewers.

Grill, covered, over medium heat for 2-4 minutes on each side or until desired doneness. Remove from grill and sprinkle with sesame seeds. **YIELD: 4 SERVINGS.**

COOKING METHODS FOR BEEF

CUT/TYPE	BRAISE	BROIL	GRILL	PAN-FRY	PAN-BROIL
BEEF STEAKS					
BOTTOM ROUND STEAK	•	•	•		
FLANK STEAK	•	•	•		
PORTERHOUSE STEAK		•	•	•	•
RIBEYE STEAK		•	•	•	•
RIB STEAK		•	•		
SIRLOIN STEAK		•	•	•	•
SKIRT STEAK	•	•	•		
T-BONE STEAK		•	•	•	•
TENDERLOIN STEAK		•	•	•	•
TOP LOIN STEAK		•	•	•	•
TOP ROUND STEAK	•	•	•		

The secret to this rib roast from our home economists is in the coffee rub. Allowing the rub to penetrate overnight heightens the flavor.

—Taste of Home Test Kitchen

COFFEE-CRUSTED PRIME RIB

- 1 tablespoon finely ground coffee
- 2 teaspoons chili powder
- 1 teaspoon onion powder
- 1 teaspoon coarsely ground pepper
- 1 teaspoon ground mustard
- 1/2 teaspoon salt
- 1/2 teaspoon garlic powder
- 1/2 teaspoon dried oregano
- 1/4 teaspoon cayenne pepper
- 1 beef ribeye roast (4 to 5 pounds)
- 2 tablespoons olive oil
- 2 cups soaked wood chips, optional

In a small bowl, combine the first nine ingredients. Tie the roast at 1-1/2- to 2-in. intervals with kitchen string. Rub seasonings over roast; cover and refrigerate for 8 hours or overnight.

Remove roast from refrigerator 1 hour before grilling; brush with oil.

Prepare grill for indirect heat, using a drip pan, adding half the wood chips if desired. Place roast over drip pan and grill, covered, over medium-low indirect heat for 2 to 2-1/2 hours or until meat reaches desired doneness (for medium-rare, a meat thermometer should read 145°; medium, 160°; well-done, 170°), adding remaining wood chips after 1 hour. Let stand for 10-15 minutes before slicing. **YIELD: 12-16 SERVINGS.**

LONDON BROIL

- 1/2 **cup water**
- 1/4 **cup red wine vinegar**
- 2 **tablespoons canola oil**
- 1 **tablespoon tomato paste**
- 1-1/2 **teaspoons garlic salt,** *divided*
- 1 **teaspoon dried thyme,** *divided*
- 1/2 **teaspoon pepper,** *divided*
- 1 **bay leaf**
- 1 **beef flank steak (1-1/2 pounds)**

In a small bowl, whisk the water, vinegar, oil, tomato paste, 1 teaspoon garlic salt, 1/2 teaspoon thyme and 1/4 teaspoon pepper; add bay leaf. Pour into a large resealable plastic bag.

Score the surface of the steak, making diamond shapes 1/4 in. deep; add to marinade. Seal bag and turn to coat; refrigerate for 3 hours or overnight, turning occasionally.

Coat grill rack with cooking spray before starting the grill. Drain and discard marinade. Pat steak dry with paper towels. Combine the remaining garlic salt, thyme and pepper; rub over both sides of steak.

Grill steak, covered, over medium-hot heat for 6-8 minutes on each side or until meat reaches desired doneness (for medium-rare, a meat thermometer should read 145°; medium, 160°; well-done, 170°). Thinly slice across the grain. **YIELD: 6 SERVINGS.**

I received this delicious recipe from my mother-in-law. Prepared on the grill, it's a real treat during warm-weather months.

—Susan Wilkins, Los Olivos, California

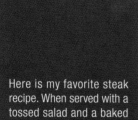

Here is my favorite steak recipe. When served with a tossed salad and a baked potato, it makes a hearty meal. I love its mild but tasty orange flavor.

—Gloria Bisek
  Deerwood, Minnesota

ORANGE FLANK STEAK

- 1/4 **cup orange juice**
- 1/4 **cup canola oil**
- 2 **tablespoons ketchup**
- 4-1/2 **teaspoons soy sauce**
- 2 **garlic cloves, minced**
- 1 **teaspoon grated orange peel**
- 1/8 **teaspoon hot pepper sauce**
- 1 **beef flank steak (1 pound)**
- 1 **medium orange, sliced**

In a large resealable plastic bag, combine the first seven ingredients. Add the beef; seal bag and turn to coat. Refrigerate for 8 hours or overnight.

Grill, covered, over medium-hot heat for 4-6 minutes on each side or until meat reaches desired doneness (for medium-rare, a meat thermometer should read 145°; medium, 160°; well-done, 170°). Let stand for 10 minutes.

Meanwhile, grill orange slices for 2 minutes. To serve, thinly slice steak across the grain. Garnish with orange slices. **YIELD: 4 SERVINGS.**

My sister served these yummy fajitas one hot summer night. They are the best I have ever tasted.

—Linere Silloway
East Charleston, Vermont

BEST BEEF FAJITAS

- 1/4   cup canola oil
- 1/3   cup chopped onion
- 2   tablespoons white wine vinegar
- 1   tablespoon lime juice
- 1   garlic clove, minced
- 1   teaspoon hot pepper sauce
- 1/8   teaspoon salt
- 1/8   teaspoon pepper

FAJITAS:

- 1   beef flank steak (1/2 pound)
- 1/2   *each* medium sweet red and green pepper, sliced
- 1   medium onion, thinly sliced
- 4   flour tortillas (8 inches), warmed

Sour cream, salsa and shredded cheddar cheese, optional

In a small bowl, combine the first eight ingredients. Pour 1/3 cup into a large resealable plastic bag; add beef. Seal bag and turn to coat. Pour remaining marinade into another large resealable plastic bag; add peppers and onion. Seal bag and turn to coat. Refrigerate beef and vegetables overnight.

Drain and discard marinade; set vegetables aside. Grill beef, covered, over medium heat for 7-8 minutes on each side or until meat reaches desired doneness (for medium-rare, a meat thermometer should read 145°; medium, 160°; well-done, 170°). Let stand for 10 minutes.

Meanwhile, place vegetables in a grill wok or basket. Grill, covered, over medium heat for 8-10 minutes or until crisp-tender, stirring frequently. Thinly slice steak across the grain; place on tortillas. Top with vegetables; roll up. Serve with sour cream, salsa and cheese if desired. **YIELD: 2 SERVINGS.**

EDITOR'S NOTE: If you do not have a grill wok or basket, use a disposable foil pan. Poke holes in the bottom of the pan with a meat fork to allow liquid to drain.

FAST GRILLED FAJITAS

IT'S EASY to enjoy the smoky flavor of charbroiled fajita meat all year. Simply grill several seasoned flank steaks at once. When cool, slice the meat and store in resealable freezer bags.

MEAL ON A STICK

8	small red potatoes
2	eggs, lightly beaten
2	teaspoons Worcestershire sauce
1-1/4	cups seasoned bread crumbs
1	teaspoon curry powder
1-1/2	pounds ground beef
24	pimiento-stuffed olives
8	plum tomatoes, halved
2	medium green peppers, cut into quarters
8	large fresh mushrooms
1/4	cup barbecue sauce

My husband and I were thrilled to receive a gas grill as a wedding gift. We love these meatball-and-veggie kabobs, which get sweetness from the barbecue sauce.

—Sundra Hauck
    Bogalusa, Louisiana

Scrub and pierce potatoes; place on a microwave-safe plate. Microwave, uncovered, on high for 3-5 minutes or until slightly tender.

Meanwhile, in a large bowl, combine the eggs, Worcestershire sauce, bread crumbs and curry powder. Crumble beef over mixture and mix well. Divide into 24 portions; shape each portion around an olive. Alternately thread meatballs and vegetables onto metal or soaked wooden skewers.

Grill kabobs, covered, over medium-hot heat for 5 minutes on each side, brushing occasionally with barbecue sauce, until meatballs are no longer pink. **YIELD: 6-8 SERVINGS.**

EDITOR'S NOTE: This recipe was tested in a 1,100-watt microwave.

6
CHICKEN

PG. 131 | **GRILLED CHICKEN VEGGIE DINNER**

ASK ANY COOK AND THEY'LL TELL YOU—IF YOU'VE GOT CHICKEN IN THE FRIDGE, YOU'VE GOT A MEAL IN MINUTES. AND WHEN YOU GRILL CHICKEN, DINNERTIME IS AS DELICIOUS AS IT IS SPEEDY! TURN HERE FOR CHICKEN RECIPES YOU'LL COME TO DEPEND ON YEAR AFTER YEAR. BEST OF ALL, EACH DISH CALLS FOR INGREDIENTS YOU PROBABLY HAVE ON HAND.

SAUCY BARBECUED CHICKEN

My aunt was affectionately called "The Barbecue Queen." As the aroma of her grilled chicken filled the air, folks in town would stop by just to sample her scrumptious food.

—Charlotte Witherspoon, Detroit, Michigan

2	cups ketchup
1/2	cup water
1/2	cup tomato sauce
1/2	cup corn syrup
1/2	cup cola
1/4	cup cider vinegar
1/4	cup butter, cubed
1/4	cup steak sauce
2	tablespoons soy sauce
1-1/2	teaspoons sugar
1	teaspoon seasoned salt
1	teaspoon hot pepper sauce
1/2	teaspoon garlic powder
1/2	teaspoon onion powder
1/2	teaspoon Liquid Smoke, optional
1	broiler/fryer chicken (3 to 3-1/2 pounds), cut up

In a large saucepan, combine the first 15 ingredients. Bring to a boil, stirring constantly. Reduce heat; simmer, uncovered, for 1 hour, stirring frequently.

Set aside 1 cup for basting. Store remaining sauce in the refrigerator for another use.

Grill chicken, covered, over medium heat for 30 minutes, turning occasionally. Baste with marinade; grill 5-10 minutes longer or until juices run clear, turning and basting frequently with marinade. **YIELD: 4 SERVINGS.**

ORANGE-MAPLE GLAZED CHICKEN

1/3	cup orange juice
1/3	cup maple syrup
2	tablespoons balsamic vinegar
1-1/2	teaspoons Dijon mustard
1	teaspoon salt, *divided*
3/4	teaspoon pepper, *divided*
1	tablespoon minced fresh basil *or* 1 teaspoon dried basil
1/2	teaspoon grated orange peel
6	boneless skinless chicken breast halves (6 ounces *each*)

Pick up a medium-size orange for the zest and juice in this tasty recipe that creatively combines citrus with maple syrup and balsamic vinegar.

—Lillian Julow, Gainesville, Florida

In a small saucepan, combine the orange juice, syrup, vinegar, mustard, 1/2 teaspoon salt and 1/4 teaspoon pepper. Bring to a boil; cook until liquid is reduced to 1/2 cup, about 5 minutes. Stir in basil and orange peel. Remove from the heat; set aside.

Sprinkle chicken with remaining salt and pepper. Grill chicken, covered, over medium heat for 5-7 minutes on each side or until a meat thermometer reads 170°, basting frequently with orange juice mixture. **YIELD: 6 SERVINGS.**

CHILI SAUCE CHICKEN

1	bottle (12 ounces) chili sauce
1/3	cup white wine *or* chicken broth
1/4	cup olive oil
10	to 12 garlic cloves, minced
4-1/2	teaspoons dried basil
1/2	teaspoon salt
1/8	teaspoon pepper
8	bone-in chicken thighs (4 ounces *each*)

In a large resealable plastic bag, combine the first seven ingredients. Remove 1/3 cup for basting; cover and refrigerate. Add chicken to bag; seal and turn to coat. Refrigerate for at least 2 hours.

Drain and discard marinade from chicken. Grill, covered, skin side down, over medium heat for 20 minutes. Baste with half the reserved marinade. Turn; grill 10 minutes longer or until a meat thermometer reads 180°, basting frequently with reserved marinade. **YIELD: 8 SERVINGS.**

Chili sauce with plenty of garlic and basil flavors these moist chicken thighs. We enjoy this tender grilled chicken not just in summertime but all year long.

—Marilyn Waltz
Idyllwild, California

TROPICAL CHICKEN KABOBS

- 1 bottle (11-1/2 ounces) sweet-and-sour sauce, *divided*
- 1/2 cup pineapple juice
- 2 tablespoons teriyaki sauce
- 2 garlic cloves, minced
- 1-1/2 pounds boneless skinless chicken breasts *or* thighs, cut into 1-1/2-inch cubes
- 2 medium sweet red peppers
- 2 medium green peppers
- 2 medium onions
- 1 fresh pineapple, washed and top removed

Crushed red pepper flakes

- 8 cherry tomatoes, optional

Hot cooked rice

For a deliciously sweet grilling dish, this recipe will exceed your expectations. It has a wonderful variety of vegetables, and even if your family doesn't like vegetables, they will love this dish.

—Taste of Home
Test Kitchen

In a bowl, combine 1/2 cup sweet-and-sour sauce, pineapple juice, teriyaki sauce and garlic. Pour half of marinade into a large resealable plastic bag; add chicken. Seal bag and turn to coat; refrigerate about 15 minutes. Set aside remaining marinade.

Meanwhile, cut peppers into 1-in. pieces and onions into wedges. Core pineapple; cut crosswise into 1/2-in. slices. Cut each slice into 4-6 wedges.

Drain chicken, discarding marinade. On metal or soaked wooden skewers, alternate meat with onions, peppers and pineapple. Brush kabobs with reserved marinade. Sprinkle with crushed red pepper flakes.

Grill, uncovered, over medium heat for 4-5 minutes on each side. Baste with marinade. Continue turning and basting 10-12 minutes longer or until chicken juices run clear, adding tomatoes to kabobs during the last 5 minutes of cooking if desired. Serve with rice. Serve remaining sweet-and-sour sauce on the side. **YIELD: 4 SERVINGS (2 KABOBS EACH).**

CHICKEN GRILLING CHART

Chicken breasts are done at 170°; whole chickens at 180° as measured in the thigh. Kabobs are done when juices run clear. Ground chicken is done at 165°. For direct grilling, turn meat halfway through grilling time. The cooking times given are a guideline. Check for doneness with a meat thermometer or other appropriate doneness test.

CUT	WEIGHT OR THICKNESS	HEAT	APPROXIMATE COOKING TIME
BROILER/FRYER, WHOLE	3 to 4 lbs.	medium/indirect	1-1/4 to 1-3/4 hours
ROASTER, WHOLE	5 to 6 lbs.	medium/indirect	1-3/4 to 2-1/4 hours
MEATY BONE-IN PIECES, BREAST HALVES, LEGS, QUARTERS	1-1/4 to 1-1/2 lbs.	medium/direct medium/indirect	35 to 45 minutes 40 to 50 minutes
BONE-IN THIGHS, DRUMSTICKS, WINGS	3 to 7 oz. each	medium-low/direct medium/indirect	15 to 30 minutes 20 to 30 minutes
BREAST HALVES, BONELESS	6 oz. each	medium/direct	10 to 15 minutes
KABOBS	1-in. cubes	medium/direct	10 to 15 minutes

As far as I'm concerned, there's no better way to spend a summer night than sitting outdoors with the family and enjoying a hot-off-the-grill meal like this.

—Sherry Schmidt, Franklin, Virginia

BASIC CHICKEN BARBECUE

1   cup white vinegar
3   tablespoons sugar
2   tablespoons salt
1   cup water
1/2 cup canola oil
1   tablespoon poultry seasoning
1   tablespoon pepper
1   broiler/fryer chicken (3 to 3-1/2 pounds), cut up

In a small bowl, whisk the vinegar, sugar and salt. Whisk in the water, oil, poultry seasoning and pepper. Reserve 1/2 cup for basting; cover and refrigerate. Pour remaining marinade into a large resealable plastic bag; add the chicken. Seal bag and turn to coat. Refrigerate for 2-4 hours.

Drain and discard marinade. Grill chicken, covered, over medium heat for 35-45 minutes or until juices run clear, turning and basting occasionally with reserved marinade. **YIELD: 4 SERVINGS.**

CHICKEN BUNDLES

- 2 boneless skinless chicken breast halves
- 2 medium red potatoes, quartered and cut into 1/2-inch slices
- 1/4 cup chopped onion
- 1 medium carrot, cut into 1/4-inch slices
- 1 celery rib, cut into 1/4-inch slices
- 1/2 teaspoon rubbed sage

Salt and pepper to taste

Fresh dill sprigs

Divide chicken and vegetables between two pieces of double-layered heavy-duty foil (about 18 in. square). Sprinkle with the sage, salt and pepper; top with dill sprigs. Fold foil around the mixture and seal tightly.

Grill, covered, over medium heat for 30 minutes or until a meat thermometer reads 170°. Open foil carefully to allow steam to escape. **YIELD: 2 SERVINGS.**

Here's an ideal dinner for two...without a lot of work. I simply season chicken and vegetables with sage and dill, then wrap them in aluminum foil, so everything grills together and cleanup is a snap.

—Cheryl Landis
Honey Brook, Pennsylvania

My father-in-law was looking for a good chicken marinade when a friend suggested mayonnaise with Italian dressing. He added the ham and cheese on his own, and we can't get enough of it! You'd never guess this BBQ is so easy and so fast!

—Jennifer Rytting
West Jordan, Utah

MAYONNAISE LOVER'S CHICKEN

- 1/2 cup Italian salad dressing
- 1-1/4 cups mayonnaise, *divided*
- 6 boneless skinless chicken breast halves (4 ounces *each*)
- 6 slices deli ham
- 6 slices Swiss cheese
- 1-1/2 teaspoons prepared mustard
- 1-1/2 teaspoons honey

In a small bowl, combine salad dressing and 1/2 cup mayonnaise. Pour 3/4 cup into a large resealable plastic bag; add chicken. Seal bag and turn to coat; refrigerate at least 30 minutes. Cover and refrigerate remaining marinade for basting.

Drain and discard marinade. Grill chicken, covered, over medium heat or broil 4 in. from the heat for 4-6 minutes on each side or until a meat thermometer reads 170°, basting frequently with reserved marinade.

Top each piece of chicken with a slice of ham and cheese. Grill, covered, 1-2 minutes longer or until cheese is melted.

In a small bowl, combine the mustard, honey and remaining mayonnaise. Serve with chicken. **YIELD: 6 SERVINGS.**

SPINACH AND MUSHROOM SMOTHERED CHICKEN

3	cups fresh baby spinach
1-3/4	cups sliced fresh mushrooms
3	green onions, sliced
2	tablespoons chopped pecans
1-1/2	teaspoons olive oil
4	boneless skinless chicken breast halves (4 ounces *each*)
1/2	teaspoon rotisserie chicken seasoning
2	slices reduced-fat provolone cheese, halved

In a large skillet, saute the spinach, mushrooms, onions and pecans in oil until mushrooms are tender. Set aside and keep warm.

Coat grill rack with cooking spray before starting the grill. Sprinkle chicken with seasoning; grill, covered, over medium heat for 4-5 minutes on each side or until a meat thermometer reads 170°.

Top with cheese. Cover and grill 2-3 minutes longer or until cheese is melted. To serve, top each chicken breast with reserved spinach mixture. **YIELD: 4 SERVINGS.**

Chicken breasts stay nice and moist with a mushroom and spinach topping tucked under a blanket of melted cheese. It's extra special to serve but is not tricky to make.

—Katrina Wagner, Grain Valley, Missouri

MAPLE BARBECUED CHICKEN

A sweet maple sauce is used to baste this chicken while grilling, with additional sauce served alongside for dipping.

—Ruth Lowen, Hythe, Alberta

3/4	cup barbecue sauce
3/4	cup maple pancake syrup
1/2	teaspoon salt
1/2	teaspoon maple flavoring
8	boneless skinless chicken breast halves (4 ounces *each*)

In a large bowl, combine the first four ingredients; reserving 3/4 cup. Grill chicken, uncovered, over medium heat for 3 minutes on each side. Grill 6-8 minutes longer or until a meat thermometer reads 170°, turning occasionally and basting with sauce. Serve with reserved sauce. **YIELD: 8 SERVINGS.**

GRILLING TIP

BONING CHICKEN BREASTS

Insert a small boning or paring knife between the ribs and breast meat. Pressing knife along bones, cut to remove meat. If desired, remove skin by pulling from breast meat.

MONTEREY CHICKEN

6	bacon strips, halved
6	boneless skinless chicken breast halves (4 ounces *each*)
1/2	cup olive oil
1/4	cup red wine vinegar
1/4	cup soy sauce
1	teaspoon minced garlic
1/2	teaspoon salt
1/2	teaspoon dried oregano
1/4	teaspoon pepper
6	thin slices sweet onion
6	thin slices tomato
6	thin slices avocado
6	thin slices Monterey Jack cheese

Cook bacon according to package directions; drain. Meanwhile, flatten chicken to 1/4-in. thickness. In a large resealable plastic bag, combine the oil, vinegar, soy sauce, garlic, salt, oregano and pepper; add chicken. Seal bag and turn to coat; refrigerate for at least 30 minutes.

Drain and discard marinade. Grill chicken, uncovered, over medium heat for 4-6 minutes on each side or until a meat thermometer reads 170°.

Move chicken to edges of grill. Top each with two bacon pieces and one slice of onion, tomato, avocado and cheese. Cover and grill 4-6 minutes longer or until cheese is melted. **YIELD: 6 SERVINGS.**

Try this chicken from the grill served in a refreshingly different way. And although the ingredient list appears long, it's a cinch to make.

—Sherri Mabry Gordon
Pickerington, Ohio

GOLDEN GLAZED FRYER

1	broiler/fryer chicken (3 to 4 pounds), cut up
1/2	cup canola oil
1/2	cup cider vinegar
1	egg, lightly beaten
4	teaspoons salt
1-1/2	teaspoon poultry seasoning
1/4	teaspoon pepper

Coat grill rack with cooking spray before starting the grill. Grill chicken, skin side down, covered, over medium heat for 15 minutes. Turn; grill 15 minutes longer.

Meanwhile, combine the remaining ingredients; brush over chicken. Grill for 5 minutes. Turn and brush with glaze; grill 5 minutes longer or until the meat juices run clear. Discard unused glaze. **YIELD: 6 SERVINGS.**

This moist, grilled chicken has a savory coating that's a nice change of pace from tomato-based sauces. The recipe has been passed down in my family for generations.

—Peggy West, Georgetown, Delaware

BARBECUED CHICKEN PIZZAS

2	boneless skinless chicken breast halves (6 ounces *each*)
1/4	teaspoon salt
1/4	teaspoon pepper
1	cup barbecue sauce, *divided*
1	tube (13.8 ounces) refrigerated pizza crust
2	teaspoons olive oil
1	medium red onion, thinly sliced
2	cups (8 ounces) shredded Gouda cheese
1/4	cup minced fresh cilantro

Coat grill rack with cooking spray before starting the grill. Sprinkle chicken with salt and pepper. Grill, covered, over medium heat for 5-7 minutes on each side or until a meat thermometer reads 170°, basting frequently with 1/2 cup barbecue sauce. Set aside and keep warm.

Divide dough in half. On a lightly floured surface, roll each portion into a 12-in. x 10-in. rectangle. Lightly brush both sides of dough with oil; place on grill. Cover and grill over medium heat for 1-2 minutes or until the bottom is lightly browned.

Remove from grill. Cut the chicken into 1/2-in. cubes. Spread the grilled side of each pizza with 1/4 cup barbecue sauce; layer with chicken, onion, cheese and cilantro. Return to grill. Cover and cook each pizza for 4-5 minutes or until the bottom is lightly browned and cheese is melted. **YIELD: 2 PIZZAS (4 PIECES EACH).**

So fast and so easy with refrigerated pizza crust, this entree will bring raves with its hot-off-the-grill, rustic flavor. Perfect for a small, spur-of-the-moment backyard pool party!

—Alicia Trevithick
  Temecula, California

LIGHT CAJUN CHICKEN PASTA

This slimmed-down dish has less sodium, calories and saturated fat than the original, but all the same rich, creamy flavor!

—Heather Privratsky
Greenfield, Wisconsin

6	boneless skinless chicken breast halves (4 ounces *each*)
2	tablespoons Cajun seasoning, *divided*
2-1/4	cups uncooked penne pasta
1	large onion, chopped
2	teaspoons olive oil
2	garlic cloves, minced
1	can (28 ounces) crushed tomatoes, drained
1/4	teaspoon pepper
1-1/2	cups half-and-half cream

Rub chicken with 1 tablespoon Cajun seasoning. Coat grill rack with cooking spray before starting the grill. Grill chicken, covered, over medium heat for 4-7 minutes on each side or until a meat thermometer reads 170°; keep warm.

Meanwhile, in a large saucepan, cook pasta according to package directions. In a Dutch oven coated with cooking spray, saute onion in oil until crisp-tender. Add garlic and remaining Cajun seasoning; cook 1 minute longer. Stir in the tomatoes and the pepper.

Drain pasta; add to the onion mixture. Stir in cream; heat through (do not boil). Serve chicken with pasta. **YIELD: 6 SERVINGS.**

SESAME CHICKEN

3/4   cup soy sauce

1/2   cup packed brown sugar

1/4   cup water

3   tablespoons sesame seeds, toasted

1   garlic clove, minced

Crushed red pepper flakes, optional

4   bone-in chicken breast halves (8 ounces *each*)

In a large resealable plastic bag, combine the first six ingredients; add chicken. Seal bag and turn to coat; refrigerate overnight.

Drain and discard marinade. Grill chicken, skin side down, uncovered, over medium heat for 6-8 minutes on each side or until a meat thermometer reads 170°. **YIELD: 4 SERVINGS.**

For flavorful, moist and tender chicken, try this no-fuss marinade. The sesame seeds cling well to season the meat. We also like this mixture on chicken wings, beef short ribs and pork.

—Julie Lake
Anchorage, Alaska

The slight spice from the jalapeno pairs well with the sweet mango and raspberry salsa in this grilled entree.

—Taste of Home Test Kitchen

CHICKEN WITH MANGO-RASPBERRY SALSA

3/4   cup chopped peeled mango

1/3   cup chopped sweet onion

1/4   cup minced fresh cilantro

3   tablespoons lime juice

1   tablespoon chopped seeded jalapeno pepper

1/2   teaspoon sugar

1   garlic clove, minced

1/2   teaspoon garlic powder

1/2   teaspoon salt

1/2   teaspoon pepper

6   boneless skinless chicken breast halves (4 ounces *each*)

3/4   cup fresh raspberries

For salsa, in a small bowl, combine the first seven ingredients. Cover and refrigerate for 1 hour.

Combine the garlic powder, salt and pepper; sprinkle over both sides of chicken.

Grill chicken, covered, over medium heat for 6-8 minutes on each side or until a meat thermometer reads 170°. Just before serving, gently fold raspberries into salsa. Serve with chicken. **YIELD: 6 SERVINGS.**

EDITOR'S NOTE: When cutting hot peppers, disposable gloves are recommended. Avoid touching your face.

GRILLED CHICKEN VEGGIE DINNER

4	bone-in chicken thighs (about 1-1/2 pounds)
1-1/2	teaspoons olive oil
1/2	teaspoon salt, *divided*
1/2	teaspoon seasoned pepper
1/2	*each* medium green, sweet red and yellow pepper, sliced
1	medium onion, halved and sliced
1-1/2	teaspoons Italian seasoning
1/4	teaspoon garlic powder
2	plum tomatoes, cut into wedges

Rub both sides of chicken with oil; sprinkle with 1/4 teaspoon salt and pepper. Place skin side down on grill rack. Grill, covered, over medium heat for 5 minutes. Turn; grill 5-6 minutes longer or until golden brown.

Place chicken on a double thickness of heavy-duty foil (about 18 in. square). Top with peppers, onion, Italian seasoning, garlic powder and remaining salt. Seal foil tightly.

Grill, covered, over indirect medium heat for 20-30 minutes. Open foil carefully; add tomatoes. Reseal foil; grill 4-5 minutes longer or until a meat thermometer reads 180°. **YIELD: 2 SERVINGS.**

Low in carbs but high in flavor, this chicken dish was created on the spur of the minute using veggies fresh from our garden. It's delicious by itself or served over buttered noodles.

—Kenneth Dunn, Bedford, Kentucky

Get ready to rock the grill with this spicy and wonderfully fragrant chicken. The zippy marinade includes hints of cinnamon, cayenne and thyme. We like to think of this dish as "chicken with attitude."

—Judy Kamalieh
Nebraska City,
Nebraska

CARIBBEAN JERK CHICKEN

4	chicken leg quarters (8-1/2 ounces *each*), skin removed
1/4	cup olive oil
2	tablespoons brown sugar
2	tablespoons reduced-sodium soy sauce
1	envelope Italian salad dressing mix
1	teaspoon dried thyme
1	teaspoon ground cinnamon
1/2	teaspoon cayenne pepper

With a sharp knife, cut leg quarters at the joints if desired. In a large resealable plastic bag, combine the remaining ingredients; add chicken. Seal bag and turn to coat; refrigerate for 2-4 hours.

Coat grill rack with cooking spray before starting the grill. Drain and discard marinade. Grill chicken, covered, over medium heat for 35-45 minutes or until a meat thermometer reads 180°, turning occasionally. **YIELD: 4 SERVINGS.**

GRILLED CHICKEN CLUB PITAS

- 3 tablespoons mayonnaise
- 3 tablespoons honey
- 3 tablespoons spicy brown mustard
- 1/4 teaspoon salt-free garlic seasoning blend
- 2 boneless skinless chicken breast halves (5 ounces *each*)
- 2 whole pita breads
- 1/2 cup shredded lettuce
- 2 bacon strips, cooked and crumbled
- 2 slices Swiss cheese

Why heat up the kitchen on warm Indian summer evenings when you can take dinner in hand with these hearty chicken pitas? I also roll up the chicken strips in flour tortillas and serve as grab-and-go wrap sandwiches. Serve any leftover chicken with mixed greens and the last of the garden tomatoes in lunch salads the next day.

—Lynne Zeigler, Odenton, Maryland

In a small bowl, combine the mayonnaise, honey, mustard and seasoning blend; set aside 3 tablespoons. Pour remaining mixture in a large resealable plastic bag; add chicken. Seal bag and turn to coat; refrigerate for at least 1 hour. Refrigerate reserved mayonnaise mixture until serving.

Grill chicken, covered, over medium heat or broil 4 in. from the heat for 5-7 minutes on each side or until a meat thermometer reads 170°. Cut chicken into 1-in. strips.

Spread reserved mayonnaise mixture over pita breads; top with the lettuce, chicken, bacon and cheese. **YIELD: 2 SERVINGS.**

HERBED BARBECUED CHICKEN

- 2 tablespoons olive oil
- 2 tablespoons reduced-sodium soy sauce
- 2 tablespoons Worcestershire sauce
- 1 garlic clove, minced
- 1 tablespoon dried parsley flakes
- 1/2 teaspoon dried rosemary, crushed
- 1/2 teaspoon rubbed sage
- 1/4 teaspoon dried oregano
- 1/4 teaspoon dried thyme
- 1/4 teaspoon pepper
- 4 boneless skinless chicken breast halves (4 ounces *each*)

In a large resealable plastic bag, combine the first 10 ingredients; add chicken. Seal bag and turn to coat; refrigerate for 8 hours or overnight.

Coat grill rack with cooking spray before starting the grill. Drain and discard marinade. Grill chicken, covered, over medium heat for 5-8 minutes on each side or until a meat thermometer reads 170°. **YIELD: 4 SERVINGS.**

Garlic, rosemary, sage and thyme help season the marinade for this moist, tender chicken. A friend gave me the recipe years ago, and my family never tires of it.

—Dawn Sowders
Harrison, Ohio

TERIYAKI GRILLED CHICKEN

Here's a super recipe you can use with any chicken pieces you like, with or without skin. Plan ahead to marinate chicken overnight for such wonderful flavor. Leftovers are fabulous the next day in a salad.

—Jennifer Nichols
Tuscon, Arizona

1/3 cup soy sauce

1/4 cup canola oil

2 green onions, thinly sliced

2 tablespoons plus 1-1/2 teaspoons honey

2 tablespoons sherry *or* chicken broth

2 garlic cloves, minced

1 teaspoon minced fresh gingerroot

6 bone-in chicken breast halves (8 ounces *each*)

In a large resealable plastic bag, combine the first seven ingredients; add the chicken. Seal bag and turn to coat; refrigerate for at least 5 hours.

Drain and discard marinade. Prepare grill for indirect heat, using a drip pan. Place chicken skin side down on grill rack. Grill, covered, over indirect medium heat for 40-50 minutes or until a meat thermometer reads 170°. **YIELD: 6 SERVINGS.**

HOT WING PIZZA

3 boneless skinless chicken breast halves (5 ounces *each*)

1 tablespoon steak seasoning

1/2 cup tomato sauce

2 tablespoons butter

2 tablespoons Louisiana-style hot sauce

1 tablespoon hot pepper sauce

1 prebaked 12-inch pizza crust

1/3 cup blue cheese salad dressing

1/2 cup shredded part-skim mozzarella cheese

3 green onions, thinly sliced

Sprinkle chicken with steak seasoning on both sides; grill, covered, over medium heat for 4-7 minutes on each side or until a meat thermometer reads 170°. Cool slightly; cut into strips.

In a small saucepan, bring the tomato sauce, butter, hot sauce and pepper sauce to a boil. Reduce heat; simmer, uncovered, for 10-15 minutes or until slightly thickened. Add chicken; heat through.

Place crust on a 12-in. pizza pan; spread with salad dressing. Top with chicken mixture, cheese and onions.

Bake at 450° for 8-10 minutes or until cheese is melted. **YIELD: 6 SLICES.**

EDITOR'S NOTE: This recipe was tested with McCormick's Montreal Steak Seasoning. Look for it in the spice aisle.

My husband loves this recipe, especially when he has a craving for hot wings. If you don't have blue cheese dressing, ranch works great, too!

—Danielle Weets, Grandview, Washington

SPICY CHICKEN BREASTS WITH PEPPER PEACH RELISH

    1/2   teaspoon salt
    1/4   teaspoon *each* ground cinnamon, cloves and nutmeg
      4   boneless skinless chicken breast halves (6 ounces *each*)

GLAZE:

    1/4   cup peach preserves
      2   tablespoons lemon juice
    1/4   teaspoon crushed red pepper flakes

RELISH:

      2   medium peaches, peeled and finely chopped
    1/3   cup finely chopped sweet red pepper
    1/3   cup finely chopped green pepper
      1   green onion, finely chopped
      2   tablespoons minced fresh mint

This summery entree is simply packed with the good-for-your-eyes vitamins found in both peaches and peppers.

—Roxanne Chan
    Albany, California

Combine the salt, cinnamon, cloves and nutmeg; rub over chicken. In a small bowl, combine the glaze ingredients; set aside. In another small bowl, combine the peaches, peppers, onion, mint and 2 tablespoons glaze; set aside.

Coat grill rack with cooking spray before starting the grill. Grill chicken, covered, over medium heat for 6-8 minutes on each side or until a meat thermometer reads 170°, basting frequently with reserved glaze. Serve with reserved relish. **YIELD: 4 SERVINGS.**

GRILLED CHICKEN AND VEGGIES

- 3/4 teaspoon dried oregano
- 1/2 teaspoon garlic salt
- 1/2 teaspoon garlic powder
- 1/2 teaspoon onion powder
- 1/2 teaspoon ground turmeric
- 1/4 teaspoon ground cumin
- 6 boneless skinless chicken breast halves (6 ounces *each*)
- 1 medium green pepper, cut into strips
- 1 medium sweet red pepper, cut into strips
- 2 medium onions, halved and sliced
- 1 tablespoon canola oil

Combine the seasonings; sprinkle over chicken and set aside. In a small bowl, toss peppers and onions with oil; transfer to a grill wok or basket.

Coat grill rack with cooking spray before starting the grill. Place chicken and grill wok on grill. Grill, covered, over medium heat for 5-8 minutes on each side or until a meat thermometer reads 170°. **YIELD: 6 SERVINGS.**

This is so easy, and people are always asking me how to make it. I often substitute adobo seasoning for the blended spices.
—Leah Lyon, Ada, Oklahoma

What better place to find a fantastic barbecue sauce than Texas, and that's where this one is from…it's my father-in-law's recipe. We've served it at many family reunions and think it's the best!
—Bobbie Morgan
   Woodstock, Georgia

FAVORITE BARBECUED CHICKEN

- 1 broiler/fryer chicken (3 pounds), cut up
- Salt and pepper to taste
- BARBECUE SAUCE:
- 1 small onion, finely chopped
- 1 tablespoon canola oil
- 1 cup ketchup
- 2 tablespoons lemon juice
- 1 tablespoon brown sugar
- 1 tablespoon water
- 1/2 teaspoon ground mustard
- 1/4 teaspoon garlic powder
- 1/8 teaspoon pepper
- Dash salt
- Dash hot pepper sauce

Sprinkle chicken with salt and pepper. Grill chicken, skin side down, uncovered, over medium heat for 20 minutes.

Meanwhile, in a small saucepan, saute the onion in oil until tender. Stir in the remaining sauce ingredients. Bring to a boil. Reduce heat; simmer, uncovered, for 10 minutes.

Turn chicken; grill 15-25 minutes longer or until juices run clear, brushing often with barbecue sauce. **YIELD: 6 SERVINGS.**

ZESTY BASIL CHICKEN

1/3 cup butter, melted

1/4 cup minced fresh basil

1 tablespoon finely chopped onion

2 garlic cloves, minced

1/2 teaspoon salt, optional

1/2 teaspoon pepper

1/2 teaspoon lemon-pepper seasoning

4 bone-in chicken breast halves, skin removed (7 ounces *each*)

2 tablespoons grated Parmesan cheese

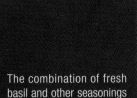

The combination of fresh basil and other seasonings gives this chicken a wonderful aroma. It's a real crowd-pleaser at picnics and potlucks...folks always come back for seconds!

—Marilyn Hamersley
 Gaithersburg, Maryland

In a small bowl, combine the butter, basil, onion, garlic and salt if desired. Rub pepper and lemon-pepper over chicken. Brush with butter mixture.

Grill chicken, covered, over medium-low heat for 15-23 minutes on each side or until a meat thermometer reads 170°, basting with marinade frequently. Before serving, sprinkle with cheese. **YIELD: 4 SERVINGS.**

I season chicken breasts with a delightful combination of herbs before topping each with veggies. Servings are individually wrapped in foil, so I can enjoy nature's beauty in my backyard while the packets cook on the grill.

—Pam Hall, Elizabeth City, North Carolina

POTATO CHICKEN PACKETS

4 boneless skinless chicken breast halves (4 ounces *each*)

1/4 cup olive oil

3 teaspoons dried rosemary, crushed

1 teaspoon dried thyme

1/2 teaspoon dried basil

1 garlic clove, minced

8 to 10 small red potatoes, quartered

2 medium yellow summer squash, cut into 1/4-inch slices

1 large onion, chopped

2 tablespoons butter, cubed

Salt and pepper to taste

Place each chicken breast on a double thickness of heavy-duty foil (about 12 in. square). Combine the oil, rosemary, thyme, basil and garlic; drizzle over chicken. Top with potatoes, squash, onion and butter. Sprinkle with salt and pepper. Fold foil over mixture and seal tightly.

Grill, covered, over medium heat for 30 minutes or until a meat thermometer reads 170°. Open foil carefully to allow steam to escape. **YIELD: 4 SERVINGS.**

Mesquite chips can be used for additional flavor when grilling this chicken. Dark stout beer doesn't usually come in 12 ounce cans, but another clean beverage can or an upright chicken roaster can be used.

—Taste of Home Test Kitchen

CHILI-HEAD CHICKEN

1-1/2	cups dark stout beer, *divided*
2	dried pasilla chilies
2	teaspoons kosher salt
2	teaspoons paprika
1	teaspoon ground cumin
1	teaspoon onion powder
1/2	teaspoon garlic powder
1/2	teaspoon dried oregano
1/2	teaspoon pepper
1/2	teaspoon cayenne pepper
2	teaspoons canola oil
1	jalapeno pepper, chopped
1	broiler/fryer chicken (3-1/2 to 4 pounds)
1	empty 12-ounce beverage can

Place 3/4 cup beer in a microwave-safe bowl; microwave, uncovered, for 1-1/2 minutes or until very hot. Remove stems and seeds from chilies; add chilies to the beer. Let stand for 20 minutes or until softened. Drain, reserving 4 tablespoons seasoned beer. Set chilies aside.

In a small bowl, combine the kosher salt, paprika, cumin, onion powder, garlic powder, oregano, pepper and cayenne; set aside 1 teaspoon of the seasoning mix.

In a blender, combine the oil, 2 tablespoons seasoned beer, jalapeno pepper, reserved chilies, and remaining seasoning mix; cover and process until a smooth thick paste forms, adding additional seasoned beer if necessary.

Loosen skin from around the chicken breast, thighs and legs. Rub the chili paste under the skin. Tuck wing tips behind the back. Rub any remaining paste into the body and neck cavities. Sprinkle chicken with reserved seasoning mix.

Prepare grill for indirect heat, using a drip pan. Poke additional holes in top of the empty can with a can opener. Pour the remaining 3/4 cup beer into the can. Holding the chicken with legs pointed down, lower chicken over the can so it fills the body cavity.

Place chicken over drip pan; grill, covered, over indirect medium heat for 1-1/4 to 1-1/2 hours or until a meat thermometer reads 180°. Remove chicken from grill; cover and let stand for 10 minutes. Remove chicken from can. **YIELD: 6 SERVINGS.**

EDITOR'S NOTE: This recipe was tested in a 1,100-watt microwave oven. When handling chilies, disposable gloves are recommended. Avoid touching your face.

CHICKEN AND ASPARAGUS KABOBS

DIPPING SAUCE:

- 2   cups mayonnaise
- 1/4   cup sugar
- 1/4   cup soy sauce
- 2   tablespoons sesame seeds, toasted
- 1   tablespoon sesame oil
- 1/2   teaspoon white pepper

KABOBS:

- 1/4   cup soy sauce
- 2   tablespoons brown sugar
- 2   tablespoons water
- 1   tablespoon sesame oil
- 1   teaspoon crushed red pepper flakes
- 1   teaspoon minced fresh gingerroot
- 1-1/2   pounds boneless skinless chicken breasts, cut into 1-1/2-inch pieces
- 1   pound fresh asparagus, trimmed and cut into 2-inch pieces
- 2   tablespoons olive oil
- 1/2   teaspoon salt

In a small bowl, combine the sauce ingredients. Cover and refrigerate for 2-4 hours.

In a large resealable plastic bag, combine the soy sauce, brown sugar, water, sesame oil, pepper flakes and ginger. Add the chicken; seal bag and turn to coat. Refrigerate for 2 hours, turning occasionally.

Drain and discard marinade. In a large bowl, toss the asparagus with olive oil and salt. On six metal or soaked wooden skewers, alternately thread one chicken piece and two asparagus pieces.

Grill, covered, over medium heat for 4-5 minutes on each side or until chicken is no longer pink and asparagus is crisp-tender. Serve with dipping sauce. **YIELD: 6 SERVINGS.**

My Asian-inspired kabobs, served with a tasty dipping sauce, are special enough to make for guests at your next backyard get-together. Sometimes I even substitute salmon for the chicken breasts.

—Kelly Townsend
   Syracuse, Nebraska

SKEWERED CHICKEN 'N' SWEET POTATOES

For a different kabob combination, try this quick and simple recipe. The unusual molasses butter sauce adds an appealing accent to the chicken, potato and sweet onion combo.

—Janice Elder
    Charlotte,
    North Carolina

4   medium sweet potatoes, peeled and cut into 1-inch cubes
2   tablespoons water
1/4   cup olive oil
2   tablespoons lemon juice
2   tablespoons Worcestershire sauce
2   garlic cloves, minced
1/2   teaspoon pepper
1/4   teaspoon salt
1-1/2   pounds boneless skinless chicken breasts, cut into 1-inch cubes
2   large sweet onions, cut into chunks

CHIPOTLE MOLASSES BUTTER:

1/2   cup butter, softened
2   tablespoons molasses
2   teaspoons minced chipotle pepper in adobo sauce
1   teaspoon grated lemon peel

Place sweet potatoes and water in a large microwave-safe dish. Cover and microwave on high for 8 minutes or until tender; drain and set aside.

In a small bowl, combine the oil, lemon juice, Worcestershire sauce, garlic, pepper and salt. Place chicken in a large resealable plastic bag; add half of the marinade. Place onions and sweet potatoes in another large resealable plastic bag; add remaining marinade. Seal bags and turn to coat; refrigerate for 30 minutes.

In a small bowl, combine the butter, molasses, chipotle peppers and lemon peel. Cover and refrigerate until serving.

Drain and discard marinade. On 12 metal or soaked wooden skewers, alternately thread the chicken, sweet potatoes and onions. Grill, covered, over medium-hot heat for 6-8 minutes on each side or until chicken is no longer pink. Serve with chipotle molasses butter. **YIELD: 6 SERVINGS.**

EDITOR'S NOTE: This recipe was tested in a 1,100-watt microwave.

SPICY BARBECUED CHICKEN

1-1/2 cups sugar

1-1/2 cups ketchup

1/2 cup water

1/4 cup lemon juice

1/4 cup cider vinegar

1/4 cup Worcestershire sauce

2 tablespoons plus 2 teaspoons chili powder

2 tablespoons plus 2 teaspoons prepared mustard

1 teaspoon salt

1/2 teaspoon crushed red pepper flakes

2 broiler/fryer chickens (3-1/2 to 4 pounds *each*), cut up

In a large saucepan, combine the first 10 ingredients; bring to a boil. Reduce heat; simmer, uncovered, for 15 minutes.

Grill chicken, covered, over medium heat for 40 minutes, turning several times. Set half of the barbecue sauce aside. Baste chicken with remaining sauce; grill 5-10 minutes longer or until juices run clear. Serve with reserved sauce. **YIELD: 8 SERVINGS.**

My grown children still beg for my grilled chicken. They like the savory barbecue sauce so much, they've been known to hover over me, trying to snitch a spoonful behind my back.

—Patricia Parker
Connelly Springs,
North Carolina

ISLAND JERK CHICKEN

3/4 cup water	2 teaspoons ground cinnamon
4 green onions, chopped	1 teaspoon salt
2 tablespoons canola oil	1 teaspoon ground nutmeg
1 tablespoon hot pepper sauce	4 boneless skinless chicken breast halves (4 ounces *each*)
4 teaspoons ground allspice	
3 garlic cloves, minced	

In a small saucepan, combine the first nine ingredients; bring to a boil. Reduce heat; simmer, uncovered, for 10 minutes. Cool to room temperature.

Pour 1/2 cup marinade into a large resealable plastic bag; add the chicken. Seal bag and turn to coat; refrigerate overnight. Transfer remaining marinade to a small bowl; cover and refrigerate for basting.

Coat grill rack with cooking spray before starting the grill. Drain and discard marinade. Grill chicken, covered, over medium heat for 4-7 minutes on each side or until a meat thermometer reads 170°, basting occasionally with reserved marinade. **YIELD: 4 SERVINGS.**

My husband is crazy about hot sauce and I'm not…luckily, we both absolutely love this chicken dish!

—Lynn Davis, St. Louis Park, Minnesota

APPLE-BUTTER BARBECUED CHICKEN

1	teaspoon salt
3/4	teaspoon garlic powder
1/4	teaspoon pepper
1/8	teaspoon cayenne pepper
1	roasting chicken (6 to 7 pounds)
1	can (11-1/2 ounces) unsweetened apple juice
1/2	cup apple butter
1/4	cup barbecue sauce

Combine the salt, garlic powder, pepper and cayenne; sprinkle over chicken.

Prepare grill for indirect heat, using a drip pan. Pour half of the apple juice into another container and save for another use. With a can opener, poke additional holes in the top of the can. Holding the chicken with legs pointed down, lower chicken over the can so it fills the body cavity. Place chicken on grill rack over drip pan.

Grill, covered, over indirect medium heat for 1-1/2 to 2 hours or until a meat thermometer reads 180°. Combine apple butter and barbecue sauce; baste chicken occasionally during the last 30 minutes. Remove chicken from grill; cover and let stand for 10 minutes. Remove chicken from can before carving. **YIELD: 6-8 SERVINGS.**

I love cooking so much I sometimes think of recipes in my sleep and wake up to write them down! This dream-inspired dish is my family's favorite way to eat chicken.

—Holly Kilbel, Akron, Ohio

BLACKENED CAJUN CHICKEN

1	tablespoon *each* paprika, brown sugar, garlic powder and ground mustard
1	teaspoon *each* onion powder, ground cumin, dried thyme and pepper
1	teaspoon crushed bay leaves
1	teaspoon dried rosemary, crushed
1/2	to 1 teaspoon cayenne pepper
1	teaspoon salt, optional
1	broiler/fryer chicken (3 to 3-1/2 pounds), cut up and skin removed

My son's a great cook who came up with a seasoning rub on his own. The rub is one of our favorite ways to flavor grilled chicken because it's nice and zesty.

—Marian Platt
  Sequim, Washington

Combine all seasonings. Place chicken in a 13-in. x 9-in. baking dish; rub with half of the seasoning mixture. Cover and refrigerate overnight.

Grill, covered, over medium heat for 15-23 minutes on each side or until juices run clear. **YIELD: 4 SERVINGS.**

EDITOR'S NOTE: Seasoning mix is enough for two chickens. It may be made ahead and stored in an airtight container until needed.

LEMON HERB CHICKEN

1/4	cup butter, softened
1	tablespoon minced fresh parsley
1	teaspoon onion powder
1	teaspoon dried thyme
1	teaspoon dried rosemary, crushed
1/2	teaspoon dried savory
1	broiler/fryer chicken (3-1/2 to 4 pounds)
1	small lemon, thinly sliced
1	empty 12-ounce beverage can
3/4	cup dry white wine

Prepare grill for indirect heat, using a drip pan. In a small bowl, combine the first six ingredients. Loosen skin from around the chicken breast, thighs and legs. Rub the butter mixture under the skin. Rub any remaining butter mixture into the body and neck cavities.

Arrange four to six lemon slices under the skin on the breast and thighs. Tuck wing tips behind the back.

Poke additional holes in top of the empty can with a can opener. Pour the wine into the can. Holding the chicken with legs pointed down, lower chicken over the can so it fills the body cavity. Place chicken over drip pan.

Grill, covered, over indirect medium heat for 1-1/4 to 1-1/2 hours or until a meat thermometer reads 180°. Remove chicken from grill; cover and let stand for 10 minutes. **YIELD: 6 SERVINGS.**

The mild flavor from grilling with apple-wood chips pairs well with the wine, herbs and citrus found in this delightful chicken entree.

—Taste of Home
Test Kitchen

APRICOT CHICKEN DRUMSTICKS

12	chicken drumsticks (3 pounds)
1	teaspoon salt
1/4	teaspoon pepper
1/4	cup canola oil
1/4	cup apricot jam, warmed
1/4	cup prepared mustard
1	tablespoon brown sugar

Sprinkle chicken with salt and pepper. For sauce, in a small bowl, combine the remaining ingredients.

Coat grill rack with cooking spray before starting the grill. Grill, covered, over medium heat for 15-20 minutes or until a meat thermometer reads 180°, turning and basting occasionally with sauce. Cool for 5 minutes. Cover and refrigerate until chilled. **YIELD: 6 SERVINGS.**

During the summer months, you can find my family gathered around the grill enjoying delicious dishes like this. You can serve these drumsticks hot off the grill or try them chilled.

—Mary Ann Sklanka
Blakely, Pennsylvania

PINEAPPLE CHICKEN KABOBS

2	cans (one 20 ounces, one 8 ounces) unsweetened pineapple chunks
1/3	cup Worcestershire sauce
8	boneless skinless chicken breast halves (4 ounces *each*)
1	package (1 pound) sliced bacon
2	large sweet onions
4	large green peppers
32	cherry tomatoes

Drain pineapple, reserving juice; set pineapple aside. In a small bowl, combine Worcestershire sauce and reserved juice. Cut each piece of chicken into four strips. Pour 1 cup marinade into a large resealable plastic bag; add chicken. Seal bag and turn to coat; refrigerate for at least 1 hour. Cover and refrigerate remaining marinade for basting.

In a large skillet, cook bacon over medium heat until partially cooked but not crisp. Remove to paper towels to drain; cut in half widthwise. Cut each onion into 16 wedges; cut each pepper into eight pieces. Drain and discard marinade. Wrap a piece of bacon around each chicken strip.

On 16 metal or soaked wooden skewers, alternately thread the bacon-wrapped chicken, vegetables and pineapple. Grill, uncovered, over medium heat for 6-8 minutes on each side or until meat is no longer pink, basting frequently with reserved marinade. **YIELD: 8 SERVINGS.**

I combined a couple of different kabob recipes to come up with this summer grilling mainstay. The marinade does a terrific job of making the chicken and vegetables so tender and tasty.

—Angela Leinenbach
Mechanicsville, Virginia

DAD'S BEST BARBECUE

2	cups white vinegar
1	cup canola oil
1	cup ketchup
1/2	cup tomato juice
2	to 3 tablespoons hot pepper sauce
1	tablespoon poultry seasoning
4-1/2	teaspoons salt
1-1/2	teaspoons pepper
3/4	teaspoon garlic powder
1	broiler/fryer chicken (3 to 4 pounds), cut up

In a large resealable storage bag, combine the first nine ingredients. Remove 1 cup for basting chicken; cover and refrigerate. Add chicken to the bag; seal and turn to coat. Refrigerate for 4 hours. Drain; discard marinade.

Grill chicken, covered, over low heat, turning and brushing with reserved marinade several times, for 60-75 minutes or until juices run clear. **YIELD: 6 SERVINGS.**

Whenever I prepare this great chicken, I fondly remember my father. He would grill his "famous" chicken frequently for picnics and other functions.
—Connie Will
Edinburg, Virginia

LEMON GRILLED CHICKEN

1/2	cup lemon juice
1/4	cup canola oil
3	tablespoons chopped onion
1/2	teaspoon salt
1/2	teaspoon pepper
1/2	teaspoon dried thyme
1	garlic clove, minced
1	broiler/fryer chicken (3 to 4 pounds), cut up

In a large resealable plastic bag, combine the first seven ingredients. Remove 1/4 cup for basting; cover and refrigerate. Add chicken to the bag; seal and turn to coat. Refrigerate for 8 hours or overnight.

Drain and discard marinade from chicken. Grill, covered, over medium heat for 20 minutes. Baste with reserved marinade. Grill 20-30 minutes longer or until a meat thermometer reads 170°, basting and turning several times. **YIELD: 4 SERVINGS.**

EDITOR'S NOTE: This recipe can also be prepared in the oven in a greased 13-in. x 9-in. x 2-in. baking dish. Bake, uncovered, at 350° for 50-60 minutes or until juices run clear.

My mother relied on this recipe when I was growing up. Its mild lemon taste reminds me of summertime.
—Ellen Seidl, Crookston, Nebraska

TROPICAL ISLAND CHICKEN

- 1/2 cup soy sauce
- 1/3 cup canola oil
- 1/4 cup water
- 2 tablespoons dried minced onion
- 2 tablespoons sesame seeds
- 1 tablespoon sugar
- 4 garlic cloves, minced
- 1 teaspoon ground ginger
- 3/4 teaspoon salt
- 1/8 teaspoon cayenne pepper
- 2 broiler/fryer chickens (3 to 4 pounds *each*), quartered

In a large resealable plastic bag, combine the first 10 ingredients. Remove 1/3 cup for basting; cover and refrigerate. Add chicken to bag; seal and turn to coat. Refrigerate for 8 hours or overnight.

Drain and discard marinade. Grill chicken, covered, over medium-hot heat for 45-60 minutes or until juices run clear, turning and basting often with reserved marinade. **YIELD: 8 SERVINGS.**

The marinade makes a savory statement in this all-time-favorite chicken recipe that I served at our son's pirate-theme birthday party. It smelled so good on the grill that guests could hardly wait to try a piece!
—Sharon Hanson, Franklin, Tennessee

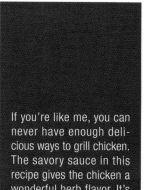

If you're like me, you can never have enough delicious ways to grill chicken. The savory sauce in this recipe gives the chicken a wonderful herb flavor. It's easy to put together a great meal when you start with these juicy golden pieces.

—Joanne Shew Chuk
St. Benedict,
Saskatchewan

BARBECUED CHICKEN

- 1/4 cup water
- 1/4 cup white vinegar
- 1/4 cup butter, cubed
- 1/4 teaspoon garlic powder
- 1/4 teaspoon dried thyme
- 1/4 teaspoon dried oregano
- 1/4 teaspoon dried rosemary, crushed
- 1/8 teaspoon salt
- 1/8 teaspoon pepper
- 1 broiler/fryer chicken (3-1/2 to 4 pounds), quartered

In a small saucepan, combine the first nine ingredients; bring to a gentle boil. Remove from the heat; cool to room temperature. Place chicken in a large resealable plastic bag; add marinade. Seal bag and turn to coat; refrigerate for 4 hours, turning once.

Drain and discard marinade. Grill chicken, covered, over medium heat for 30-40 minutes or until juices run clear. **YIELD: 4 SERVINGS.**

HONEY-MUSTARD CHICKEN

1	cup pineapple juice
3/4	cup honey
1/2	cup Dijon mustard
1	teaspoon ground ginger
2	tablespoons cornstarch
1/4	cup cold water
1	broiler/fryer chicken (3-1/2 to 4 pounds), cut up

If my family had their wish, I'd serve chicken on the grill every night. This sweet and tangy glaze is an appealing alternative to traditional grilling sauces.

—Heidi Holmes, Renton, Washington

In a small saucepan, combine the pineapple juice, honey, mustard and ginger; bring to a boil. Combine cornstarch and water; gradually whisk into honey mixture. Cook and stir for 2-3 minutes or until thickened. Reserve 3/4 cup to serve with chicken if desired.

Baste chicken with remaining glaze. Grill, covered, over medium-low heat for 30 minutes. Turn chicken; brush again with glaze. Grill, uncovered, for 20 minutes or until juices run clear. Serve with reserved glaze if desired. **YIELD: 4 SERVINGS.**

SOUTH-OF THE-BORDER THIGHS

1	cup olive oil
4-1/2	teaspoons chili powder
1	tablespoon lime juice
2	teaspoons ground cumin
1	teaspoon ground coriander
1	teaspoon salt
1/2	teaspoon ground cloves
1/2	teaspoon cayenne pepper
1/2	teaspoon pepper
6	garlic cloves, minced
6	bone-in chicken thighs (about 2-1/4 pounds)

We may not live anywhere near the border, but we favor Mexican food! Served with warm tortillas and chili beans, this is a much-requested dish whenever we fire up the grill.

—Patricia Collins
Imbler, Oregon

In a small bowl, combine the first 10 ingredients. Set aside half of marinade for basting; cover and refrigerate. Pour remaining marinade in a large resealable plastic bag; add chicken. Seal bag and turn to coat; refrigerate for at least 4 hours.

Drain and discard marinade. Grill chicken, uncovered, over medium-low heat, for 20-40 minutes or until a meat thermometer reads 180°, turning and basting frequently with reserved marinade. **YIELD: 4-6 SERVINGS.**

EDITOR'S NOTE: Watch closely; chicken may burn easily.

GRILLED CHICKEN WITH CHUTNEY

My husband didn't like plums until he tasted them cooked with peaches, dried cranberries and spices in this robust chutney. It's also great with pork tenderloin.

—Gilda Lester
Wilmington,
North Carolina

- 3 medium plums, chopped
- 2/3 cup sugar
- 1/2 cup white wine vinegar
- 3 tablespoons balsamic vinegar
- 2 tablespoons dried cranberries
- 1 garlic clove, minced
- 1 teaspoon minced fresh gingerroot
- 1/4 teaspoon ground allspice
- 1/4 teaspoon crushed red pepper flakes
- 2 cups chopped peeled peaches
- 1/4 cup finely chopped red onion
- 1 teaspoon Dijon mustard
- 1/2 teaspoon minced seeded jalapeno pepper
- 6 boneless skinless chicken breast halves (5 ounces *each*)
- 2 tablespoons olive oil
- 1 tablespoon Tex-Mex chili seasoning mix

Red leaf lettuce

Additional chopped jalapenos, optional

For chutney, in a large saucepan, combine the first nine ingredients. Bring to a boil; cook and stir for 6-8 minutes or until thickened. Stir in the peaches, onion, mustard and jalapeno. Cool to room temperature.

Brush chicken with oil; sprinkle with chili seasoning mix. Grill chicken, covered, over medium heat for 5-6 minutes on each side or until a meat thermometer reads 170°. Slice chicken; serve on lettuce leaves with chutney. Sprinkle with additional jalapenos if desired. **YIELD: 6 SERVINGS.**

EDITOR'S NOTE: When cutting hot peppers, disposable gloves are recommended. Avoid touching your face.

SPICED CHICKEN WITH MELON SALSA

1/4	teaspoon salt
1/4	teaspoon ground ginger
1/4	teaspoon ground nutmeg
1/8	to 1/4 teaspoon crushed red pepper flakes
2	boneless skinless chicken breast halves (5 ounces *each*)

SALSA:

1/3	cup *each* diced cantaloupe, honeydew and watermelon
2	tablespoons diced celery
1	green onion, finely chopped
2	teaspoons minced fresh mint *or* 1/4 teaspoon dried mint
2	teaspoons chopped candied ginger
2	teaspoons lime juice
2	teaspoons honey
1/4	teaspoon grated lime peel

Both sweet and spicy, this summery entree can be grilled or broiled. To speed up preparation, I buy a container of mixed melon pieces at the supermarket.

—Roxanne Chan
  Albany, California

In a small bowl, combine the salt, ginger, nutmeg and pepper flakes; rub over chicken. Grill, covered, over medium heat or broil 6 in. from the heat for 6 minutes on each side or until a meat thermometer reads 170°.

Meanwhile, in a small bowl, combine the salsa ingredients. Serve with chicken.
YIELD: 2 SERVINGS.

BLUEBERRY CHUTNEY FOR GRILLED CHICKEN

2	cups fresh *or* frozen blueberries
1/2	cup chopped dried apricots
1/3	cup packed brown sugar
1/3	cup finely chopped onion
3	tablespoons cider vinegar
3	teaspoons minced fresh gingerroot
1/2	teaspoon minced garlic
1/4	teaspoon ground coriander
1/2	cup Italian salad dressing
6	boneless skinless chicken breast halves (6 ounces *each*)

Fresh blueberries and dried apricots are tossed with brown sugar and other tasty ingredients, then lightly simmered to create a delicious berry chutney. Serve this treat warm or even at room temperature.

—Taste of Home
Test Kitchen

For chutney, in a large saucepan, combine the first eight ingredients. Bring to a boil. Reduce heat to medium-low; cook, uncovered, for 20-25 minutes or until thickened, stirring occasionally.

Meanwhile, pour salad dressing into a large resealable plastic bag; add the chicken. Seal bag and turn to coat; refrigerate for 20 minutes.

Cool chutney to room temperature. Drain and discard marinade. Grill chicken, covered, over medium heat for 5-6 minutes on each side or until a meat thermometer reads 170°. Serve with chutney. **YIELD: 6 SERVINGS.**

ZESTY MUSTARD CHICKEN

1/2	cup prepared mustard
1/2	cup honey
1	tablespoon salt-free seasoning blend
1	tablespoon Worcestershire sauce
1	broiler/fryer chicken (3 pounds), cut in half

In a small bowl, combine the mustard, honey, seasoning blend and Worcestershire sauce. Carefully loosen the skin of the chicken; spoon some of the mustard mixture under the skin.

Coat grill rack with cooking spray before starting the grill. Place chicken skin side up on grill rack. Grill, covered, over indirect medium heat for 20-30 minutes on each side or until juices run clear and a meat thermometer reads 180°, basting occasionally with remaining mustard mixture.

Cover chicken and let stand for 5 minutes before cutting into serving-size pieces. **YIELD: 6 SERVINGS.**

Halved chicken is a perfect choice for winter grilling. Cooked over indirect heat, it virtually eliminates grill flare-ups. This version features a tangy four-ingredient mustard sauce you can whip up in minutes.

—Michael Everidge
Morristown, Tennessee

CAMPFIRE CASSEROLES

- 6 bone-in chicken breast halves (8 ounces *each*)
- 6 sheets heavy-duty aluminum foil (18 inches x 12 inches)
- 6 carrots, cut into 1/4-inch slices
- 3 medium potatoes, cut into 1/4-inch slices
- 1/2 pound fresh mushrooms, quartered
- 1 medium onion, sliced
- 6 tablespoons butter
- 1 can (10-3/4 ounces) condensed cream of chicken soup, undiluted

Salt and pepper to taste

Place each chicken breast in the center of a piece of foil. Divide carrots, potatoes, mushrooms and onion equally and place on top and around each piece of chicken. Top each with 1 tablespoon butter and about 2 tablespoons soup. Sprinkle with salt and pepper.

Bring opposite long edges of foil together over the top of each breast and fold down several times. Fold the short ends toward the food and crimp tightly to prevent leaks.

Grill, covered, over medium-low heat for 50-60 minutes or until a meat thermometer reads 170°. To serve, carefully unwrap packets to allow steam to escape; spoon contents onto individual plates. **YIELD: 6 SERVINGS.**

Because they make individual portions, you can tailor these chicken and vegetable "casseroles" to suit everyone's tastes. They're great when camping in a group.

—Julie Wilson
   Fort Collins, Colorado

BARBECUE JACK CHICKEN

- 4 boneless skinless chicken breast halves (6 ounces *each*)
- 4 slices pepper Jack cheese
- 1 cup barbecue sauce

Carefully cut a pocket in each chicken breast half. Fill with cheese; secure with metal or soaked wooden skewers.

Grill chicken, covered, over medium heat or broil 4 in. from the heat for 6-8 minutes on each side or a meat thermometer reads 170°, basting frequently with barbecue sauce. **YIELD: 4 SERVINGS.**

Pepper Jack cheese from the deli and bottled barbecue sauce are all you need to dress up these simple grilled chicken breasts.

—Taste of Home Test Kitchen

CHICKEN WITH BLACK BEAN SALSA

There's nothing timid about the flavors in this Southwestern-style entree. Prepared on the grill, it's a fast, fun meal for a busy weeknight or a weekend get-together with friends.

—Trisha Kruse
Eagle, Idaho

1	can (15 ounces) black beans, rinsed and drained
1	can (8 ounces) unsweetened crushed pineapple, drained
1	small red onion, chopped
1	plum tomato, chopped
1	garlic clove, minced
2	tablespoons lime juice
1/4	teaspoon salt
1/4	teaspoon coarsely ground pepper

RUB:

1	tablespoon brown sugar
1	teaspoon hot pepper sauce
1/2	teaspoon garlic powder
1/2	teaspoon salt
1/2	teaspoon coarsely ground pepper
4	boneless skinless chicken breast halves (4 ounces *each*)

For salsa, in a large bowl, combine the first eight ingredients; refrigerate until serving. Combine the brown sugar, pepper sauce, garlic powder, salt and pepper; rub over both sides of chicken.

If grilling the chicken, coat grill rack with cooking spray before starting the grill. Grill chicken, covered, over medium heat or broil 4 in. from the heat for 4-7 minutes on each side or until a meat thermometer reads 170°. Serve with salsa. **YIELD: 4 SERVINGS.**

SUPREME KABOBS

3/4	cup canola oil
1/3	cup soy sauce
1/4	cup red wine vinegar
1/4	cup lemon juice
2	tablespoons Worcestershire sauce
2	teaspoons ground mustard
1	teaspoon pepper
1	teaspoon dried parsley flakes
2	pounds boneless skinless chicken breasts, cut into 1-inch cubes
12	ounces small fresh mushrooms
1	medium green *or* sweet red pepper, cut into 1-inch pieces
2	small onions, cut into 1-inch pieces
1	can (8 ounces) pineapple chunks, drained

I first prepared these splendid skewers at a birthday party...they were an instant success! I especially enjoy serving them for casual weekend meals with friends.
—Karla Gleason
Waterville, Ohio

In a small bowl, combine the first eight ingredients. Place half of the marinade in two large resealable plastic bags. Add chicken to one bag and the mushrooms, pepper and onions to the second bag. Seal bags and turn to coat; refrigerate for at least 6 hours.

Drain and discard marinade from chicken and vegetables. Thread the chicken, vegetables and pineapple alternately on skewers.

Grill, covered, over medium-low heat, turning frequently, for 16-20 minutes or until chicken is no longer pink. **YIELD: 8 SERVINGS.**

CHIPOTLE CHICKEN FAJITAS

1	bottle (12 ounces) chili sauce
1/4	cup lime juice
4	chipotle peppers in adobo sauce
1	pound boneless skinless chicken breasts, cut into strips
1/2	cup cider vinegar
1/3	cup packed brown sugar
1/3	cup molasses
4	medium green peppers, cut into 1-inch pieces
1	large onion, cut into 1-inch pieces
1	tablespoon olive oil
1/8	teaspoon salt
1/8	teaspoon pepper
10	flour tortillas (8 inches)
1-1/2	cups chopped tomatoes
1	cup (4 ounces) shredded Mexican cheese blend

I've had this recipe for 3 years, and my husband and I just love it. Be careful with the chipotle peppers as they can be very hot. I changed it up a little to fit our taste. You may want to adjust the amount to your preference.

—Melissa Thomeczek
  Hannibal, Missouri

Place the chili sauce, lime juice and chipotle peppers in a food processor; cover and process until blended. Transfer 1/2 cup to a large resealable plastic bag; add chicken. Seal bag and turn to coat; refrigerate for 1-4 hours.

Pour remaining marinade into a small bowl; add the vinegar, brown sugar and molasses. Cover and refrigerate.

On six metal or soaked wooden skewers, alternately thread chicken, green peppers and onion. Brush with oil; sprinkle with salt and pepper. Grill, covered, over medium heat for 10-16 minutes or until chicken is no longer pink, turning occasionally.

Unskewer chicken and vegetables into a large bowl; add 1/2 cup chipotle-molasses mixture and toss to coat. Keep warm.

Grill tortillas, uncovered, over medium heat for 45-55 seconds on each side or until warmed. Top with chicken mixture, tomatoes, cheese and remaining chipotle-molasses mixture. **YIELD: 5 SERVINGS.**

TEXAS-STYLE FRYER

1	tablespoon seasoned salt
1	teaspoon pepper
1	broiler/fryer chicken (3 to 3-1/2 pounds)
2	garlic cloves, minced
1/2	cup butter
1/2	cup chicken broth
1/4	cup lemon juice

Combine seasoned salt and pepper; rub inside and outside of chicken. Place chicken on rotisserie rod on grill with a drip pan according to manufacturer's directions.

In a small saucepan, saute garlic in butter for 1 minute. Stir in broth and lemon juice.

Pour into drip pan and place under chicken. Baste with sauce every 15 minutes for 1 to 1-1/2 hours or until a meat thermometer reads 180°. Additional broth may be added to basting sauce if necessary. **YIELD: 4 SERVINGS.**

Spring is a special season for us. That's when we invite family and friends over to see the beautiful wildflowers in our backyard and to sample this tender, juicy chicken.

—Molly Koepp
   Canyon Lake, Texas

MAPLE MUSTARD CHICKEN

For make-ahead convenience, I marinate these chicken breasts overnight. Their sweet-mustard flavor goes well with baked potatoes. They make delightful chicken sandwiches, too.

—Lynda Ebel, Medicine Hat, Alberta

1/2	cup maple syrup
3	tablespoons red wine vinegar
2	tablespoons Dijon mustard
1	tablespoon canola oil
2	garlic cloves, minced
3/4	to 1 teaspoon pepper
6	boneless skinless chicken breast halves (about 1-1/2 pounds)

In a small bowl, combine the first six ingredients. Reserve 1/4 cup for basting; cover and refrigerate. Pour remaining marinade into a large resealable plastic bag; add chicken. Seal bag and turn to coat; refrigerate for 4-8 hours, turning occasionally. Drain and discard marinade.

Grill, uncovered, over medium heat for 3 minutes on each side. Grill 6-8 minutes longer or until a meat thermometer reads 170°, basting with the reserved marinade and turning occasionally. **YIELD: 6 SERVINGS.**

GRILLED LEMON CHICKEN

3/4	cup thawed lemonade concentrate
1/3	cup soy sauce
1	garlic clove, minced
1	teaspoon seasoned salt
1/2	teaspoon celery salt
1/8	teaspoon garlic powder
2	broiler/fryer chickens (3 to 3-1/2 pounds *each*), quartered

In a bowl, whisk the first six ingredients until combined. Pour half into a shallow glass dish. Cover and refrigerate remaining sauce.

Dip chicken on both sides into sauce; discard sauce. Grill chicken, covered, over medium heat for 30 minutes, turning occasionally. Brush with reserved sauce. Continue basting and turning chicken several times for 10-15 minutes more or until juices run clear. **YIELD: 8 SERVINGS.**

The secret behind the citrus flavor in my chicken is simply lemonade concentrate.

—Linda Nilsen, Anoka, Minnesota

7
TURKEY

PG. 163 | **BRINED GRILLED TURKEY BREAST**

PROVING IT'S NOT JUST FOR THANKSGIVING ANYMORE, TURKEY HAS BECOME A DINNERTIME STAPLE IN HOMES FROM COAST TO COAST. NOW IT'S EASIER THAN EVER TO ENJOY THE SUCCULENT FLAVOR OF TURKEY ALL YEAR. JUST CONSIDER THESE FINGER-LICKING IDEAS THAT GRILL THE BIG BIRD TO PERFECTION EACH AND EVERY TIME.

SAVORY GRILLED TURKEY

My family likes this recipe so much that we even fire up the grill for it during winter. We truly enjoy this juicy, grilled bird all year long.

—Karen Buenting, Livermore, Iowa

1	**turkey (12 pounds)**
1	**cup butter, cubed**
1/2	**cup cider vinegar**
1/2	**cup lemon juice**
1	**tablespoon Worcestershire sauce**
1	**tablespoon A.1 steak sauce**
1	**teaspoon salt**
1	**teaspoon pepper**
1	**teaspoon Louisiana-style hot sauce**

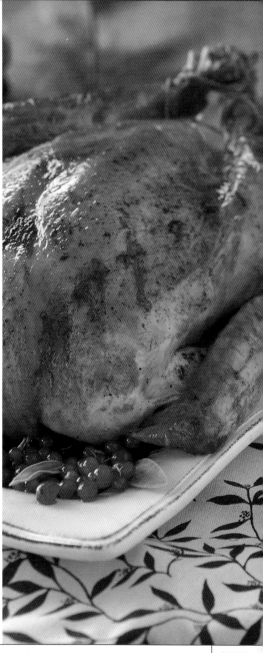

Remove giblets from turkey (discard or save for another use). Coat grill rack with cooking spray before starting the grill. Prepare grill for indirect heat, using a drip pan. Skewer turkey openings; tie drumsticks together.

Place turkey over drip pan; grill, covered, over indirect medium heat for 1 hour.

Meanwhile, in a small saucepan, combine the remaining ingredients. Bring to a boil. Reduce heat; simmer for 10 minutes, stirring occasionally. Remove the sauce from the heat. Set aside 2/3 cup for serving.

Grill turkey 1-2 hours longer or until a meat thermometer reads 180°, basting frequently with remaining sauce. Cover and let stand for 15 minutes before carving. Serve with reserved sauce. **YIELD: 12 SERVINGS.**

This is a combination of several favorite family recipes. People who try it for the first time are amazed to find that it's not only flavorful but healthy as well.

—Mary Relyea, Canastota, New York

PEPPERY GRILLED TURKEY BREAST

2	tablespoons light brown sugar
1	tablespoon salt
2	teaspoons ground cinnamon
1	teaspoon cayenne pepper
1/2	teaspoon ground mustard
1	bone-in turkey breast (5 pounds)
1	cup reduced-sodium chicken broth
1/4	cup white vinegar
1/4	cup jalapeno pepper jelly
2	tablespoons olive oil

In a small bowl, combine the brown sugar, salt, cinnamon, cayenne and mustard. With fingers, carefully loosen the skin from both sides of turkey breast. Spread half of spice mixture under turkey skin; secure skin to underside of breast with wooden toothpicks. Spread remaining spice mixture over the skin.

Coat grill rack with cooking spray before starting the grill. Prepare grill for indirect heat, using a drip pan. Place turkey over drip pan. Grill, covered, over indirect medium heat for 30 minutes.

In a small saucepan, combine the broth, vinegar, jelly and oil. Cook and stir over medium heat for 2 minutes or until jelly is melted. Set aside 1/2 cup. Baste turkey with some of the remaining jelly mixture. Grill 1 to 1-1/2 hours longer or until a meat thermometer reads 170°, basting every 15 minutes.

Cover and let stand for 10 minutes. Remove and discard turkey skin if desired. Brush with reserved jelly mixture before slicing. **YIELD: 15 SERVINGS.**

SIMPLE TURKEY BREAST

1	bone-in wild turkey breast (about 1-1/2 pounds), split
1	bottle (8 ounces) fat-free honey Dijon salad dressing

Place turkey in a large resealable plastic bag; add salad dressing. Seal bag and turn to coat; refrigerate overnight, turning occasionally.

Drain and discard marinade. Grill turkey, covered, over indirect medium heat for 45-55 minutes or until a meat thermometer reads 170°. **YIELD: 2 SERVINGS.**

With only two ingredients, this is definitely the easiest recipe I have for cooking the wild turkey that my husband brings home during spring hunting season. The grilled meat takes on a wonderful sweet smoky flavor we just love.

—Michelle Kaase
 Tomball, Texas

TURKEY TENDERLOINS FOR TWO

I frequently serve these turkey tenderloins with grilled potatoes and rosemary or grilled summer vegetables. A marinade of fragrant herbs and soy sauce create a terrific flavor combination.

—Pamela Anderson
Noblesville, Indiana

1/4 cup canola oil

1/4 cup reduced-sodium soy sauce

1/2 teaspoon dried basil

1/2 teaspoon dried marjoram

1/2 teaspoon dried thyme

2 turkey breast tenderloins (6 ounces *each*)

In a small bowl, combine the oil, soy sauce, basil, marjoram and thyme. Pour 1/3 cup into a large resealable plastic bag; add turkey. Seal bag and turn to coat; refrigerate for up to 4 hours. Cover and refrigerate remaining marinade for basting.

Coat grill rack with cooking spray before starting the grill. Drain and discard marinade from turkey. Grill turkey, covered, over medium heat for 12-14 minutes or until a meat thermometer reads 170°, turning twice and basting occasionally with reserved marinade. **YIELD: 2 SERVINGS.**

HONEY-GINGER TURKEY KABOBS

- 2 tablespoons chopped green onion
- 2 tablespoons soy sauce
- 1 tablespoon honey
- 1 tablespoon minced fresh gingerroot
- 1 teaspoon lime juice
- 2 garlic cloves, minced
- 1 pound turkey breast tenderloins, cut into 1-inch cubes
- 2 cups cubed fresh pineapple
- 1 medium sweet red pepper, cut into 1-inch pieces
- 1 medium red onion, cut into chunks
- 1 medium lime, cut into wedges

PINEAPPLE RICE:

- 2-1/2 cups water
- 1 cup uncooked long grain rice
- 1/2 cup chopped dried pineapple
- 2 teaspoons butter
- 1/2 teaspoon grated lime peel
- 1/4 teaspoon salt
- 1/4 cup minced fresh cilantro
- 1/4 cup chopped green onions
- 2 tablespoons lime juice

Lime juice and fresh pineapple lend an island flair to these fun kabobs, served with well-seasoned rice. I got the recipe from a friend and make it often.

—Pam Thomas
Marion, Iowa

In a large resealable plastic bag, combine the first six ingredients; add turkey. Seal bag and turn to coat; refrigerate for at least 2 hours.

Drain and discard marinade. On eight metal or soaked wooden skewers, alternately thread the turkey, pineapple, red pepper, red onion and lime wedges; set aside.

In a large saucepan, bring water to a boil. Stir in the rice, dried pineapple, butter, lime peel and salt. Reduce heat; cover and simmer for 15-20 minutes or until tender.

Meanwhile, grill kabobs, covered, over medium heat or broil 4-6 in. from the heat for 4-6 minutes on each side or until turkey is no longer pink and vegetables are tender. Stir the cilantro, onions and lime juice into the rice. Serve with kabobs. **YIELD: 4 SERVINGS.**

GRILLING TIP

GINGERROOT is the perfect addition to marinades and bold basting sauces. Look for fresh gingerroot in the produce section of your supermarket. Tightly wrapped, gingerroot can be frozen for 2 months.

MUSTARD TURKEY CUTLETS

- 2 teaspoons cornstarch
- 1/2 teaspoon salt, *divided*
- 1/8 teaspoon plus 1/4 teaspoon pepper, *divided*
- 1/2 cup thawed apple juice concentrate
- 1/4 cup Dijon mustard
- 1-1/2 tablespoons minced fresh rosemary *or* 1-1/2 teaspoons dried rosemary, crushed
- 1 package (17.6 ounces) turkey breast cutlets
- 1 teaspoon olive oil

In a small saucepan, combine the cornstarch, 1/4 teaspoon salt and 1/8 teaspoon pepper. Gradually whisk in the concentrate, mustard and rosemary until blended. Cook and stir over medium-high heat until thickened and bubbly. Reduce heat; cook and stir 2 minutes longer. Set aside 1/4 cup sauce.

Coat grill rack with cooking spray before starting the grill. Brush turkey with oil; sprinkle with remaining salt and pepper. Grill, covered, over medium heat for 2-3 minutes on each side or until no longer pink, basting occasionally with remaining sauce. Brush with reserved sauce before serving. **YIELD: 4 SERVINGS.**

Grilled turkey cutlets are treated with a slightly sweet sauce that mustard-lovers will thoroughly enjoy. This recipe feels fancy, but it's ideal for a weeknight.
—Deborah Williams, Peoria, Arizona

TURKEY WITH CRANBERRY-GRAPE SAUCE

- 1 teaspoon cornstarch
- 1/2 cup orange juice
- 1/4 cup dried cranberries
- 4-1/2 teaspoons honey
- 1 tablespoon lemon juice
- 2 turkey breast tenderloins (12 ounces *each*) , halved widthwise
- 2 teaspoons olive oil
- 1 teaspoon coarsely ground pepper
- 1/2 teaspoon salt
- 1-1/2 cups green grapes, halved

In a small saucepan, combine the first five ingredients until smooth. Bring to a boil; cook and stir for 1-2 minutes or until thickened. Cover and refrigerate.

Coat grill rack with cooking spray before starting the grill. Flatten turkey to 3/4-in. thickness. Combine oil, pepper and salt; rub over both sides of turkey. Grill turkey, covered, over direct medium heat or broil 4-6 in. from the heat for 5-7 minutes on each side or until no longer pink.

Just before serving, stir grapes into sauce. Serve turkey with cranberry-grape sauce. **YIELD: 4 SERVINGS.**

Our son-in-law brought home wild turkey, which inspired this delectable main dish. The sauce stirs up very quickly...and you can grill the turkey in just a few minutes.

—Marguerite Shaeffer
Sewell, New Jersey

GINGER TURKEY TENDERLOINS

1/4   **cup reduced-sodium soy sauce**

4   **teaspoons canola oil**

1   **teaspoon sugar**

1   **garlic clove, minced**

1/2   **teaspoon ground ginger**

1/2   **teaspoon ground mustard**

3/4   **pound turkey breast tenderloins**

In a small bowl, combine the soy sauce, oil, sugar, garlic, ginger and mustard. Pour 1/4 cup marinade into a large resealable plastic bag; add turkey. Seal bag and turn to coat; refrigerate for up to 4 hours. Cover and refrigerate remaining marinade for basting.

Coat grill rack with cooking spray before starting the grill. Drain and discard marinade from turkey. Grill turkey, covered, over medium heat for 8-10 minutes or until a meat thermometer reads 170°, turning twice and basting occasionally with reserved marinade. Cut into slices. **YIELD: 2 SERVINGS.**

I've been using this recipe for 10 years—we love it! I am a high school teacher, and a student actually gave me the recipe.

—Debra Holt
   Franklin, Virginia

This is a citrusy treat for the grill; it's very easy to prepare and absolutely delicious. Best of all, it's a healthy kabob for summer picnics and family get-togethers.

—Edie DeSpain, Logan, Utah

TURKEY FRUIT KABOBS

3/4   **cup thawed lemonade concentrate**

3   **tablespoons canola oil**

3   **tablespoons reduced-sodium soy sauce**

1   **pound turkey breast tenderloins, cut into 1-in. cubes**

1   **honeydew half, seeded, peeled and cut into 1-1/2-in. cubes**

1   **medium mango, peeled and cut into 1-1/2-in. cubes**

In a small bowl, combine the lemonade concentrate, oil and soy sauce. Pour 1/2 cup marinade into a large resealable plastic bag; add turkey. Seal bag and turn to coat; refrigerate for 2 hours. Cover and refrigerate remaining marinade.

Coat grill rack with cooking spray before starting the grill. Drain and discard marinade. On four metal or soaked wooden skewers, alternately thread turkey and fruits.

Grill, covered, over medium-hot heat for 3-4 minutes on each side or until meat is no longer pink, basting frequently with reserved marinade. **YIELD: 4 SERVINGS.**

BRINED GRILLED TURKEY BREAST

You'll want to give thanks for this mouthwatering turkey! Moist, slightly sweet and a hint of spice make this one of our best turkeys ever.

—Tina Repak-Mirilovich
Johnstown,
Pennsylvania

2	quarts cold water, *divided*
1/2	cup kosher salt
1/2	cup packed brown sugar
1	tablespoon whole peppercorns
1	boneless skinless turkey breast half (2 to 3 pounds)

BASTING SAUCE:

1/4	cup canola oil
1/4	cup sesame oil
1/4	cup reduced-sodium soy sauce
3	tablespoons lemon juice
2	tablespoons honey
3	garlic cloves, minced
1/4	teaspoon dried thyme
1/4	teaspoon crushed red pepper flakes

GRILLING TIP

BRINING soaks meat in a solution of water and salt (such as kosher, sea or table salt). Brining tenderizes lean meats so they do not dry out as easily when grilled. A brine can be flavored with sugars or seasonings.

In a large saucepan, combine 1 quart water, salt, brown sugar and peppercorns. Bring to a boil. Cook and stir until salt and sugar are dissolved. Remove from the heat. Add the remaining cold water to cool the brine to room temperature.

Place a large resealable plastic bag inside a second plastic bag; add turkey breast. Carefully pour cooled brine into bag. Squeeze out as much air as possible; seal bags and turn to coat. Place in a pan. Refrigerate for 4-6 hours.

Prepare grill for indirect heat, using a drip pan. Meanwhile, combine basting sauce ingredients. Place turkey over drip pan and grill, covered, over indirect medium heat for 1-1/4 to 1-1/2 hours or until a meat thermometer reads 170°, basting occasionally with sauce. Cover and let stand for 10 minutes before slicing. **YIELD: 6 SERVINGS.**

EDITOR'S NOTE: This recipe was tested with Morton brand kosher salt. It is best not to use a prebasted turkey breast for this recipe. However, if you do, be sure to omit the salt in the recipe.

CITRUS GRILLED TURKEY CUTLETS

2	tablespoons *each* lemon, lime and orange juices
1	tablespoon minced fresh cilantro
1	tablespoon canola oil
1	tablespoon honey
1	small garlic clove, minced
1/2	teaspoon salt
1/2	teaspoon chili powder
1/4	teaspoon ground cumin
1/4	teaspoon pepper
1	package (17.6 ounces) turkey breast cutlets

In a large resealable plastic bag, combine the juices, cilantro, oil, honey, garlic and seasonings; add turkey. Seal bag and turn to coat; refrigerate for 2 hours.

Coat grill rack with cooking spray before starting the grill. Drain and discard marinade.

Grill turkey, covered, over medium heat for 2-4 minutes on each side or until no longer pink. **YIELD: 4 SERVINGS.**

My family loves this turkey recipe year-round, but it's especially nice in the summer as an alternative to grilled chicken. Add a green salad, grilled onions and peppers, plus some crusty bread for a great dinner.

—Janice Mentzer, Sharpsburg, Maryland

ROMANO BASIL TURKEY BREAST

4	ounces Romano cheese, cubed
1/2	cup fresh basil leaves, torn
4	lemon slices
4	garlic cloves, minced
1	bone-in turkey breast (4 to 5 pounds)
2	tablespoons olive oil
1/2	teaspoon salt
1/4	teaspoon pepper

Combine the cheese, basil, lemon slices and garlic. With fingers, carefully loosen skin from the turkey breast; place mixture under the skin. Secure skin to underside of breast with toothpicks. Rub skin with oil and sprinkle with salt and pepper.

Prepare grill for indirect heat, using a drip pan. Place turkey over drip pan. Grill, covered, over indirect medium heat for 1-1/2 to 2 hours or until a meat thermometer reads 170°. Remove toothpicks. Cover and let stand for 10 minutes before slicing. **YIELD: 8 SERVINGS.**

Guests will be impressed when you slice this golden, grilled turkey breast, dressed up with a flavorful layer of basil and cheese under the skin.

—Darlene Markham
Rochester, New York

MARINATED TURKEY SLICES

- 1/2 **cup soy sauce**
- 1/2 **cup canola oil**
- 1/2 **teaspoon prepared horseradish**
- 1/4 **teaspoon garlic powder**
- 1 **cup lemon-lime soda**
- 3 **pounds boneless skinless turkey breast halves, cut into 1/4-inch slices**

In a blender, combine soy sauce, oil, horseradish and garlic powder; cover and blend on high until smooth. Add soda; cover and blend on high until smooth.

Pour into several large resealable plastic bags. Add turkey; toss gently to coat. Cover and refrigerate overnight, turning once.

Drain and discard marinade. Grill turkey, covered, over medium-hot heat for 5-6 minutes or until no longer pink, turning occasionally. **YIELD: 12 SERVINGS.**

We love to entertain and have found this recipe makes plenty for a large get-together. The tender, flavorful turkey slices are always popular.

—Shavon Hoopes
Vernal, Utah

DILLY BARBECUED TURKEY

- 1 **cup plain yogurt**
- 1/2 **cup lemon juice**
- 1/3 **cup canola oil**
- 1/2 **cup minced fresh parsley**
- 1/2 **cup chopped green onions**
- 4 **garlic cloves, minced**
- 4 **tablespoons minced fresh dill *or* 4 teaspoons dill weed**
- 1 **teaspoon dried rosemary, crushed**
- 1 **teaspoon salt**
- 1/2 **teaspoon pepper**
- 1 **turkey breast half with bone (2-1/2 to 3 pounds)**

In a large bowl, combine the first 10 ingredients. Pour half into a large resealable plastic bag; add turkey. Seal bag and turn to coat. Cover and refrigerate for 6-8 hours or overnight. Cover and refrigerate remaining yogurt.

Drain and discard marinade from turkey. Grill turkey, covered, over medium-hot heat, basting often with reserved marinade, for 1 to 1-1/4 hours or until a meat thermometer reads 180°. **YIELD: 6 SERVINGS.**

This is one of my brother-in-law's special cookout recipes. The onions, garlic and herbs in the marinade make a tasty, tender turkey, and the tempting aroma prompts the family to gather around the grill.

—Sue Walker, Greentown, Indiana

GRILLED JERK TURKEY

1/4	cup rice vinegar
1/4	cup orange juice
2	tablespoons canola oil
2	tablespoons reduced-sodium soy sauce
2	green onions, chopped
2	garlic cloves, minced
4	teaspoons chopped jalapeno pepper
1	tablespoon Caribbean jerk seasoning
1-1/2	teaspoons packed brown sugar
1-1/2	teaspoons minced fresh gingerroot
1/2	teaspoon salt
1	package (20 ounces) turkey breast tenderloins

Moist and seasoned with ginger, Caribbean jerk spices and jalapeno pepper, this simple grilled entree is more tangy than hot and spicy. It's wonderful for backyard get-togethers with family and friends.

—Diane Halferty
   Corpus Christi, Texas

In a small bowl, combine the first 11 ingredients. Pour 1/2 cup marinade into a large resealable plastic bag; add turkey. Seal bag and turn to coat; refrigerate for 2 hours. Cover and refrigerate remaining marinade.

Coat grill rack with cooking spray before starting the grill. Drain and discard marinade from the turkey. Grill, covered, over medium heat for 7-10 minutes on each side or until a meat thermometer reads 170°, basting occasionally with reserved marinade. Cut into slices. **YIELD: 4 SERVINGS.**

EDITOR'S NOTE: When cutting hot peppers, disposable gloves are recommended. Avoid touching your face.

TANGY TURKEY KABOBS

- 12 small red potatoes, cut in half
- 1/2 cup honey mustard salad dressing
- 2 teaspoons dried rosemary, crushed
- 1 package (17.6 ounces) turkey breast cutlets, cut into 1-inch strips
- 2 medium green apples, cut into 1-inch pieces

Place potatoes in a large saucepan and cover with water. Bring to a boil; cook for 5 minutes or until crisp-tender; drain. Meanwhile, in a small bowl, combine salad dressing and rosemary; set aside.

Fold turkey strips in thirds; thread onto four metal or soaked wooden skewers alternately with potatoes and apples.

Spoon half of the dressing over kabobs. Grill, uncovered, over medium-hot heat for 5-7 minutes on each side or until no longer pink, basting and turning occasionally with remaining dressing. **YIELD: 4 SERVINGS.**

Unlike traditional kabobs, these call for turkey breast slices, potatoes and apple chunks. The flavorful honey-mustard salad dressing shines through in each delicious bite.

—Taste of Home Test Kitchen

This is a recipe my son brought home from college. It's definitely become a summer grilling favorite with my gang.

—Shirley Glaesman
 Pelican Rapids,
 Minnesota

GRILLED TURKEY TENDERLOINS

- 1 can (12 ounces) lemon-lime soda
- 1/4 cup soy sauce
- 1/4 cup canola oil
- 1 teaspoon garlic powder
- 4 turkey breast tenderloins (8 ounces *each*)

In a large resealable plastic bag, combine the soda, soy sauce, oil and garlic powder; add turkey. Seal bag and turn to coat; refrigerate for 8 hours or overnight, turning occasionally.

Drain and discard marinade. Grill tenderloins, covered, over medium heat for 7-10 minutes on each side or until a meat thermometer reads 170°. Cut into 1/2-in. slices. **YIELD: 6 SERVINGS.**

HICKORY TURKEY

2	cups packed brown sugar
3/4	cup salt
1	jar (6 ounces) pickled ginger slices, drained
4	bay leaves
2	whole garlic bulbs, halved
2	tablespoons minced fresh marjoram *or* 2 teaspoons dried marjoram
2	tablespoons minced fresh thyme *or* 2 teaspoons dried thyme
2	tablespoons minced fresh sage
2	teaspoons crushed red pepper flakes
3	quarts water
1-1/2	cups reduced-sodium soy sauce
1	cup maple syrup
1	turkey (12 to 14 pounds)
4	cups soaked hickory wood chips
1	large onion, cut into wedges
1	large navel orange, cut into wedges
6	garlic cloves, peeled
1/4	cup canola oil
2	tablespoons sesame oil

In a stockpot, bring the first 12 ingredients to a boil. Cook and stir until sugar and salt are dissolved. Remove from the heat; cool to room temperature.

Remove giblets from turkey; discard. Place a turkey-size oven roasting bag inside a second roasting bag; add turkey. Carefully pour cooled marinade into bag. Squeeze out as much air as possible; seal bags and turn to coat. Place in a roasting pan. Refrigerate for 18-24 hours, turning several times.

Prepare grill for indirect heat, using a drip pan. Add wood chips to grill according to manufacturer's directions. Drain turkey and discard brine. Rinse turkey under cold water; pat dry. Place the onion, orange and peeled garlic inside cavity. Skewer turkey openings; tie drumsticks together. Combine oils; rub over skin.

Place turkey over the drip pan. Grill, covered, over indirect medium heat for 1 hour. Tent turkey with foil; grill 1-2 hours longer or until a meat thermometer reads 180°. Cover and let stand for 15 minutes before carving. **YIELD: 12 SERVINGS.**

EDITOR'S NOTE: It is best not to use a prebasted turkey for this recipe. However, if you do, omit the salt in the recipe.

Marjoram, thyme, sage and maple syrup help make this grilled turkey simply unforgettable. It's a wonderful way to celebrate special occasions any time of the year.

—Kim Russell
North Wales,
Pennsylvania

GRILLING TIP

WOOD CHIPS impart incredible richness to grilled foods. For turkey and chicken dishes that are slightly sweet, use apple, cherry and peach wood types. For hearty dishes, use hickory, maple and pecan chips.

KIELBASA APPLE KABOBS

1/4 cup sugar

1 tablespoon cornstarch

3/4 cup cranberry juice

2 tablespoons cider vinegar

2 teaspoons soy sauce

1 pound smoked turkey kielbasa, cut into 1-1/2-inch pieces

2 medium tart apples, cut into wedges

1 medium sweet red pepper, cut into 1-inch pieces

1 medium green pepper, cut into 1-inch pieces

In a large saucepan, combine sugar and cornstarch. Stir in cranberry juice, vine-gar and soy sauce. Bring to a boil; cook and stir for 1-2 minutes or until sauce is thickened.

On eight metal or soaked wooden skewers, alternately thread sausage, apples and peppers. Grill, uncovered, over indirect heat for 8 minutes or until heated through, turning and brushing with glaze occasionally. **YIELD: 8 SERVINGS.**

MARINATED TURKEY TENDERLOINS

1 cup lemon-lime soda

1/4 cup soy sauce

2 tablespoons lemon juice

2 garlic cloves, minced

1 teaspoon prepared horseradish

1/2 teaspoon lemon-pepper seasoning

1/4 teaspoon curry powder

1/4 teaspoon ground ginger

1/4 teaspoon paprika

1/4 teaspoon crushed red pepper flakes

2 pounds turkey breast tenderloins

In a large bowl, combine the first 10 ingredients. Pour 1 cup into a large resealable plastic bag; add turkey. Seal bag and turn to coat; re-frigerate 8 hours or overnight, turning occasionally. Cover and refrig-erate remaining marinade for serving.

Drain and discard marinade from turkey. Grill, covered, over medium-hot heat for 10-12 minutes on each side or until a meat thermome-ter reads 170°. Serve with reserved marinade. **YIELD: 8 SERVINGS.**

8

PORK, LAMB & MORE

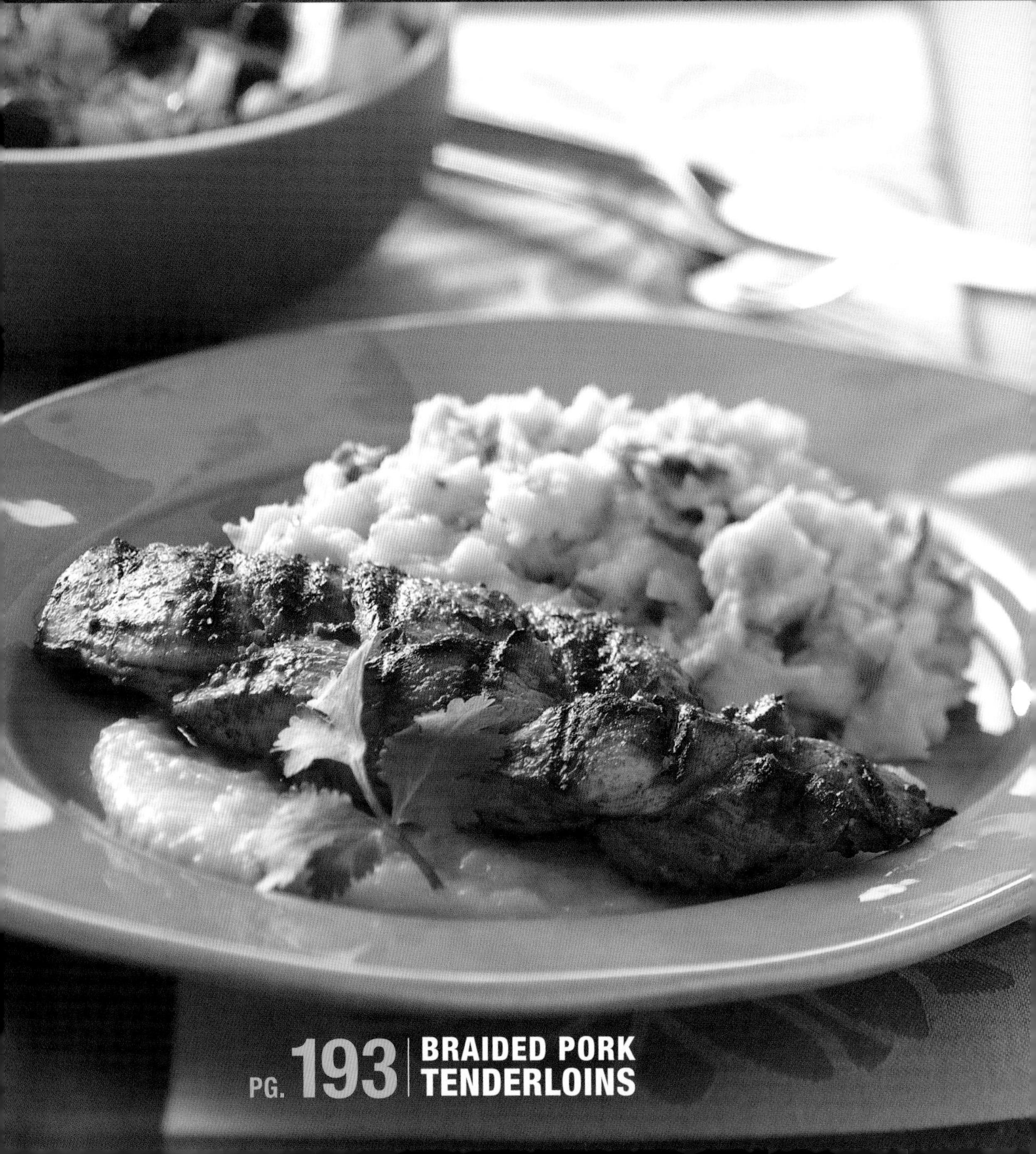

PG. 193 | BRAIDED PORK TENDERLOINS

SIZZLING STRIPS OF PORK TENDERLOIN, JUICY LAMB CHOPS, TANGY HAM STEAKS…THESE ARE JUST A FEW OF THE MOUTHWATERING SPECIALTIES YOU'LL FIND IN THIS POPULAR CHAPTER. WITH THEIR THICK AND HEARTY CONSISTENCY, PORK PRODUCTS ARE A NATURAL FIT FOR FLAME-BROILED MENUS. CONSIDER ANY OF THESE 43 RECIPES TO SEE WHAT WE MEAN!

ORANGE BARBECUED HAM

This recipe decreases the amount of time I spend in the kitchen…because my husband does the grilling!
—Lucy Kampstra, Bradenton, Florida

1/2	cup ketchup
1/3	cup orange marmalade
2	tablespoons finely chopped onion
2	tablespoons canola oil
1	tablespoon lemon juice
1	to 1-1/2 teaspoons ground mustard
3	to 5 drops hot pepper sauce
1	boneless fully cooked ham slice (1-1/2 pounds and 3/4 inch thick)

In a small bowl, combine the first seven ingredients. Pour half of the sauce into a microwave-safe bowl; set aside. Grill ham, covered, over indirect heat for 3-4 minutes on each side, basting occasionally with the remaining sauce.

Grill 6-8 minutes longer or until heated through, turning and basting occasionally. Cover and microwave reserved sauce on high for 30 seconds or until heated through. Serve with ham. **YIELD: 6 SERVINGS.**

Salsa gives Mom's delicious roast a zesty accent. It's so simple to make and always comes out tender and juicy. It will melt in your mouth!

—June Dress, Boise, Idaho

DUTCH OVEN PORK ROAST

- 1 **boneless whole pork loin roast (3 to 4 pounds)**
- 1 **jar (16 ounces) salsa**
- 1 **can (16 ounces) kidney beans, undrained**
- 1/4 **teaspoon salt**
- 1/4 **teaspoon pepper**

Prepare grill or campfire for low heat, using 20-24 charcoal briquettes or large wood chips.

Line a Dutch oven with heavy-duty aluminum foil; add pork. Combine the salsa, kidney beans, salt and pepper; pour over pork.

Cover Dutch oven. When briquettes or wood chips are covered with white ash, place Dutch oven directly on top of 10-12 of them. Using long-handled tongs, place remaining briquettes on pan cover.

Cook for 1-1/4 to 1-1/2 hours or until a meat thermometer reads 160°. To check for doneness, use the tongs to carefully lift the cover. **YIELD: 9 SERVINGS (3 CUPS SAUCE).**

LAMB KABOBS WITH BULGUR PILAF

- 30 **garlic cloves, crushed (1-1/2 to 2 bulbs)**
- 1/2 **cup balsamic vinegar**
- 3/4 **cup chopped fresh mint** *or* **1/4 cup dried mint**
- 1/4 **cup olive oil**
- 2 **pounds lean boneless lamb, cut into 1-1/2-inch cubes**

PILAF:
- 1/2 **cup butter, cubed**
- 1 **large onion, chopped**
- 1 **cup uncooked mini spiral pasta**
- 2 **cups bulgur**
- 3 **cups beef broth**

In a large resealable plastic bag, combine the garlic, vinegar, mint and oil; add lamb. Seal bag and turn to coat; refrigerate for several hours or overnight.

For pilaf, in a large skillet, melt butter. Add onion and pasta; saute until pasta is lightly browned. Add bulgur and stir to coat. Stir in broth. Bring to a boil. Reduce heat; cover and simmer for 25-30 minutes or until tender. Remove from the heat; let stand for 5 minutes. Fluff with a fork.

Drain and discard marinade. Thread onto six metal or soaked wooden skewers.

Grill kabobs, covered, over medium heat for 8-10 minutes or until meat reaches desired doneness, turning frequently. Serve with pilaf. **YIELD: 6 SERVINGS.**

EDITOR'S NOTE: This recipe was tested with Barilla brand mini fusilli pasta.

This is a great old family recipe that shows my Armenian heritage. The tender, slightly sweet lamb is complemented perfectly by the savory bulgur pilaf.

—Ruth Hartunian-
  Alumbaugh
  Willimantic,
  Connecticut

MARINATED GRILLED LAMB

1	boneless leg of lamb (3 to 4 pounds), trimmed
1/4	cup lemon juice
1/4	cup dry white wine *or* chicken broth
3	tablespoons olive oil
8	garlic cloves, minced
3	tablespoons minced fresh rosemary
1	tablespoon minced fresh thyme
1	tablespoon minced fresh oregano
1	teaspoon salt
1/2	teaspoon coarsely ground pepper
1	sprig fresh rosemary

Additional salt and pepper

If leg of lamb is tied, untie it. In a large resealable plastic bag, combine the lemon juice, wine, oil, garlic, rosemary, thyme, oregano, salt and pepper; add lamb. Seal bag and turn to coat. Refrigerate for 4 hours.

Drain and discard marinade. Prepare grill for indirect medium heat. Place rosemary sprig on lamb; roll up and tie with kitchen string, leaving a small section of the sprig exposed. Sprinkle with additional salt and pepper.

Grill lamb, covered, over indirect medium heat for 1-1/2 to 2 hours or until meat reaches desired doneness (for medium-rare, a meat thermometer should read 145°; medium, 160°; well-done, 170°). Remove rosemary sprig. Let meat stand for 10 minutes before slicing. **YIELD: 10 SERVINGS.**

SAUSAGE VEGGIE GRILL

- 1 **pound Italian sausage links, cut into 1/2-inch slices**
- 1 **medium zucchini, cut into 1-inch slices**
- 1 **medium yellow summer squash, cut into 1-inch slices**
- 1 **medium sweet red pepper, sliced**
- 1 **medium onion, cut into wedges**
- 1 **cup quartered fresh mushrooms**
- 1/4 **cup olive oil**
- 1 **tablespoon dried oregano**
- 1 **tablespoon dried parsley flakes**
- 1 **teaspoon garlic salt**
- 1 **teaspoon paprika**

In a large bowl, combine the first six ingredients. In a small bowl, combine the oil, oregano, parsley, garlic salt and paprika. Pour over sausage mixture; toss to coat. Divide between two pieces of heavy-duty foil (about 14 in. x 12 in.). Fold foil around sausage mixture and seal tightly.

Grill, covered, over medium heat for 25-30 minutes or until meat is no longer pink and vegetables are tender. Open foil carefully to allow steam to escape. **YIELD: 4 SERVINGS.**

With sausage, fresh vegetables and herbs, these grill packets are bursting with color and flavor. They're very easy to put together and taste yummy for a summer get-together on the patio.

—Laura Hillyer
Bayfield, Colorado

Spiedis (pronounced "speedeez") are a type of grilled meat sandwich considered a local specialty. This recipe is my own, but there are many variations in our area. In nearby Binghamton, Spiedi-Fest is held in August, featuring this delicious dish made of all different kinds of meat. Thousands of people attend. I hope you enjoy my pork version.

—Beatrice Riddell
Chenango Bridge, New York

PORK SPIEDIS

- 2 **cups tomato juice**
- 2 **large onions, finely chopped**
- 4 **to 5 garlic cloves, minced**
- 2 **tablespoons Worcestershire sauce**
- 2 **teaspoons chopped fresh basil** *or* 1 **teaspoon dried basil**

Pepper to taste

- 4 **pounds pork tenderloin, cut into 1-inch cubes**
- 12 **slices Italian bread**

In a large resealable plastic bag, combine the first six ingredients; add pork. Seal bag and turn to coat; refrigerate overnight.

Drain and discard marinade. Thread pork on small metal or soaked wooden skewers. Grill or broil for 15-20 minutes, turning occasionally, until meat is no longer pink.

To serve, wrap a slice of bread around about five pork cubes and pull off skewer. **YIELD: 12 SERVINGS.**

PORK FAJITA KABOBS

2	teaspoons paprika
1-1/2	teaspoons ground cumin
1-1/2	teaspoons dried oregano
1	teaspoon garlic powder
1/8	to 1/4 teaspoon crushed red pepper flakes
1-1/2	pounds boneless pork loin chops, cut into 1-inch cubes
1	small green pepper, cut into 1-inch pieces
1	small onion, cut into eight wedges
8	large fresh mushrooms
16	grape tomatoes
8	flour tortillas (8 inches), warmed
3/4	cup chunky salsa

In a large resealable plastic bag, combine the paprika, cumin, oregano, garlic powder and pepper flakes; add pork. Seal bag and toss to coat. On eight metal or soaked wooden skewers, alternately thread the pork, green pepper, onion, mushrooms and tomatoes.

Grill kabobs, covered, over medium heat for 5-8 minutes on each side or until meat is no longer pink and vegetables are tender. Place each kabob in a tortilla; remove skewers and fold tortillas in half. Serve with salsa. **YIELD: 4 SERVINGS.**

This has become my favorite way to cook pork loin. The grilled vegetable and meat chunks, seasoned with a homemade Southwestern-style spice blend, are appropriately served in a flour tortilla. Just top with salsa and enjoy!

—Bea Westphal, Slidell, Louisiana

Slow-cook the ribs during the day, and they will be ready to finish on the grill when you get home.

—Taste of Home Test Kitchen

BABY BACK RIBS

2-1/2	pounds pork baby back ribs, cut into eight pieces
5	cups water
1	medium onion, sliced
2	celery ribs, cut in half
2	teaspoons minced garlic, *divided*

1	teaspoon whole peppercorns
1/2	cup barbecue sauce
1/4	cup plum sauce
Dash	hot pepper sauce

Place the ribs in a 5-qt. slow cooker. Add the water, onion, celery, 1 teaspoon garlic and peppercorns. Cover and cook on low for 6 hours or until meat is tender.

In a small saucepan, combine the barbecue sauce, plum sauce, hot pepper sauce and remaining garlic. Cook and stir over medium heat for 5 minutes or until heated through. Remove ribs. Discard cooking juices and vegetables.

Coat grill rack with cooking spray before starting the grill. Brush ribs with sauce. Grill, uncovered, over medium-low heat for 8-10 minutes or until browned, turning occasionally and brushing with remaining sauce. **YIELD: 4 SERVINGS.**

PORK GRILLING CHART

Pork, fresh pork sausages and ground pork are done at 160°. Cooked sausages are done when heated through. For direct grilling, turn meat halfway through grilling time. The cooking times given are a guideline. Check for doneness with a meat thermometer.

CUT	WEIGHT OR THICKNESS	HEAT	APPROXIMATE COOKING TIME
LOIN OR RIB CHOP, BONE-IN	3/4 to 1 in.	medium/direct	8 to 10 minutes
	1-1/4 to 1-1/2 in.	medium/direct	12 to 18 minutes
LOIN CHOP, BONELESS	3/4 to 1 in.	medium/direct	8 to 10 minutes
	1-1/4 to 1-1/2 in.	medium/direct	12 to 18 minutes
BACK RIBS OR SPARERIBS	3 to 4 lbs.	medium/indirect	1-1/2 to 2 hours
TENDERLOIN	3/4 to 1 lb.	medium-hot/indirect	25 to 40 minutes
LOIN ROAST, BONE-IN OR BONELESS	3 to 5 lbs.	medium/indirect	1-1/4 to 1-3/4 hours
KABOBS	1-in. cubes	medium/direct	10 to 15 minutes
SAUSAGE, COOKED	—	medium/direct	3 to 7 minutes or until heated through
SAUSAGE, FRESH	4 oz.	medium/indirect	20 to 30 minutes
PORK PATTIES	4 oz. and 1/2 in.	medium/direct	8 to 10 minutes

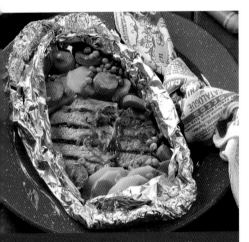

Kids enjoy making this simple dinner as much as eating it. I got the recipe years ago at a camp I stayed at.

—Louise Graybiel, Toronto, Ontario

DINNER IN A PACKET

- 1 boneless pork loin chop (4 ounces)
- 1 medium potato, sliced
- 1 large carrot, sliced
- 1/4 cup frozen peas
- 1 tablespoon onion soup mix

Place the pork chop on a double thickness of heavy-duty foil (about 18 in. x 14 in.). Top with potato, carrot and peas. Sprinkle with soup mix. Seal foil tightly.

Grill, covered, over medium heat for 30-35 minutes or until meat juices run clear, turning occasionally. Carefully remove foil to allow steam to escape. **YIELD: 1 SERVING.**

HAM & SWEET POTATO KABOBS

- 1 large sweet potato, peeled and cubed
- 1 can (20 ounces) unsweetened pineapple chunks
- 1/4 cup butter, melted
- 4 teaspoons brown sugar
- 1 pound fully cooked boneless ham, cut into 1-inch cubes
- 2 yellow summer squash, cut into 3/4-in. slices
- 2 large apples, cubed

Place sweet potato in a small saucepan; cover with water. Bring to a boil. Reduce heat; cover and cook for 10-15 minutes or until almost tender. Drain and set aside.

Drain pineapple, reserving juice; set pineapple aside. In a small bowl, combine the butter, brown sugar and reserved juice. Place the ham, squash, apples, sweet potato and pineapple in a large resealable plastic bag; add the juice mixture. Seal bag and turn to coat; refrigerate for 1 hour.

Drain and discard marinade. On eight metal or soaked wooden skewers, alternately thread the ham, sweet potato, squash, apples and pineapple. Grill, covered, over medium heat for 15-20 minutes or until apples are tender, turning occasionally. **YIELD: 8 KABOBS.**

I like to serve these kabobs with a green salad for an easy, thrifty meal. The buttery, brown sugar marinade highlights everything on the skewer.

—Sandra Hill, Wilson, New York

HERB-MARINATED PORK LOIN

- 1/2 cup tomato juice
- 1/2 cup canola oil
- 1/2 cup finely chopped onion
- 1/4 cup lemon juice
- 1/4 cup chopped fresh parsley
- 1 garlic clove, minced
- 1 teaspoon salt
- 1 teaspoon dried marjoram
- 1 teaspoon dried thyme
- 1/2 teaspoon pepper
- 1 boneless pork loin roast (3 pounds)

In a large resealable plastic bag, combine the first 10 ingredients; add pork. Seal bag and turn to coat; refrigerate overnight, turning meat occasionally.

Drain and discard marinade. Grill, covered, over indirect heat, turning occasionally, for 1-1/4 to 1-3/4 hours or until a meat thermometer reads 160°. Let stand for 5 minutes before slicing. **YIELD: 10-12 SERVINGS.**

I use pork quite often in many recipes, but this pork loin is a real favorite. The mildly seasoned marinade appeals to everyone who's ever sampled this tender meat.

—Jean Ham Evenson
Osage, Iowa

GRILLED PORK TENDERLOIN SATAY

1	small onion, chopped
1/4	cup packed brown sugar
1/4	cup water
3	tablespoons reduced-sodium soy sauce
2	tablespoons reduced-fat creamy peanut butter
4-1/2	teaspoons canola oil
2	garlic cloves, minced
1/4	teaspoon ground ginger
1	pork tenderloin (1 pound)

In a small saucepan, bring the first eight ingredients to a boil. Reduce heat; simmer, uncovered, for 10-12 minutes or until thickened. Set aside 1/2 cup mixture for sauce.

Cut pork in half widthwise; cut each half into thin strips. Thread pork strips onto eight metal or soaked wooden skewers. Grill, uncovered, over medium-hot heat for 2-3 minutes on each side or until no longer pink, basting occasionally with remaining mixture. Serve with reserved sauce. **YIELD: 8 SKEWERS (1/2 CUP SAUCE).**

My dad made this often when grilling for the family. I love this served on roasted veggies and yellow rice. Peanut butter and soy sauce come together for great Asian flavor.

—Gayle Jefferson
Las Vegas, Nevada

MARINATED HAM STEAKS

This recipe, which was given to me by a friend, is an old stand-by. It wins rave reviews from all of my neighborhood friends.

—Judy Grimes
Brandon, Mississippi

1/2	cup ginger ale	1/4	teaspoon ground ginger
1/2	cup orange juice	1/8	teaspoon ground cloves
1/4	cup packed brown sugar	4	individual boneless fully cooked ham steaks (about 5 ounces *each*)
1	tablespoon canola oil		
1-1/2	teaspoons white vinegar		
1	teaspoon ground mustard		

In a large resealable plastic bag, combine the first eight ingredients. Add ham steaks; seal bag and turn to coat. Refrigerate for 8 hours or overnight.

Prepare grill for indirect heat. Drain and discard marinade. Grill ham, covered, over indirect medium heat for 3-4 minutes on each side or until heated through. **YIELD: 4 SERVINGS.**

CORDON BLEU PORK CHOPS

- 2 **bone-in pork loin chops (8 ounces *each*)**
- 1/4 **cup water**
- 1/4 **cup ketchup**
- 2 **tablespoons white vinegar**
- 1 **tablespoon dried minced onion**
- 1 **tablespoon brown sugar**
- 1 **tablespoon Worcestershire sauce**
- 1-1/2 **teaspoons lemon juice**
- 1-1/2 **teaspoons reduced-sodium soy sauce**
- 1/2 **teaspoon garlic powder**
- 1/2 **teaspoon ground mustard**
- 2 **slices part-skim mozzarella cheese (3/4 ounce *each*)**
- 2 **slices deli ham (3/4 ounce *each*)**

Cut a pocket in each chop by slicing almost to the bone; set aside.

In a small bowl, combine the water, ketchup, vinegar, onion, brown sugar, Worcestershire sauce, lemon juice, soy sauce, garlic powder and mustard. Pour 1/2 cup marinade into a large resealable plastic bag; add pork. Seal bag and turn to coat; refrigerate overnight. Cover and refrigerate remaining marinade.

Drain and discard marinade. Place a cheese slice on each slice of ham; roll up jelly-roll style. Insert into each pocket; secure with toothpicks.

Grill pork chops, covered, over medium heat for 6-8 minutes on each side or until a meat thermometer reads 160°, basting occasionally with reserved marinade. Remove toothpicks. **YIELD: 2 SERVINGS.**

Perfect for a backyard barbecue or an afternoon tailgate, these cheesy chops will hit the spot at any time and any place!

—Marcia Obenhaus, Princeton, Illinois

GLAZED PORK TENDERLOIN

1/4 teaspoon salt

1/4 teaspoon pepper

1 pork tenderloin (1-1/4 pounds)

2 sprigs fresh rosemary

1/2 cup pineapple preserves

1 tablespoon prepared horseradish

Combine salt and pepper; rub over pork. Coat grill rack with cooking spray before starting the grill. Prepare grill for indirect heat. Place one sprig of rosemary under the pork and one on top. Grill, covered, over medium-hot indirect heat for 15 minutes.

Meanwhile, in a small saucepan, heat preserves and horseradish until preserves are melted; stir until blended. Remove and discard top rosemary sprig. Set aside 1/4 cup pineapple mixture for serving; brush pork with the remaining mixture.

Grill 10-20 minutes longer or until a meat thermometer reads 160°. Let stand for 5 minutes before slicing. Serve with the reserved sauce. **YIELD: 4 SERVINGS.**

This pork tenderloin is outstanding on the grill, but I can bake it in the oven, too. A simple sauce of pineapple preserves and horseradish gives the pork a tasty treatment. The brand of horseradish you select will determine the "heat" level of the sauce.

—Bernice Dean
Garland, Texas

SOUTHWESTERN LAMB CHOPS

1 cup orange juice

2 jalapeno peppers, seeded and finely chopped

1 teaspoon ground cumin

1/2 teaspoon salt, optional

Dash pepper

3/4 cup halved sliced sweet onion

4 teaspoons cornstarch

1/4 cup cold water

1 cup fresh orange sections

2 tablespoons minced fresh cilantro

8 lamb loin chops (1 inch thick and 4 ounces *each*)

In a small saucepan, combine the orange juice, jalapeno, cumin, salt if desired and pepper. Cook over medium-high heat until mixture begins to simmer. Stir in onion.

Combine cornstarch and water until smooth; gradually add to the sauce. Bring to a boil over medium heat; cook and stir for 2 minutes or until thickened and bubbly. Remove from the heat. Stir in oranges and cilantro; keep warm.

Grill lamb chops, covered, over medium heat or broil 4-6 in. from the heat for 4-9 minutes on each side or until meat reaches desired doneness (for medium-rare, a meat thermometer should read 145°; medium, 160°; well-done, 170°). Serve with orange sauce. **YIELD: 4 SERVINGS.**

This flavorful yet not too spicy sauce for tender lamb is our family's favorite. It's tasty with any choice of grilled meat.

—Margaret Pache, Mesa, Arizona

TANGY PORK KABOBS

- 1 cup canola oil
- 3 tablespoons honey
- 2 tablespoons onion powder
- 2 tablespoons soy sauce
- 2 pork tenderloins (1 pound *each*), cut into 1-inch cubes
- 1-1/2 teaspoons seasoned salt
- 1/2 teaspoon pepper

HORSERADISH RASPBERRY SAUCE:

- 1 jar (18 ounces) seedless raspberry preserves, warmed
- 1/4 cup red wine vinegar
- 3 tablespoons prepared horseradish
- 2 tablespoons soy sauce
- 3 teaspoons garlic powder
- 1-1/2 teaspoons ketchup

In a large resealable plastic bag, combine the oil, honey, onion powder and soy sauce; add pork. Seal bag and turn to coat; refrigerate overnight.

Coat grill rack with cooking spray before starting the grill. Prepare grill for indirect heat. Drain and discard marinade. Sprinkle pork with seasoned salt and pepper; thread onto six metal or soaked wooden skewers. In a small bowl, combine the sauce ingredients.

Grill kabobs, covered, over medium heat for 8-10 minutes or until juices run clear, turning occasionally and brushing with some of the sauce during the last minute. Serve remaining sauce with kabobs. **YIELD: 6 SERVINGS (1-1/2 CUPS SAUCE).**

Tasters at a recent Horseradish Festival rooted for Julia Piper Jung. They got a culinary kick out of her grilled kabobs made sweetly sassy with horseradish raspberry glaze.

—Horseradish Festival, Collinsville, Illinois

BARBECUED RIBS

- 1 teaspoon salt
- 1 teaspoon Italian seasoning
- 1/2 teaspoon pepper
- 1 rack pork spareribs (3 to 4 pounds)
- 1 bottle (12 ounces) beer
- 2/3 cup barbecue sauce

These ribs are so simple to make, you will want to make them often. They always are juicy and have a wonderful taste.

—Catherine Santich
Alamo, California

Rub the salt, Italian seasoning and pepper over ribs and place in a shallow roasting pan; add beer. Cover and bake at 325° for 2 hours.

Coat grill rack with cooking spray before starting the grill. Drain ribs. Spoon some of the sauce over ribs. Grill, covered, over medium heat for 8-10 minutes or until browned, turning occasionally and basting with sauce. **YIELD: 3 SERVINGS.**

SALSA CHORIZO PIZZAS

SALSA:

- 3 cups chopped seeded tomatoes
- 1 medium onion, chopped
- 2 jalapeno peppers, seeded and chopped
- 1 poblano pepper, seeded and chopped
- 1/3 cup minced fresh cilantro
- 1/4 cup lime juice
- 1 tablespoon olive oil
- 1 garlic clove, minced
- 1 teaspoon chili powder
- 1 teaspoon ground cumin
- 1/2 teaspoon salt

PIZZAS:

- 1 loaf (1 pound) frozen bread dough, thawed
- 3 tablespoons olive oil
- 2 cups (8 ounces) shredded Mexican cheese blend
- 1/2 pound chorizo, cooked and crumbled

Grilled pizza is a snap when starting with frozen bread dough. This version with a Mexican twist features a fresh homemade salsa and chorizo, which is a highly seasoned, coarsely ground pork sausage.

—Taste of Home
  Test Kitchen

In a large bowl, combine the salsa ingredients; set aside.

Divide dough into fourths. On a lightly floured surface, roll each portion into an 8-in. circle. Lightly brush both sides of dough with oil; place on grill. Cover and grill over medium heat for 1-2 minutes or until the bottom is lightly browned.

Remove from the grill. Top the grilled side of each pizza with 1/2 cup cheese, 1/4 cup chorizo and 1/2 cup salsa. Return to the grill. Cover and cook for 4-5 minutes or until the bottom is browned and cheese is melted. Refrigerate remaining salsa. **YIELD: 4 SERVINGS.**

EDITOR'S NOTE: When cutting hot peppers, disposable gloves are recommended. Avoid touching your face.

PRICELESS BBQ RIBS

The name of this dish says it all. One taste and you'll see why it's a favorite.

—Edgar Wright
New Orleans, Louisiana

16	cups water	1	bay leaf
2	racks pork baby back ribs (2-1/2 pounds *each*)		**BARBECUE SAUCE:**
1/3	cup sugar	1	cup barbecue sauce
1/3	cup onion powder	1/4	cup packed brown sugar
1/3	cup seafood seasoning	1	tablespoon honey
2	tablespoons garlic powder	1	tablespoon Liquid Smoke, optional

In a stock pot, combine the first seven ingredients; bring to a boil. Reduce heat; cover and simmer for 1 hour.

Remove from the heat; let stand for 30 minutes. Drain and discard cooking liquid.

In a small bowl, combine the barbecue sauce ingredients. Brush half of sauce over ribs. Grill ribs, covered, over medium heat for 4-5 minutes or until heated through, basting with remaining barbecue sauce. **YIELD: 5 SERVINGS.**

MARINATED LAMB CHOPS

- 1 **small onion, sliced**
- 2 **tablespoons red wine vinegar**
- 1 **tablespoon lemon juice**
- 1 **tablespoon olive oil**
- 2 **teaspoons minced fresh rosemary** *or* 3/4 **teaspoon dried rosemary, crushed**
- 2 **teaspoons Dijon mustard**
- 1 **garlic clove, minced**
- 1/2 **teaspoon pepper**
- 1/4 **teaspoon salt**
- 1/4 **teaspoon ground ginger**
- 8 **lamb loin chops (3 ounces** *each***)**

In a large resealable plastic bag, combine the first 10 ingredients; add lamb chops. Seal bag and turn to coat; refrigerate for several hours or overnight.

Drain and discard marinade and onion. Coat grill rack with cooking spray before starting the grill. Grill chops, covered, over medium heat for 5-7 minutes on each side or until meat reaches desired doneness (for medium-rare, a meat thermometer should read 145°; medium, 160°; well-done, 170°). **YIELD: 4 SERVINGS.**

These lean little lamb chops are packed with the flavors of rosemary, ginger and mustard. Marinating makes them so tender. They're something special.

—Jill Heatwole, Pittsville, Maryland

TERIYAKI PINEAPPLE & PORK CHOPS

- 1 **cup unsweetened pineapple juice**
- 4 **bone-in pork loin chops (8 ounces** *each***)**
- 1 **tablespoon minced fresh rosemary** *or* **1 teaspoon dried rosemary, crushed**
- 1 **teaspoon garlic powder**
- 1/2 **teaspoon salt**
- 1/4 **teaspoon pepper**
- 1 **fresh pineapple**
- 1/2 **cup teriyaki sauce**
- 1 **package (9 ounces) fresh baby spinach**

Place pineapple juice in a large resealable plastic bag; add pork chops. Seal bag and turn to coat; refrigerate for up to 2 hours.

Drain and discard marinade. Combine the rosemary, garlic powder, salt and pepper; sprinkle over chops.

Peel and core pineapple; cut into eight spears. Grill chops and pineapple, covered, over medium heat for 4-6 minutes on each side or until a meat thermometer reads 160° and pineapple is tender, basting occasionally with teriyaki sauce.

Arrange spinach on a serving platter; top with pineapple and chops. **YIELD: 4 SERVINGS.**

Pork chops are wonderful on the grill. Adding the pineapple and teriyaki makes them even better! This dish reminds me of Hawaii!
—Alaina Showalter, Clover, South Carolina

ROCKY MOUNTAIN GRILL

- 2 **tablespoons water**
- 2 **tablespoons red wine vinegar**
- 2 **tablespoons canola oil**
- 1-1/2 **teaspoons rubbed sage**
- 1 **teaspoon grated onion**
- 1/2 **teaspoon lemon-pepper seasoning**
- 1/2 **teaspoon Dijon mustard**
- 1/8 **to 1/4 teaspoon cayenne pepper**
- 4 **lamb loin chops (1 pound)**

In a large resealable plastic bag, combine the first eight ingredients. Remove 3 tablespoons for basting; refrigerate. Add lamb chops to the remaining marinade. Seal bag and turn to coat. Refrigerate overnight.

Drain and discard marinade. Grill chops, covered, over medium-hot heat for 4 minutes. Turn; baste with reserved marinade. Grill for 4 minutes. Turn and grill 1 minute longer or until meat reaches desired doneness (for medium-rare, a meat thermometer should read 145°; medium, 160°; well-done, 170°). **YIELD: 4 SERVINGS.**

These flavorful lamb chops simply marinate overnight, then grill up in only 10 minutes or so. The Dijon mustard and cayenne pepper add a delicious zip to this entree, which was shared by the American Lamb Council.

—Rick Wertheimer
American Lamb Council
Englewood, Colorado

SWEET 'N' SPICY COUNTRY RIBS

3/4	cup unsweetened apple juice
1/2	cup canola oil
1/2	cup cola
1/4	cup packed brown sugar
1/4	cup honey
1	tablespoon minced garlic
1	tablespoon Worcestershire sauce
2	teaspoons Liquid Smoke, optional
1	teaspoon salt
1	teaspoon dried thyme
1	teaspoon pepper
1/2	teaspoon cayenne pepper
1/2	teaspoon ground nutmeg
3	to 4 pounds boneless country-style pork ribs

My friends have asked me to bottle my barbecue sauce, rub and marinades. My favorite saying is, "You cook it, and they will come." And they sure will with these tender ribs on the menu!

—Allan Stackhouse Jr.
  Jennings, Louisiana

In a small bowl, combine the apple juice, oil, cola, brown sugar, honey, garlic, Worcestershire sauce, Liquid Smoke if desired and seasonings.

Pour 1-1/2 cups marinade into a large resealable plastic bag; add the ribs. Seal bag and turn to coat; refrigerate for 5 hours or overnight, turning once. Cover and refrigerate remaining marinade for basting.

Coat grill rack with cooking spray before starting the grill. Prepare grill for indirect heat. Drain and discard marinade. Grill ribs, covered, over indirect medium heat for 10 minutes on each side, basting occasionally.

Grill 20-25 minutes longer or until meat is tender, turning and basting occasionally with remaining marinade. **YIELD: 12 SERVINGS.**

FRUIT-GLAZED PORK CHOPS

1/3	cup hickory smoke-flavored barbecue sauce
1/2	cup apricot *or* peach preserves
1	tablespoon corn syrup
1	teaspoon prepared mustard
1/4	teaspoon ground cloves
6	bone-in pork loin chops (3/4 inch thick and 8 ounces *each*)
1/2	teaspoon salt
1/2	teaspoon pepper

In a small bowl, combine the barbecue sauce, preserves, corn syrup, mustard and cloves; set aside.

Coat grill rack with cooking spray before starting the grill. Sprinkle pork chops with salt and pepper. Grill, covered, over medium heat for 6-8 minutes on each side or until a meat thermometer reads 160°, basting frequently with sauce mixture. **YIELD: 6 SERVINGS.**

Here's a fast and simple way to grill chops. Your meal can be ready in half an hour, and other fruit preserves easily can be substituted. The chops are also nice quickly broiled in the oven!

—Edie DeSpain
Logan, Utah

SWEET 'N' SMOKY KANSAS CITY RIBS

- 1/3   cup packed brown sugar
- 2   teaspoons chicken bouillon granules
- 2   teaspoons paprika
- 2   teaspoons chili powder
- 1   teaspoon ground cumin
- 3/4   teaspoon garlic powder
- 1/2   teaspoon *each* minced fresh basil, rosemary and sage
- 1/2   teaspoon ground celery seed
- 1/4   teaspoon ground coriander
- 1/8   teaspoon fennel seed, crushed
- 2   pork baby back ribs (about 5 pounds)
- 2   cups soaked wood chips (mequite, hickory *or* alder), optional

SAUCE:

- 1   large onion, chopped
- 2   tablespoons olive oil
- 1   tablespoon butter
- 2   tablespoons brown sugar
- 1   tablespoon Worcestershire sauce
- 1   teaspoon *each* minced fresh basil, marjoram and rosemary, crushed
- 1   teaspoon *each* minced fresh dill, sage and cilantro
- 1   teaspoon minced chives
- 1   bottle (18 ounces) barbecue sauce

In a small bowl, combine the brown sugar, bouillon, seasonings and herbs; rub over ribs. Let stand for 15 minutes.

Prepare grill for indirect heat, using a drip pan. Add 1 cup of soaked wood chips if desired. Place ribs in a disposable foil pan. Grill, covered, over indirect medium heat for 30 minutes. Remove ribs from pan and place on grill rack over drip pan. Add remaining wood chips. Grill 30 minutes longer, turning occasionally.

Meanwhile, in a small saucepan, saute onion in oil and butter until tender. Stir in the brown sugar, Worcestershire sauce and herbs; cook and stir for 1 minute. Add barbecue sauce. Bring to a boil. Reduce heat; simmer, uncovered, for 5 minutes. Baste ribs with sauce; grill for 10-15 minutes or until meat is tender, turning and basting occasionally. **YIELD: 5 SERVINGS.**

Tender and juicy, these saucy ribs are packed with a big smoky punch. The seasonings rubbed on the meat and that go into the sauce ensure these finger-licking ribs are requested again and again!

—Gloria Warczak, Cedarburg, Wisconsin

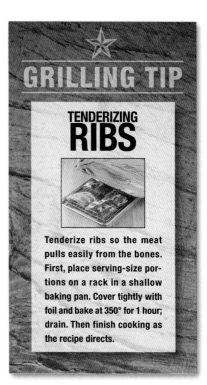

GRILLING TIP

TENDERIZING
RIBS

Tenderize ribs so the meat pulls easily from the bones. First, place serving-size portions on a rack in a shallow baking pan. Cover tightly with foil and bake at 350° for 1 hour; drain. Then finish cooking as the recipe directs.

When my son and his wife were married in our backyard, I served this special roast at the rehearsal dinner. It can be prepared on the grill or in the oven, but grilling enhances the flavors. The fruit salsa goes nicely with the pork's tasty herbal rub.

—B.J Wall, Lanexa, Virginia

PORK ROAST WITH MANGO SALSA

3	tablespoons paprika
1	tablespoon garlic powder
2	teaspoons dried oregano
2	teaspoons dried thyme
3/4	teaspoon cayenne pepper
1/2	teaspoon salt
1/2	teaspoon ground cumin
1/2	teaspoon pepper
1/4	teaspoon ground nutmeg
1	boneless whole pork loin roast (2-1/2 pounds)

SALSA:

1	medium mango, peeled and chopped
1/2	cup chopped seeded plum tomatoes
1/2	cup chopped red onion
1/2	cup chopped peeled cucumber
1/4	cup lime juice
2	tablespoons minced fresh cilantro
1	tablespoon olive oil
1	tablespoon dry red wine *or* cider vinegar
1	teaspoon ground cumin

In a small bowl, combine the first nine ingredients. Rub over the roast. Place in a shallow baking dish; cover and refrigerate for 3 hours or overnight. In a large bowl, combine the salsa ingredients; cover and refrigerate until serving.

If grilling the roast, coat grill rack with cooking spray before starting the grill. Prepare grill for indirect heat. If baking the roast, place on a rack in a shallow roasting pan.

Grill pork, covered, over indirect medium heat for 1-1/4 hours or bake, uncovered, at 350° for 1-1/2 hours or until a meat thermometer reads 160°.

Cover loosely with foil and let stand for 15 minutes before slicing. Serve with salsa. **YIELD: 8 SERVINGS.**

SWITCH UP WITH SALSA

FEW THINGS complement the flavor of grilled meats like colorful salsas. Get creative when making salsa, and remember that a salsa from one recipe might be perfect with different grilled dishes.

POLYNESIAN SAUSAGE KABOBS

1/2	cup lemon juice
1/2	cup soy sauce
1/3	cup water
1/3	cup honey
1/4	teaspoon salt
1-1/2	pounds smoked kielbasa *or* Polish sausage, cut into 1-1/2-inch pieces
1	small pineapple, cut into 1-inch cubes
1	small cantaloupe, cut into 1-inch cubes
2	medium green peppers, cut into 1-inch pieces

In a large bowl, combine the first five ingredients. Set aside half of the marinade for basting; cover and refrigerate. Pour remaining marinade into a large resealable plastic bag; add sausage. Seal bag and turn to coat. Refrigerate for 3 hours.

Drain and discard the marinade from sausage. On metal or soaked wooden skewers, alternate the sausage, pineapple, cantaloupe and green peppers. Grill, uncovered, over medium heat for 10 minutes or until sausage is browned, turning and basting frequently with reserved marinade. **YIELD: 5 SERVINGS.**

Here's a meal on a skewer with a unique twist. The pineapple, cantaloupe and peppers complement the sausage perfectly. I frequently fire up the grill for these simple kabobs in summer.

—Patricia Eggemeyer, Ellis Grove, Illinois

MAPLE-GLAZED RIBS

3	pounds pork spareribs, cut into serving-size pieces
1	cup maple syrup
3	tablespoons orange juice concentrate
3	tablespoons ketchup
2	tablespoons soy sauce
1	tablespoon Worcestershire sauce
1	tablespoon Dijon mustard
1	teaspoon curry powder
1	garlic clove, minced
2	green onions, minced
1	tablespoon sesame seeds, toasted

Place ribs, meaty side up, on a rack in a greased 15-in. x 10-in. x 1-in. baking pan. Cover pan tightly with foil. Bake at 350° for 1-1/4 hours or until tender; drain.

Meanwhile, combine the next nine ingredients in a small saucepan. Bring to a boil over medium heat. Reduce heat; simmer, uncovered, for 15 minutes, stirring occasionally.

Coat grill rack with cooking spray before starting the grill. Grill ribs, covered, over medium heat for 15-20 minutes, brushing with glaze twice. Sprinkle with sesame seeds just before serving. **YIELD: 6 SERVINGS.**

I love maple syrup and so does my family, so I gave this recipe a try. It's well worth the effort! I make these ribs often, and I never have leftovers. With two teenage boys who like to eat, this main dish is a real winner.

—Linda Kobeluck
Ardrossan, Alberta

LOW COUNTRY GRILL

2	tablespoons olive oil
1	teaspoon salt, *divided*
1	teaspoon garlic powder, *divided*
1	teaspoon seafood seasoning, *divided*
12	small red potatoes, quartered
1/3	cup butter, melted
1	pound smoked kielbasa *or* Polish sausage
3	medium ears sweet corn, cut in half
1-1/2	pounds uncooked medium shrimp, peeled and deveined

In a large bowl, combine the oil with 1/4 teaspoon each of salt, garlic powder and seafood seasoning. Add potatoes; toss to coat. Spoon onto a greased double thickness of heavy-duty foil (about 18 in. square).

Fold foil around potatoes and seal tightly. Grill, covered, over medium heat for 30-35 minutes or until tender, turning once. Set aside and keep warm.

In a small bowl, combine butter with remaining salt, garlic powder and seafood seasoning. Grill kielbasa and corn, covered, over medium heat for 10-12 minutes or until kielbasa is heated through and corn is tender, turning occasionally and basting corn with half of the butter mixture. Keep warm.

Thread shrimp onto four metal or soaked wooden skewers; grill, covered, over medium heat for 3-4 minutes on each side or until shrimp turn pink, basting with remaining butter mixture. Slice kielbasa into six pieces before serving. Carefully open foil from the potatoes to allow steam to escape. **YIELD: 6 SERVINGS.**

Grilling is one of my family's favorite ways of cooking. This recipe contains many different ingredients, but they come together quickly.

—Alaina Showalter
 Clover, South Carolina

LAMB & CHICKEN KABOBS

In summer, I fire up the grill and toss on these great kabobs. In the winter, I use my trusty indoor grill to make them.

—Weda Mosellie
Phillipsburg,
New Jersey

- 6 ounces sirloin lamb roast, cut into 1-inch pieces
- 1 boneless skinless chicken breast (5 ounces), cut into 1-inch pieces
- 1 large portobello mushroom, quartered
- 1/2 small sweet red pepper, cut into 1-inch pieces
- 2 green onions, cut into 2-inch pieces
- 1/2 teaspoon garlic powder
- 1/8 teaspoon salt

Dash pepper

- 2 tablespoons lemon juice
- 2 tablespoons olive oil
- 2 fresh basil leaves, thinly sliced

On two metal or soaked wooden skewers, alternately thread the lamb, chicken and vegetables. Sprinkle with garlic powder, salt and pepper. In a small bowl, combine the lemon juice, oil and basil; set aside.

Grill kabobs, covered, over medium heat for 4-5 minutes on each side or until chicken is no longer pink, basting frequently with lemon mixture. **YIELD: 2 SERVINGS.**

BARBECUED PORK CHOPS

- 1/2 **cup hickory smoke-flavored barbecue sauce**
- 1/2 **cup A.1. steak sauce**
- 1/2 **cup sherry *or* unsweetened apple juice**
- 3 **tablespoons honey**
- 6 **bone-in pork loin chops (3/4 inch thick and 8 ounces *each*)**
- 3/4 **teaspoon salt**
- 1/2 **teaspoon pepper**

Coat grill rack with cooking spray before starting the grill. In a small bowl, combine the barbecue sauce, steak sauce, sherry or apple juice and honey. Transfer 1/3 cup sauce to another bowl; set aside for serving.

Sprinkle pork chops with salt and pepper. Grill, covered, over medium heat for 4-5 minutes on each side or until a meat thermometer reads 160°, basting frequently with remaining sauce. Serve with reserved sauce. **YIELD: 6 SERVINGS.**

Sherry, honey, barbecue and steak sauces combine to give these chops a beautiful glaze and a real dressed-up flavor. The sauce works well on chicken breasts, too, and couldn't be much easier to put together.

—LaJuana Kay Holland
Amarillo, Texas

BRAIDED PORK TENDERLOINS

- 2 pork tenderloins (1 pound *each*)
- 1/2 cup mango nectar
- 1/4 cup plus 1 tablespoon spiced rum *or* additional mango nectar, *divided*
- 2 tablespoons olive oil
- 2 tablespoons Caribbean jerk seasoning, *divided*
- 2 garlic cloves, minced
- 1 tablespoon heavy whipping cream
- 1 cup chopped peeled mango

Cut tenderloins in half lengthwise; cut each half into three strips to within 1 in. of one end. In a large resealable plastic bag, combine the mango nectar, 1/4 cup rum, oil, 1 tablespoon jerk seasoning and garlic; add pork. Seal bag and turn to coat; refrigerate for up to 4 hours.

Drain and discard marinade. Place tenderloin halves on a clean cutting board and braid; secure loose ends with toothpicks. Sprinkle with remaining jerk seasoning.

Grill braids, covered, over medium heat for 4-5 minutes on each side or until a meat thermometer reads 160°. Discard toothpicks. Let stand for 5 minutes before slicing.

Meanwhile, place the cream, remaining rum and mango in a food processor. Cover and process until smooth. Transfer to a small saucepan; heat through. Serve with pork. **YIELD: 8 SERVINGS (3/4 CUP SAUCE).**

For a summertime family dinner, I served a jerk-spiced, marinated pork tenderloin. Braiding the meat, which is easy to do, makes for an attractive presentation.

—Jim Rude, Janesville, Wisconsin

Even folks who don't prefer lamb can't resist these tender chops. The seasoning blend is easy to prepare and really complements the lamb.

—DeLea Lonadier
Montgomery, Louisiana

GRILLED LAMB CHOPS

- 1/2 cup vegetable oil
- 1/4 cup finely chopped onion
- 2 tablespoons lemon juice
- 1 teaspoon ground mustard
- 1/2 teaspoon garlic salt
- 1/2 teaspoon dried tarragon
- 1/8 teaspoon pepper
- 6 lamb loin chops (1-1/4 inches thick and 6 ounces *each*)

In a large resealable plastic bag, combine the first seven ingredients; add lamb chops. Seal bag and turn to coat; refrigerate for 10-15 minutes.

Drain and discard marinade. Grill chops, covered, over medium-hot heat for 7 minutes on each side or until meat reaches desired doneness (for medium-rare, a meat thermometer should read 145°; medium, 160°; well-done, 170°). **YIELD: 3 SERVINGS.**

We love these full-flavored kabobs and fix them often, even in winter. A sweet sauce is used to baste and later serve alongside the colorful combination of sausage, bacon, shrimp, vegetables and pineapple.
—Gloria Warczak, Cedarburg, Wisconsin

SAUSAGE SHRIMP KABOBS

1	can (8 ounces) pineapple chunks
4	bacon strips
8	large fresh mushrooms
8	uncooked large shrimp, peeled and deveined
8	large cherry tomatoes
8	ounces smoked sausage, cut into 1/2-inch slices
1	large sweet onion, cut into 8 wedges
1	large green pepper, cut into 1-inch pieces
1/2	cup barbecue sauce
1/3	cup corn syrup
1/4	cup ketchup
3	tablespoons soy sauce
1	tablespoon lime juice
1/2	teaspoon maple flavoring
1/4	teaspoon garlic powder
1/4	teaspoon ground ginger
1/8	teaspoon dried coriander

Drain pineapple, reserving juice. Cut bacon strips in half; wrap each around a mushroom. On metal or soaked wooden skewers, alternately thread the shrimp, pineapple chunks, tomatoes, sausage, bacon-wrapped mushrooms, onion and green pepper.

In a large bowl, combine the barbecue sauce, corn syrup, ketchup, soy sauce, lime juice, maple flavoring, seasonings and reserved pineapple juice. Set aside 2/3 cup for serving.

Grill kabobs, covered, over medium heat for 10-15 minutes or vegetables are tender and shrimp turn pink, turning and basting occasionally with remaining sauce. Serve with reserved sauce. **YIELD: 4 SERVINGS.**

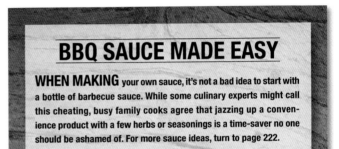

BBQ SAUCE MADE EASY

WHEN MAKING your own sauce, it's not a bad idea to start with a bottle of barbecue sauce. While some culinary experts might call this cheating, busy family cooks agree that jazzing up a convenience product with a few herbs or seasonings is a time-saver no one should be ashamed of. For more sauce ideas, turn to page 222.

CHIPOTLE-TERIYAKI PORK CHOPS

1/4	cup lime juice
1/4	cup orange juice
2	tablespoons soy sauce
2	tablespoons grated onion
1	tablespoon teriyaki sauce
1	chipotle pepper in adobo sauce, drained
1	garlic clove, peeled
1/8	teaspoon ground ginger
2	tablespoons ground ancho pepper
2	tablespoons olive oil
1	teaspoon salt
1/2	teaspoon dried oregano
1/2	teaspoon coarsely ground pepper
1/4	teaspoon ground cumin
4	boneless pork loin chops (8 ounces *each*)
1/2	cup queso fresco *or* shredded Monterey Jack cheese

These flavorful pork chops have both Southwestern and Asian flair—with the chipotle and ancho pepper, and the teriyaki and soy sauce. They're topped with queso fresco—a white, fresh Mexican cheese that has a fine-grained texture and mild flavor.

—Kathleen Boulanger
Williston, Vermont

For sauce, combine the first eight ingredients in a blender; cover and process until smooth. Transfer to a small bowl; set aside. Combine the ancho pepper, oil, salt, oregano, pepper and cumin; gently rub over both sides of pork chops.

Grill chops, covered, over medium-hot heat for 5-7 minutes on each side or until a meat thermometer reads 160°, basting occasionally with 1/3 cup of the sauce. Sprinkle with queso fresco; grill 2-3 minutes longer or until cheese is softened. Serve with remaining sauce. **YIELD: 4 SERVINGS.**

GERMAN BRATWURST

1	teaspoon cornstarch
1/4	cup chicken broth
2	tablespoons Dijon mustard
1	tablespoon brown sugar
1	tablespoon white wine *or* additional chicken broth
1	tablespoon cider vinegar
1/8	teaspoon celery seed
5	uncooked bratwurst links

The tangy mustard and brown sugar make this quick-and-easy German Bratwurst recipe something special.

—Taste of Home
Test Kitchen

In a small saucepan, combine the first seven ingredients. Bring to a boil; cook and stir until thickened. Cool. Cover and refrigerate until serving.

Grill bratwurst, covered, over medium heat for 15-20 minutes or until no longer pink, turning frequently. In a small disposable foil pan, heat mustard mixture. Add bratwurst and turn to coat. **YIELD: 5 SERVINGS.**

BARBECUED LAMB CHOPS

2	to 3 cups olive oil
1/4	cup chopped garlic
4	teaspoons salt
1	teaspoon minced fresh rosemary *or* 1/2 teaspoon dried rosemary, crushed
1	teaspoon salt-free garlic and herb seasoning
1	teaspoon pepper
18	lamb rib chops (1 inch thick and 4 ounces *each*)

In a large resealable plastic bag, combine the oil, garlic and seasonings; add lamb chops. Seal bag and turn to coat; refrigerate overnight, turning occasionally.

Drain and discard marinade. Grill the chops, uncovered, over medium heat for 5-9 minutes on each side or until meat reaches desired doneness (for medium-rare, a meat thermometer should read 145°; medium 160°; well-done, 170°). **YIELD: 9 SERVINGS.**

At Eastertime and for other holidays, I often get requests for these lamb chops. The moist and tender chops aren't difficult to make, but they taste special. Even people who don't care for lamb like it prepared this way.

—Chris Nash
  Berthoud, Colorado

This pork tenderloin beats all at a cookout! The recipe came from a family member and is such a treat. Fresh strawberries and avocado in the salsa help cool the tasty heat of the pork.

—Priscilla Gilbert
  Indian Harbour Beach, Florida

CHIPOTLE PORK TENDERLOINS

1	cup sliced onion
1/2	cup chipotle peppers in adobo sauce, chopped
1/4	cup lime juice
1-1/2	teaspoons minced garlic
3	pork tenderloins (1 pound *each*)

STRAWBERRY SALSA:

5	cups sliced fresh strawberries
1/4	cup thinly sliced green onions
1/4	cup minced fresh cilantro
1/4	cup lime juice
1/4	teaspoon salt
1	medium ripe avocado, peeled and chopped

In a large resealable plastic bag, combine the onion, chipotle peppers, lime juice and garlic; add pork. Seal bag and turn to coat; refrigerate for at least 1 hour.

Prepare grill for indirect heat. Drain and discard marinade. Grill pork, covered, over indirect medium heat for 10-13 minutes on each side or until a meat thermometer reads 160°. Let stand for 5 minutes before slicing.

For salsa, in a large bowl, combine the strawberries, green onions, cilantro, lime juice and salt. Gently stir in avocado. Serve with pork. **YIELD: 9 SERVINGS (5 CUPS SALSA).**

ASIAN-STYLE BABY BACK RIBS

1-1/2	pounds pork baby back ribs
4-1/2	teaspoons molasses
1	tablespoon garlic salt
1	teaspoon onion powder
1	teaspoon Worcestershire sauce

GLAZE:

1/2	cup reduced-sodium soy sauce
3	tablespoons thawed pineapple juice concentrate
2	tablespoons rice vinegar
2	tablespoons hoisin sauce
2	tablespoons ketchup
1	teaspoon lemon juice
1	teaspoon whole grain mustard
1	teaspoon Worcestershire sauce
1	teaspoon minced fresh gingerroot
1/2	teaspoon minced garlic

Chopped green onion

Pat ribs dry. Combine the molasses, garlic salt, onion powder and Worcestershire sauce; spoon over meat. Place ribs on a rack in a small shallow roasting pan. Cover and bake at 300° for 1 hour or until tender.

In a small saucepan, combine the soy sauce, pineapple juice concentrate, vinegar, hoisin sauce, ketchup, lemon juice, mustard, Worcestershire sauce, ginger and garlic. Bring to a boil. Reduce heat; simmer, uncovered, for 10 minutes or until slightly thickened, stirring occasionally.

Coat grill rack with cooking spray before starting the grill. Brush ribs with some of the glaze; grill over medium heat for 8-12 minutes or until browned, turning frequently and brushing with additional glaze. Serve remaining glaze on the side. Garnish with onion. **YIELD: 2 SERVINGS.**

The combination of tender grilled pork and an irresistible sauce will have you licking your fingers. Be ready to add this dish to your list of summer favorites!

—Esther Danielson
San Marcos, California

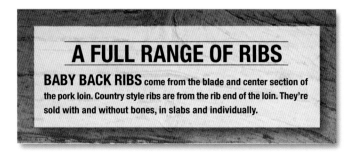

A FULL RANGE OF RIBS

BABY BACK RIBS come from the blade and center section of the pork loin. Country style ribs are from the rib end of the loin. They're sold with and without bones, in slabs and individually.

GRILLED PORK ROAST

2/3	cup canola oil
1/3	cup soy sauce
1/4	cup red wine vinegar
2	tablespoons lemon juice
2	tablespoons Worcestershire sauce
2	garlic cloves, minced
1	to 2 tablespoons ground mustard
1	to 2 teaspoons pepper
1	teaspoon salt
1	boneless pork loin roast (2-1/2 to 3 pounds)

We enjoy the mild mustard flavor of this juicy, tender pork roast. With a little advance preparation, this roast is simple since it creates no dirty dishes, and I get the rest of the meal ready while it cooks.

—Myra Innes, Auburn, Kansas

In a large resealable plastic bag, combine the first nine ingredients; add pork. Seal bag and turn to coat. Refrigerate overnight.

Prepare grill for indirect heat. Drain and discard marinade. Grill roast, covered, over indirect heat for 1-1/2 hours or until a meat thermometer reads 160°. Let stand for 10 minutes before slicing. **YIELD: 8 SERVINGS.**

LAMB KABOBS WITH YOGURT SAUCE

1/2	cup white wine *or* chicken broth
2	tablespoons olive oil
2	teaspoons ground coriander
1	teaspoon ground ginger
1/2	teaspoon salt
1/4	teaspoon ground cinnamon
1/2	pound sirloin lamb roast, cut into 1-inch cubes
1/2	cup plain yogurt
6	medium fresh mushrooms
1	medium zucchini, cut into 1/2-inch slices
1-1/2	cups hot cooked couscous

In a small bowl, combine the first six ingredients. Pour 1/3 cup marinade into a large resealable plastic bag; add lamb. Seal bag and turn to coat; refrigerate for 15 minutes.

Pour 1 tablespoon marinade into a small bowl. Stir in yogurt; cover and refrigerate. Cover and refrigerate remaining marinade for basting. Drain and discard marinade from lamb. On two metal or soaked wooden skewers, alternately thread lamb, mushrooms and zucchini.

Grill kabobs, covered, over medium heat for 5-6 minutes on each side or until lamb reaches desired doneness (for medium-rare, a meat thermometer should read 145°; medium, 160°; well-done, 170°), basting frequently with reserved marinade. Serve with couscous and yogurt mixture. **YIELD: 2 SERVINGS.**

I make these whenever I find lamb stew chunks at the meat counter. I've served it to people who aren't fond of lamb but enjoyed the flavor of these kabobs.

—L. Foringer
 Los Angeles, California

CHERRY-STUFFED PORK CHOPS

Grilled pork chops have a lovely stuffing of couscous, cherries and seasonings in this quick and elegant main dish. Served with a salad, it's perfect for special occasions, but speedy enough for everyday family suppers.

—Taste of Home
 Test Kitchen

- 1 **package (5.6 ounces) couscous with toasted pine nuts**
- 6 **boneless pork loin chops (1 inch thick and 6 ounces *each*)**
- 1/2 **cup dried cherries**
- 1 **tablespoon brown sugar**
- 1 **tablespoon butter, melted**
- 1/2 **teaspoon minced fresh gingerroot**
- 1/2 **teaspoon garlic powder**
- 1/2 **teaspoon pepper**

Prepare couscous according to package directions. Meanwhile, cut a deep slit in each pork chop, forming a pocket. Stir the cherries, brown sugar, butter and ginger into prepared couscous. Stuff 1/3 cup into each chop; secure with toothpicks. Sprinkle with garlic powder and pepper.

Grill pork chops, covered, over medium heat for 10-12 minutes on each side or until a meat thermometer reads 160°. Discard toothpicks. **YIELD: 6 SERVINGS.**

9
FISH & SEAFOOD

PG. 217 **TOMATO-BASIL SHRIMP SKEWERS**

LOOKING FOR A REFRESHING MEAL THAT NOT ONLY OFFERS A TASTY CHANGE OF PACE BUT COMES TOGETHER IN MOMENTS? GRILL UP A FEW FISH FILLETS, MARINATED SHRIMP OR WELL-SEASONED SCALLOPS. SEAFOOD IS A HEALTHY CHOICE THAT COOKS QUICKLY ON THE GRILL. TRY ONE OF THESE 30 RECIPES TONIGHT.

ZUCCHINI-WRAPPED SCALLOPS

My citrus marinade is the perfect choice for these scallops that are wrapped in thin zucchini strips.
—Julie Gwinn, Hershey, Pennsylvania

2	tablespoons orange juice
1	tablespoon olive oil
1	teaspoon Caribbean jerk seasoning
1	teaspoon grated orange peel
1/8	teaspoon crushed red pepper flakes
1-1/2	pounds sea scallops (about 16)
2	medium zucchini

In a small bowl, combine the orange juice, oil, seasoning, orange peel and red pepper flakes; set aside 1 tablespoon for basting. Pour the remaining marinade into a large resealable plastic bag; add the scallops. Seal bag and turn to coat; refrigerate for 30 minutes.

Using a vegetable peeler or metal cheese slicer, cut zucchini into very thin lengthwise strips. Drain and discard marinade. Wrap a zucchini strip around each scallop. Secure by threading where the zucchini ends overlap onto metal or soaked wooden skewers.

Coat grill rack with cooking spray before starting the grill. Grill skewers, covered, over medium heat for 3-4 minutes on each side or until scallops are opaque, brushing once with reserved marinade. **YIELD: 4 SERVINGS.**

GRILLED ROSEMARY SWORDFISH

- 1 tablespoon lemon juice
- 1 tablespoon olive oil
- 2 garlic cloves, minced
- 1 teaspoon minced fresh rosemary *or* 1/4 teaspoon dried rosemary, crushed
- 1 teaspoon grated lemon peel
- 1/4 teaspoon salt
- 1/4 teaspoon pepper
- 2 swordfish steaks (5 ounces *each*)

In a large resealable plastic bag, combine the first seven ingredients; add the swordfish. Seal bag and turn to coat; refrigerate for 1 hour.

Drain and discard marinade. Coat grill rack with cooking spray before starting the grill. Grill swordfish, covered, over medium-high heat for 4-6 minutes on each side or until fish just turns opaque. **YIELD: 2 SERVINGS.**

My husband loves swordfish, and this is how he likes to have it—moist, tender and perked up with herbs. Tuna is a good substitute for swordfish. Its firm texture stands up to grilling.

—Lorie Rice
Liverpool, New York

A ripe nectarine inspired me to put together a fruity salsa to serve with fish fillets. I received six thumbs up from our three children for this easy, nutritious main dish.

—Michelle Augustine, Cincinnati, Ohio

MAHI MAHI WITH NECTARINE SALSA

- 1 medium nectarine, peeled and chopped
- 1/4 cup chopped onion
- 2 tablespoons chopped cucumber
- 1 tablespoon minced fresh cilantro
- 2 teaspoons chopped seeded jalapeno pepper
- 2 teaspoons lime juice
- 1/4 teaspoon salt
- 1/4 teaspoon pepper
- 1/4 teaspoon Louisiana-style hot sauce

FISH FILLETS:
- 2 mahi mahi fillets (6 ounces *each*)
- 1 tablespoon olive oil

Dash salt

For salsa, in a small bowl, combine the first nine ingredients. Cover and refrigerate until serving.

If grilling the fish, coat grill rack with cooking spray before starting the grill. Drizzle fillets with oil; sprinkle with salt. Grill fillets, covered, over medium heat or broil 4-6 in. from the heat for 3-5 minutes on each side or until fish just turns opaque. Serve with salsa. **YIELD: 2 SERVINGS.**

EDITOR'S NOTE: When cutting hot peppers, disposable gloves are recommended. Avoid touching your face.

FISH & SEAFOOD GRILLING CHART

Fish is done when it turns opaque in the thickest portion and flakes into sections. Scallops are done when they turn opaque, and shrimp are done when they turn pink. Watch closely to avoid overcooking. For direct grilling, turn steaks, whole fish, shrimp and scallops halfway through grilling time. Fillets generally do not need to be turned. To ease turning, use a grill basket. The cooking times given are a guideline. Check for doneness with a meat thermometer or other appropriate doneness test.

CUT	WEIGHT OR THICKNESS	HEAT	APPROXIMATE COOKING TIME (IN MINUTES)
FISH			
FILLETS OR STEAKS	1/4 to 1/2 in.	high/direct	3 to 5
	1/2 to 1 in.	high/direct	5 to 10
DRESSED FISH	1 lb.	medium/direct	10 to 15
	2 to 2-1/2 lbs.	medium/indirect	20 to 30
KABOBS	1-in. cubes	medium/direct	8 to 12
SHELLFISH			
SEA SCALLOPS	1 lb.	medium/direct	5 to 8
SHRIMP, MEDIUM	1 lb.	medium/direct	5 to 8

HONEY GRILLED SHRIMP

- 1   bottle (8 ounces) Italian salad dressing
- 1   cup honey
- 1/2   teaspoon minced garlic
- 2   pounds uncooked medium shrimp, peeled and deveined

In a small bowl, combine the salad dressing, honey and garlic; set aside 1/2 cup. Pour remaining marinade into a large resealable plastic bag; add the shrimp. Seal bag and turn to coat; refrigerate for 30 minutes. Cover and refrigerate reserved marinade for basting.

Coat grill rack with cooking spray before starting the grill. Drain and discard marinade. Thread shrimp onto eight metal or soaked wooden skewers. Grill, uncovered, over medium heat for 1 to 1-1/2 minutes on each side. Baste with reserved marinade. Grill 3-4 minutes longer or until shrimp turn pink, turning and basting frequently. **YIELD: 8 SERVINGS.**

My husband was given this super-simple idea by a man who sold shrimp at the fish market. It's now become our absolute favorite shrimp recipe. We've even served it to company with great success.

—Lisa Blackwell
  Henderson,
  North Carolina

I love beef and lamb kabobs, but my doctor says I need to eat more fish. Since I also love grilling, these kabobs are a healthy alternative. They're great year-round.

—Weda Mosellie
  Phillipsburg, New Jersey

SWORDFISH SHRIMP KABOBS

1/4	cup olive oil
2	tablespoons balsamic vinegar
1/2	teaspoon crushed red pepper flakes
1/2	teaspoon dried oregano
1/4	teaspoon salt
1/8	teaspoon pepper
1/2	pound swordfish steak, skin removed and cut into 1-inch chunks
8	uncooked large shrimp, peeled and deveined
8	cherry tomatoes
1/2	medium red onion, cut into 4 wedges
1/2	medium sweet yellow pepper, cut into 8 chunks

In a small bowl, combine the oil, vinegar and seasonings. Place 3 tablespoons in a large resealable plastic bag; add swordfish and shrimp. Seal bag and turn to coat; refrigerate for up to 1 hour. Set remaining marinade aside for basting.

On four metal or soaked wooden skewers, thread the swordfish, tomatoes, shrimp, onion and yellow pepper.

Coat grill rack with cooking spray before starting grill. Grill kabobs, uncovered, over medium heat for 3 minutes, turning once. Baste with some of reserved marinade. Grill 3-4 minutes longer or until fish just turns opaque and shrimp turn pink, turning and basting frequently. **YIELD: 2 SERVINGS.**

GRILLING TIP

HAVE LEFTOVERS? Grilled foods can be just as tasty the next day. Consider Swordfish Shrimp Kabobs for example.

For a delicious dish the next day, remove the items from the skewers, toss with salad greens and top with a simple dressing. Or, reheat the items in the microwave with a bit of dressing or salsa and roll them up in a flour tortilla for a handheld treat. You can also serve the leftovers over rice for a no-fuss seafood dinner.

ORANGE ROUGHY WITH TARTAR SAUCE

You'll never buy tartar sauce again once you've tasted this super-easy recipe! Wrapped in a foil packet, the fish comes out moist, flaky and perfect every time—and cleanup is a cinch. I love it alongside baked beans.

—Michelle Stromko
 Forest Hill, Maryland

6   **orange roughy fillets (6 ounces *each*)**

1   **tablespoon seafood seasoning**

2   **tablespoons butter, cubed**

TARTAR SAUCE:

  2/3   **cup chopped dill pickles**

  1/2   **cup mayonnaise**

  3   **tablespoons finely chopped onion**

Dash pepper

Place three fillets on each of two double thickness of heavy-duty foil (about 18 in. square). Sprinkle each with seasoning; dot with butter.

Fold foil around fish and seal tightly. Grill, covered, over medium heat for 10-15 minutes or until fish flakes easily with a fork. Open foil carefully to allow steam to escape.

In a small bowl, combine the sauce ingredients; serve with fish. **YIELD: 6 SERVINGS (1 CUP SAUCE).**

GLAZED SALMON FILLET

- 1-1/2 cups packed brown sugar
- 6 tablespoons butter, melted
- 3 to 6 tablespoons lemon juice
- 2-1/4 teaspoons dill weed
- 3/4 teaspoon cayenne pepper
- 1 salmon fillet (about 2 pounds)
- Lemon-pepper seasoning

In a small bowl, combine the first five ingredients; mix well. Remove 1/2 cup to a saucepan; simmer until heated through. Set aside remaining mixture for basting.

Sprinkle salmon with lemon-pepper. Place on grill with skin side down. Grill, covered, over medium heat for 5 minutes. Brush with the reserved brown sugar mixture. Grill 10-15 minutes longer, basting occasionally. Serve with the warmed sauce. **YIELD: 6-8 SERVINGS.**

My husband caught a lot of salmon when we lived in Alaska, so I had to learn how to cook it. Basted with a sweet glaze, this tasty fillet is a staple in our house. Our kids love it.

—Jerilyn Colvin
Foxboro, Massachusetts

This entree assembles quickly and has very little preparation or cleanup. It's so delicious…and impressive enough to serve for guests. My family always shows up for this change-of-pace meal!

—Amy Hammons, Martinez, Georgia

FIERY SHRIMP FAJITAS

- 1/2 pound sliced bacon
- 1/2 pound uncooked medium shrimp, peeled and deveined
- 1 medium green pepper, cut into 1-inch pieces
- 1 medium sweet red pepper, cut into 1-inch pieces
- 1 medium onion, cut into 1-inch pieces
- 1/2 cup barbecue sauce
- 6 flour tortillas (8 inches), warmed
- 1 cup shredded lettuce
- 1 medium tomato, diced
- 1/2 cup shredded cheddar cheese

In a large skillet, cook bacon over medium heat until cooked but not crisp. Drain on paper towels. Wrap a strip of bacon around each shrimp; secure ends with toothpicks.

On six metal or soaked wooden skewers, alternately thread shrimp, peppers and onion. Grill, covered, over medium heat or broil 4 in. from the heat for 2-3 minutes on each side or until shrimp turn pink and vegetables are tender, basting frequently with barbecue sauce.

Remove shrimp and vegetables from skewers; discard toothpicks. Place on one side of each tortilla. Top with lettuce, tomato and cheese; fold over. **YIELD: 6 SERVINGS.**

TILAPIA WITH PINEAPPLE SALSA

2	cups cubed fresh pineapple
2	green onions, chopped
1/4	cup finely chopped green pepper
1/4	cup minced fresh cilantro
4	teaspoons plus 2 tablespoons lime juice, *divided*
1/8	teaspoon plus 1/4 teaspoon salt, *divided*

Dash cayenne pepper

1	tablespoon canola oil
8	tilapia fillets (4 ounces *each*)
1/8	teaspoon pepper

I found this recipe in a seafood cookbook years ago, and it's been one of my favorites. The refreshing, slightly spicy salsa is a delightful complement to the fish.

—Beth Fleming
  Downers Grove,
  Illinois

In a small bowl, combine the pineapple, onions, green pepper, cilantro, 4 teaspoons lime juice, 1/8 teaspoon salt and cayenne. Chill until serving.

Combine oil and remaining lime juice; drizzle over fillets. Sprinkle with pepper and remaining salt.

Coat grill rack with cooking spray before starting the grill. Grill fish, covered, over medium heat for 3-4 minutes on each side or until fish flakes easily with a fork. Serve with salsa. **YIELD: 8 SERVINGS (2 CUPS SALSA).**

SCALLOP KABOBS

- 3 **tablespoons lemon juice**
- 3 **tablespoons reduced-sodium soy sauce**
- 2 **tablespoons canola oil**

Dash garlic powder

Dash pepper

- 1-1/2 **pounds sea scallops**
- 3 **medium green peppers, cut into 1-1/2-inch pieces**
- 2 **cups cherry tomatoes**

In a small bowl, combine the first five ingredients. Pour 1/4 cup into a large resealable plastic bag; add scallops. Seal bag and turn to coat; refrigerate for 20 minutes. Cover and refrigerate remaining marinade for basting.

Meanwhile, in a large saucepan, bring 3 cups water to a boil. Add peppers; cover and boil for 2 minutes. Drain and immediately place peppers in ice water. Drain and pat dry.

Coat grill rack with cooking spray before starting the grill. Drain and discard marinade. On eight metal or soaked wooden skewers, alternately thread the tomatoes, scallops and peppers.

Grill, covered, over medium heat for 3-5 minutes on each side or until scallops are firm and opaque, basting occasionally with reserved marinade. **YIELD: 4 SERVINGS.**

I'm always on the lookout for recipes that are lower in fat and heart-healthy, too. These kabobs fit the bill. I like to serve them with a fruit salad and a light dessert.

—Edie DeSpain
 Logan, Utah

BALSAMIC-GLAZED TUNA STEAKS

4	tuna steaks (3/4 inch thick and 6 ounces *each*)
1-1/4	teaspoons pepper
1/4	teaspoon salt
4	teaspoons dark brown sugar
1/2	teaspoon cornstarch
1/4	cup chicken broth
1	tablespoon balsamic vinegar
1	tablespoon soy sauce

Sprinkle tuna with pepper and salt. If grilling the fish, coat grill rack with cooking spray before starting the grill. Grill fish, covered, over medium heat or broil 4-6 in. from the heat for 3-5 minutes on each side for medium-rare or until slightly pink in the center.

Meanwhile, in a small saucepan, combine the remaining ingredients until smooth. Bring to a boil; cook and stir for 1 minute or until thickened. Serve with fish. **YIELD: 4 SERVINGS.**

Simple to prepare but full of flavor, these tuna steaks have a slight sweetness, thanks to the delicious balsamic glaze. Ready in minutes, they're perfect for hectic days.
—Laura McDowell, Lake Villa, Illinois

GRILLING TIP

TESTING FOR DONENESS

For fish fillets, check for doneness by inserting a fork at an angle into the thickest portion of the fish and gently parting the meat. When it flakes into sections, it is cooked completely. Whole fish or steaks are done when the flesh is easily removed from the bones. Cooked fish is opaque in color and the juices are milky white.

CAMPFIRE FRIED FISH

Five ingredients are all you need to spruce up fish fillets in this no-fuss recipe. Prepared on a grill-proof skillet, the fried fish promises to be a hit with your gang any night of the week.
—Taste of Home Test Kitchen

2	eggs
3/4	cup all-purpose flour
1/2	cup cornmeal
1	teaspoon salt
1	teaspoon paprika
3	pounds walleye, bluegill *or* perch fillets

Canola oil

In a shallow bowl, whisk eggs. In a large resealable plastic bag, combine the flour, cornmeal, salt and paprika. Dip fillets in eggs, then roll in flour mixture.

Add 1/4 in. of oil to a large cast-iron skillet; place skillet on grill rack over medium-hot heat. Fry fillets in oil in batches for 3-4 minutes on each side or until fish flakes easily with a fork. **YIELD: 6 SERVINGS.**

GRILLED SALMON WITH GARLIC MAYO

3	tablespoons plus 1 teaspoon olive oil, *divided*
1/2	teaspoon dried rosemary, crushed
4	salmon fillets (6 ounces *each*)
8	garlic cloves, peeled
1	tablespoon lemon juice
3/4	cup mayonnaise
2	tablespoons plain yogurt
1	tablespoon Dijon mustard

Coat grill rack with cooking spray before starting the grill. Combine 3 tablespoons oil and rosemary; drizzle over salmon. Place salmon skin side down on grill rack.

Grill, covered, over medium heat for 10-12 minutes or until fish flakes easily with a fork.

Meanwhile, in a small microwave-safe bowl, combine garlic and remaining oil. Microwave, uncovered, on high for 20-30 seconds or until softened; transfer to a blender. Add the remaining ingredients. Cover and process until blended. Serve with salmon. **YIELD: 4 SERVINGS.**

This is my stand-by for a quick, elegant midweek dinner!

—Donna Noel
Gray, Maine

BUTTERY GRILLED SHRIMP

1/2	cup butter, melted
3	tablespoons lemon juice
2	teaspoons chili powder
1	teaspoon ground ginger
1/4	teaspoon salt
2	pounds uncooked jumbo shrimp, peeled and deveined

In a small bowl, combine the first five ingredients; set aside 1/4 cup. Thread shrimp onto eight metal or soaked wooden skewers.

Grill shrimp, covered, over medium heat for 3-5 minutes on each side or until shrimp turn pink, basting occasionally with butter mixture. Remove from the grill; brush with reserved butter mixture. **YIELD: 8 SERVINGS.**

This is easy and delicious! These shrimp are great with steak, but for a special occasion, brush the sauce on lobster tails you prepare on the grill.

—Sheryl Shenberger
Albuquerque, New Mexico

BACON HONEY WALLEYE

16	bacon strips, partially cooked
4	walleye fillets (2-1/2 pounds)
1	cup thinly sliced onion
1/4	cup butter, melted
2	tablespoons honey
1/2	teaspoon salt
1/4	teaspoon pepper

Fold four 18-in. x 15-in. pieces of heavy-duty aluminum foil in half; fold up edges to make pans about 12 in. x 7 in. Place four strips of bacon in each foil pan; top each with a fillet and 1/4 cup onion. Drizzle with butter and honey. Sprinkle with salt and pepper.

Grill, covered, over medium heat for 12-15 minutes or until fish flakes easily with a fork. Cut fillets in half; serve each with two bacon strips. **YIELD: 8 SERVINGS.**

The texture and flavor of walleye is only enhanced by this recipe's savory-sweet topping. It takes only a few minutes to grill.

—Linda Neumann, Algonac, Michigan

For a beautiful seafood dinner that's impressive enough to serve to company, try this delicious dish. The marinade has such a wonderful Asian flavor that you'll want to serve this time and again.

—Taste of Home
Test Kitchen

SESAME ASIAN SNAPPER

1/4	cup rice vinegar	1/4	teaspoon cayenne pepper
1/4	cup sherry	1/4	teaspoon freshly ground pepper
1/4	cup soy sauce	1	whole red snapper (3 pounds)
2	tablespoons lemon juice	1	small onion, sliced
2	tablespoons sesame oil	6	sprigs fresh cilantro
1	tablespoon minced fresh gingerroot		
2	teaspoons sugar		
2	garlic cloves, minced		

In a small bowl, combine the first 10 ingredients; set aside 1/4 cup for serving. Make three or four deep, parallel slashes to the bone on each side of fish; place in a 2-gallon resealable plastic bag. Add remaining marinade; seal bag and refrigerate for 1 hour.

Meanwhile, rub grill rack with oil or coat with cooking spray before starting grill. Drain and discard marinade from fish. Place onion and cilantro in the fish cavity.

Grill, covered, over indirect medium-high heat for 15-17 minutes on each side or until fish flakes easily with a fork. Remove onion and cilantro; drizzle with reserved soy mixture. **YIELD: 4 SERVINGS.**

WALLEYE DELIGHT

1	pound walleye, pike, perch *or* trout fillets
2	teaspoons butter, softened
1	tablespoon lemon juice
1	tablespoon minced fresh basil *or* 1/2 to 1 teaspoon dried basil
1	teaspoon lemon-pepper seasoning
1/2	teaspoon garlic salt
1-3/4	cups sliced fresh mushrooms

Coat an 18-in. square piece of heavy-duty foil with cooking spray. Place fillets on foil. Spread with butter. Sprinkle with lemon juice, basil, lemon-pepper and garlic salt. Top with mushrooms.

Seal foil tightly. Grill, covered, over medium-hot heat for 5-7 minutes on each side or until fish flakes easily with a fork. Carefully remove foil to allow steam to escape. **YIELD: 4 SERVINGS.**

I love fish and think grilling is one of the best ways to prepare it. The combination of lemon juice, basil and other seasonings in this recipe is fantastic.

—Connie Reilly
  Stanchfield,
  Minnesota

GRILLED MAHI MAHI

3/4   cup reduced-sodium teriyaki sauce

2   tablespoons sherry *or* pineapple juice

2   garlic cloves

8   mahi mahi fillets (6 ounces *each*)

TROPICAL FRUIT SALSA:

1   medium mango, peeled and diced

1   cup chopped seeded peeled papaya

3/4   cup chopped green pepper

1/2   cup cubed fresh pineapple

1/2   medium red onion, chopped

1/4   cup minced fresh cilantro

1/4   cup minced fresh mint

1   tablespoon chopped seeded jalapeno pepper

1   tablespoon lime juice

1   tablespoon lemon juice

1/2   teaspoon crushed red pepper flakes

In a large resealable plastic bag, combine the teriyaki sauce, sherry or pineapple juice and garlic; add mahi mahi. Seal bag and turn to coat; refrigerate for 30 minutes.

Meanwhile, in a large bowl, combine the salsa ingredients. Cover and refrigerate salsa until serving.

Coat grill rack with cooking spray before starting the grill. Drain and discard marinade. Grill mahi mahi, covered, over medium heat for 4-5 minutes on each side or until fish flakes easily with a fork. Serve with salsa. **YIELD: 8 SERVINGS.**

EDITOR'S NOTE: When cutting hot peppers, disposable gloves are recommended. Avoid touching your face.

GRILLED SNAPPER WITH CAPER SAUCE

1/3	cup lime juice		2	tablespoons water
1	jalapeno pepper, seeded		2	teaspoons red wine vinegar
3	garlic cloves, peeled		1/2	cup fresh cilantro leaves
1-1/4	teaspoons fresh thyme leaves *or* 1/4 teaspoon dried thyme		1	shallot, peeled
1	teaspoon salt		1	tablespoon capers, drained
1	teaspoon pepper		1-1/2	teaspoons chopped seeded jalapeno pepper
4	red snapper fillets (6 ounces *each*)		1	garlic clove, peeled and halved

SAUCE:

3	tablespoons lime juice
3	tablespoons olive oil

1/4	teaspoon pepper

There is snapper in this recipe, but if you prefer another fish, try mahi mahi. It is a deliciously firm, mild fish that won't fall apart on the grill.

—Alaina Showalter
Clover, South Carolina

In a small food processor, combine the first six ingredients; cover and process until blended. Pour into a large resealable plastic bag. Add the fillets; seal bag and turn to coat. Refrigerate for 30 minutes.

Coat grill rack with cooking spray before starting the grill. Drain and discard marinade. Grill fillets, covered, over medium heat for 3-5 minutes on each side or until fish flakes easily with a fork.

Meanwhile, combine sauce ingredients in a small food processor. Cover and process until blended. Serve with fish. **YIELD: 4 SERVINGS.**

EDITOR'S NOTE: When cutting hot peppers, disposable gloves are recommended. Avoid touching your face.

SKILLET-GRILLED CATFISH

1/4	cup all-purpose flour
1/4	cup cornmeal
1	teaspoon onion powder
1	teaspoon dried basil
1/2	teaspoon garlic salt
1/2	teaspoon dried thyme
1/4	to 1/2 teaspoon white pepper
1/4	to 1/2 teaspoon cayenne pepper
1/4	to 1/2 teaspoon pepper
4	catfish fillets (6 to 8 ounces *each*)
1/4	cup butter

In a large resealable bag, combine the first nine ingredients. Add catfish, one fillet at a time, and shake to coat.

Place a large cast-iron skillet on a grill rack over medium-hot heat. Melt butter in the skillet; add catfish. Grill, covered, for 6-8 minutes on each side or until fish flakes easily with a fork. **YIELD: 4 SERVINGS.**

I suggest catfish or haddock for this dinner. The Cajun flavor is great, and everyone finds it a nice change of pace!

—Traci Wynne, Clayton, Delaware

PINEAPPLE SHRIMP PACKETS

6	canned pineapple slices
1-1/2	pounds uncooked medium shrimp, peeled and deveined
1/3	cup chopped sweet red pepper
1/3	cup packed brown sugar
1	tablespoon seafood seasoning
3	tablespoons butter, cubed

For each packet, place a pineapple slice on a double thickness of heavy-duty foil (about 12 in. square). Top with shrimp and red pepper. Combine the brown sugar and seafood seasoning; sprinkle over shrimp. Dot with butter. Fold foil around mixture and seal tightly.

Grill, covered, over medium heat for 10-15 minutes or until shrimp turn pink. **YIELD: 6 SERVINGS.**

Your family and friends will delight in receiving these individual grilled shrimp packets. The foil makes cleanup a breeze.

—Nancy Zimmerman
Cape May Court House,
New Jersey

STUFFED SALMON

1	**whole salmon (8 pounds)**
2	**teaspoons salt,** *divided*
1-1/4	**teaspoons pepper,** *divided*
2	**cups unseasoned stuffing cubes**
1	**cup shredded carrots**
1	**cup sliced mushrooms**
1	**large onion, finely chopped**
1/2	**cup minced fresh parsley**
3/4	**cup butter, melted,** *divided*
1/4	**cup egg substitute**
4-1/2	**teaspoons plus 1/4 cup lemon juice,** *divided*
1	**garlic clove, minced**
2	**tablespoons canola oil**

Remove head and tail from salmon if desired. Sprinkle the cavity with 1 teaspoon each salt and pepper.

In a large bowl, combine the stuffing cubes, carrots, mushrooms, onion, parsley, 1/4 cup butter, egg substitute, 4-1/2 teaspoons lemon juice, garlic and remaining salt and pepper; stuff cavity. Secure with metal skewers. Drizzle salmon with oil.

Coat grill rack with cooking spray before starting the grill. Prepare grill for indirect heat. Grill salmon, covered, over indirect medium heat for 40-50 minutes or until fish flakes easily with a fork and a meat thermometer reads 165° for stuffing.

In a small bowl, combine remaining butter and lemon juice. Serve with salmon. **YIELD: 12 SERVINGS.**

KEEP FRESH FISH FRESH

FRESH FISH is highly perishable and should be prepared within a day or two after it is caught or purchased. Freshly caught fish should be pan-dressed, washed in cold water, blotted dry with paper towels, placed in an airtight container or heavy-duty plastic bag and refrigerated. For long-term storage, wrap fish in freezer paper, heavy-duty foil or heavy-duty plastic bags and freeze no longer than 3 months for fatty or oily fish (such as salmon, whitefish, mackerel) or 6 months for lean fish (such as sole, catfish, cod, orange roughy).

TOMATO-BASIL SHRIMP SKEWERS

1/3	cup olive oil
1/4	cup tomato sauce
2	tablespoons minced fresh basil
2	tablespoons red wine vinegar
1-1/2	teaspoons minced garlic
1/4	teaspoon cayenne pepper
2	pounds uncooked jumbo shrimp, peeled and deveined

In a large resealable plastic bag, combine the first six ingredients; add shrimp. Seal bag and turn to coat; refrigerate for up to 30 minutes.

Drain and discard marinade. Thread shrimp onto six metal or soaked wooden skewers. Grill, covered, over medium heat for 3-5 minutes on each side or until shrimp turn pink. **YIELD: 6 SERVINGS.**

I promise you that these are the best, most perfectly seasoned shrimp you will ever eat. My husband doesn't normally care for shrimp, but he raves over these!

—Jennifer Fulk, Moreno Valley, California

GRILLED TILAPIA WITH MANGO

4	tilapia fillets (6 ounces *each*)
1	tablespoon olive oil
1/2	teaspoon salt
1/2	teaspoon dill weed
1/4	teaspoon pepper
1	tablespoon grated Parmesan cheese
1	medium lemon, sliced
1	medium mango, peeled and thinly sliced

Coat grill rack with cooking spray before starting the grill. Brush fillets with oil; sprinkle with salt, dill and pepper.

Grill tilapia, covered, over medium heat for 5 minutes. Turn tilapia; top with cheese, lemon and mango. Grill 4-6 minutes longer or until fish flakes easily with a fork. **YIELD: 4 SERVINGS.**

Here is a different twist on tilapia that I created for my wife. She enjoyed the combination of mango with the Parmesan. There's nothing like eating this out on the deck with a cold glass of iced tea.

—Gregg May
  Columbus, Ohio

THAI TILAPIA

1-1/2	cups cooked rice
1/3	cup chopped green onions
1/3	cup chopped sweet red pepper
1	tablespoon minced fresh basil
2	tilapia fillets (6 ounces *each*)
1	cup fresh snow peas
1/3	to 1/2 cup Thai peanut sauce

Prepare grill for indirect heat. Combine the rice, onions, red pepper and basil; place on a greased double thickness of heavy-duty foil (about 15 in. square). Top with the tilapia, snow peas and peanut sauce. Fold foil around mixture and seal tightly.

Grill, covered, over indirect medium-hot heat for 8-10 minutes or until fish flakes easily with a fork. Open foil carefully to allow steam to escape. **YIELD: 2 SERVINGS.**

You can take a taste trip to Asia even on a hectic weeknight with this no-fuss meal-in-one. The sauce adds a mellow, peanutty flavor and a bit of a kick.

—Taste of Home
  Test Kitchen

GARLIC-HERB FISH

2	tablespoons lemon juice
2	red snapper fillets *or* orange roughy fillets (7 ounces *each*)
2	teaspoons grated lemon peel
1/2	teaspoon salt
1/2	teaspoon garlic powder
1/2	teaspoon dried chervil
1/4	teaspoon dill weed
1/4	teaspoon pepper

Spoon lemon juice over both sides of fillets. Combine the lemon peel and seasonings; sprinkle over fillets.

If grilling the fish, coat grill rack with cooking spray before starting the grill. Grill fish, uncovered, over medium heat or broil 4-6 in. from the heat for 3 minutes on each side or until fish flakes easily with a fork. **YIELD: 2 SERVINGS.**

My husband likes to grill seafood, and this delightful entree is a favorite of both of ours.

—Nancy Mueller
   Menomonee Falls,
   Wisconsin

FIRECRACKER SALMON STEAKS

1/4	cup balsamic vinegar
1/4	cup chili sauce
1/4	cup packed brown sugar
3	garlic cloves, minced
2	teaspoons minced fresh parsley
1	teaspoon minced fresh gingerroot
1/4 to 1/2	teaspoon cayenne pepper
1/4 to 1/2	teaspoon crushed red pepper flakes, optional
4	salmon steaks (6 ounces *each*)

Coat grill rack with cooking spray before starting the grill. In a small bowl, combine the vinegar, chili sauce, sugar, garlic, parsley and seasonings. Grill salmon, covered, over medium heat for 4-5 minutes on each side or until fish flakes easily with a fork, brushing occasionally with sauce. **YIELD: 4 SERVINGS.**

Red pepper flakes and cayenne provide fiery flavor that gives these salmon steaks their name. Basting the fish with the zippy sauce while grilling creates a glossy glaze.

—Phyllis Schmalz, Kansas City, Kansas

EASY GREEK CATFISH

- **6** catfish fillets (8 ounces *each*)
- **Greek seasoning to taste**
- **4** ounces feta cheese, crumbled
- **1** tablespoon dried mint
- **2** tablespoons olive oil

Sprinkle both sides of the fillets with Greek seasoning. Sprinkle each fillet with 1 rounded tablespoon feta cheese and 1/2 teaspoon mint. Drizzle 1 teaspoon oil over each. Roll up fillets and secure with toothpicks.

Grill over medium heat for 20-25 minutes or until fish flakes easily with a fork. Or, place fillets in a greased baking dish and bake at 350° for 30-35 minutes or until fish flakes easily with a fork. **YIELD: 6 SERVINGS.**

Temperatures here on the Gulf Coast are moderate year-round, so we grill out a lot. My husband, Larry, came up with this recipe by experimenting. Our whole family likes the unique taste of his specialty.

—Rita Futral
    Starkville, Mississippi

GRILLED DIJON FISH

- **1/4** cup butter, cubed
- **1** tablespoon lemon juice
- **1** tablespoon Dijon mustard
- **1/4** teaspoon salt
- **2** orange roughy fillets (6 ounces *each*)
- **Dash paprika**

In a small saucepan, melt butter. Remove from the heat; stir in the lemon juice, mustard and salt. Remove 2 tablespoons; set aside. Pour remaining marinade into a large resealable plastic bag; add the fillets. Seal bag and turn to coat; set aside for 20 minutes.

If grilling the fish, coat grill rack with cooking spray before starting the grill. Drain and discard marinade. Grill fish, covered, over medium heat or broil 4-6 in. from the heat for 7-10 minutes or until fillets flake easily with a fork. To serve, arrange fish on a plate. Drizzle with reserved marinade; sprinkle with paprika. **YIELD: 2 SERVINGS.**

This mild dish is ideal for a quick summer meal. The simple marinade has just enough flavor to complement the fish without overwhelming its delicate taste.

—Phyllis Schmalz, Kansas City, Kansas

FISH WITH BRUSCHETTA DINNER

Tender, flaky red snapper is topped with mustard-glazed onions for a delicious dish. Paired with the unique bruschetta side, this is one supper that will delight and surprise.

—Taste of Home
   Test Kitchen

- 1   medium onion, thinly sliced
- 6   tablespoons lime juice
- 2   tablespoons brown sugar
- 2   tablespoons butter
- 1   tablespoon prepared mustard
- 4   red snapper fillets (6 ounces *each*)

BRUSCHETTA:
- 1/4   cup olive oil
- 8   slices French bread (1 inch thick)
- 8   ounces Havarti cheese, sliced
- 2   cups salsa

In a small skillet over medium heat, cook and stir the onion, lime juice, brown sugar, butter and mustard for 4-5 minutes or until onion is tender and liquid is almost evaporated.

Place each fillet on a double thickness of heavy-duty foil (about 12 in. square). Top with onion mixture. Fold foil over fish and seal tightly. Grill, covered, over medium heat for 6-8 minutes or until fish flakes easily with a fork.

Meanwhile, brush oil over both sides of bread. Grill for 30-60 seconds on each side or until lightly browned. Top each slice of bread with a slice of cheese; grill 1 minute longer or until cheese is melted. Top with salsa.

Open foil packets carefully to allow steam to escape. Serve fish with bruschetta. **YIELD: 4 SERVINGS.**

10
SAUCES & SEASONINGS

PG. **231** CHERRY
BARBECUE
SAUCE

IT'S EASY TO SPICE UP GRILLED FARE WITH THE RIGHT BARBECUE SAUCE, SEASONING BLEND OR MARINADE. WHETHER YOU'RE LOOKING FOR A ZESTY RELISH FOR HOT DOGS OR AN HERBED BUTTER FOR CORN ON THE COB, THIS CHAPTER PROMISES SIMPLE IDEAS SURE TO JAZZ UP YOUR FLAME-BROILED SPECIALTIES.

ALL-AMERICAN RUB

This wonderful salt-free rub is great on steaks, pork and chicken. Try shaking the quick, spicy-sweet combination on popcorn, too!
—Heather Bonser, Laurel, Montana

1/2	cup packed brown sugar
2	tablespoons dried minced onion
1	tablespoon garlic powder
1	tablespoon ground mustard
1/2	teaspoon cayenne pepper
1/8	teaspoon ground nutmeg

In a small bowl, combine all of the ingredients; store in an airtight container.

Rub over meat or poultry; cover and refrigerate for up to 4 hours before grilling or broiling. **YIELD: 3/4 CUP.**

★ GRILLING TIP

MAKING A RUB is a snap. Crush your family's favorite herbs or seasonings into a small bowl. Sprinkle the mixture over the meat. Rub the mixture into the surface of the meat. Many recipes instruct you to cover and refrigerate the meat a bit, allowing the flavors to combine.

PEPPERED SQUASH RELISH

3	pounds yellow summer squash, finely chopped
3	pounds zucchini, finely chopped
6	large onions, finely chopped
3	medium green peppers, finely chopped
3	medium sweet red peppers, finely chopped
1/4	cup salt
2	cups sugar
2	cups packed brown sugar
2	cups white vinegar
4	teaspoons celery seed
1	teaspoon ground turmeric
1	teaspoon ground mustard

In a large bowl, combine the first six ingredients. Cover and refrigerate overnight.

Drain vegetable mixture. Rinse in cold water and drain again. Place vegetables in a Dutch oven. Add the sugars, vinegar, celery seed, turmeric and mustard. Bring to a boil. Reduce heat; simmer, uncovered, for 15-20 minutes or until liquid is clear.

Remove from the heat; cool. Spoon into containers. Cover and refrigerate for up to 3 weeks. **YIELD: 4 QUARTS.**

I cook for a local middle school and have been making this relish more than 25 years. Whenever I take it to a dinner or picnic, it is sure to go fast, and I get lots of requests for the recipe. Sometimes I put it into gift baskets with other homemade goodies.
—Rose Cole, Salem, West Virginia

RHUBARB KETCHUP

4	cups diced fresh *or* frozen rhubarb
3	medium onions, chopped
1	cup white vinegar
1	cup packed brown sugar
1	cup sugar
1	can (28 ounces) diced tomatoes, undrained
2	teaspoons salt
1	teaspoon ground cinnamon
1	tablespoon pickling spice

In a large saucepan, combine all ingredients. Cook for 1 hour or until thickened. Cool. Refrigerate in covered containers. **YIELD: 6-7 CUPS.**

I received this recipe from a friend about 15 years ago. It is a nice surprise for ketchup lovers, and so easy to prepare. The spicy flavor makes this one of the tastiest ketchups I've ever had!
—Faith McLillian
Rawdon, Quebec

GRILLED ONION MEDLEY

This mouthwatering medley, seasoned with garlic and rosemary, is great on grilled burgers or sausages. You can even serve it on its own as a change-of-pace side dish.

—Mary Lou Wayman
　Salt Lake City, Utah

1/2	sweet onion, cut into four wedges
1/2	small red onion, cut into four wedges
1	medium leek (white portion only), sliced
2	garlic cloves, peeled and sliced
1-1/2	teaspoons olive oil
1	to 2 teaspoons minced fresh rosemary
1/4	teaspoon salt
1/8	teaspoon pepper

Paprika

In a large bowl, combine the onions, leek and garlic. Add oil; toss to coat. Pour into a grill wok or basket. Grill, uncovered, over medium heat for 15-19 minutes or until tender, stirring occasionally.

Transfer onion mixture to a bowl. Sprinkle with rosemary, salt, pepper and paprika. Serve warm. **YIELD: 2 SERVINGS.**

CLOCKWISE FROM TOP: COOK-OFF BARBECUE SAUCE, DILLY SWEET ONION RELISH, HONEY BARBECUE SAUCE, GARLIC-PEPPER RUB

COOK-OFF BARBECUE SAUCE

2/3	cup ketchup
1	medium pepperoncini, finely chopped
1	tablespoon dried minced onion
1	tablespoon brown sugar
1	tablespoon cider vinegar
1	tablespoon lime juice
1	tablespoon Worcestershire sauce
1	teaspoon garlic powder
1	teaspoon lemon juice
1	teaspoon Dijon mustard
1	teaspoon honey
1/2	teaspoon ground cumin
1/4	to 1/2 teaspoon hot pepper sauce
1/4	teaspoon white pepper

In a small saucepan, combine all the ingredients; heat through. Serve with chicken or pork. **YIELD: 1 CUP.**

EDITOR'S NOTE: Look for pepperoncinis (pickled peppers) in the pickle and olive section of your grocery store.

After looking for the perfect BBQ sauce for 12 years, I tried making my own. After many attempts, I hit on the magic combination. Everyone who's tried this version agrees that it's a winner.

—Phil Maine
   Truckee, California

DILLY SWEET ONION RELISH

6	large sweet onions, thinly sliced (about 3-1/2 pounds)
1/4	cup olive oil
3/4	cup chicken broth
1/4	cup white balsamic vinegar
1/4	cup snipped fresh dill or 4 teaspoons dill weed
2	tablespoons honey
1/4	teaspoon salt
1/4	teaspoon pepper

This is absolutely the best sweet relish I've tasted. It can be served warm, cold or at room temperature. My aunt swore by this relish, and I can see why it cannot be matched!

—Denise Patterson
Bainbridge, Ohio

In a large skillet, saute onions in oil until tender. Add broth and vinegar. Bring to a boil; cook until liquid is reduced by half.

Remove from the heat; stir in the remaining ingredients. Serve at room temperature. Refrigerate leftovers. **YIELD: 4-1/2 CUPS.**

HONEY BARBECUE SAUCE

This sauce is my own recipe that my whole family enjoys, especially my father. It is a quick and easy mixture that can be made ahead and refrigerated.

—Karene Donnay, Glencoe, Minnesota

1	can (8 ounces) tomato sauce
2	tablespoons brown sugar
2	tablespoons honey
1	tablespoon lemon juice
1	tablespoon molasses
1-1/2	teaspoons Worcestershire sauce
1-1/2	teaspoons prepared mustard
1	garlic clove, minced
1/4	teaspoon dried oregano
1/4	teaspoon chili powder
1/8	teaspoon pepper

In a small saucepan, combine all ingredients. Bring to a boil. Serve with chicken or pork. **YIELD: 1-1/3 CUPS.**

GARLIC-PEPPER RUB

Here's a no-fuss rub that adds a tasty mix of garlic, pepper and lemon to any burger. It's a great way to spice up grilled goods.

—Ann Marie Moch, Kintyre, North Dakota

6	tablespoons lemon-pepper seasoning
2	tablespoons dried thyme
2	tablespoons paprika
2	teaspoons garlic powder
1	teaspoon sugar
1/2	teaspoon salt
1/4	teaspoon ground coriander
1/8	teaspoon ground cumin
1/8	teaspoon cayenne pepper

In a large bowl, combine all the ingredients; store in a covered container. Rub over meat or poultry; let stand for at least 30 minutes before grilling or broiling. **YIELD: 2/3 CUP.**

CONEY ISLAND SAUCE

- 1/2 pound ground beef
- 1/4 cup chopped onion
- 2 tablespoons chopped celery
- 1 can (8 ounces) tomato sauce
- 2 tablespoons brown sugar
- 1 tablespoon lemon juice
- 2-1/4 teaspoons Worcestershire sauce
- 3/4 teaspoon chili powder
- 1/2 teaspoon prepared mustard
- 1/4 teaspoon salt
- 8 hot dogs
- 8 hot dog buns, split

In a large skillet, cook the beef, onion and celery over medium heat until meat is no longer pink; drain. Stir in the tomato sauce, brown sugar, lemon juice, Worcestershire sauce, chili powder, mustard and salt. Bring to a boil. Reduce heat; simmer, uncovered, for 15-20 minutes or until the sauce is thickened, stirring occasionally.

Grill or cook hot dogs according to package directions. Place hot dogs in buns; top with sauce. **YIELD: 8 SERVINGS.**

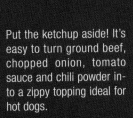

Put the ketchup aside! It's easy to turn ground beef, chopped onion, tomato sauce and chili powder into a zippy topping ideal for hot dogs.

—Shirley Heston
Pickerington, Ohio

My mother gave me this seasoned butter recipe several years ago. It's simple and is perfect for garlic bread made on the grill. Try it over veggies, too.

—Marla Pinson, Granbury, Texas

GARLIC BUTTER TOPPING

- 3 tablespoons butter, softened
- 1/2 teaspoon garlic powder
- 1/4 teaspoon dried thyme

GARLIC BREAD:
- 4 hoagie buns, split
- 1/4 cup grated Parmesan cheese

In a small microwave-safe bowl, combine the butter, garlic powder and thyme. Cover and microwave on high until butter is melted. **YIELD: 3 TABLESPOONS.**

FOR GARLIC BREAD: Brush butter topping over cut sides of buns. Place cut side down on grill. Grill, uncovered, over medium heat for 1 minute or until toasted. Sprinkle with cheese. **YIELD: 4 SERVINGS.**

EDITOR'S NOTE: This recipe was tested in a 1,100-watt microwave.

TANGY BARBECUE SAUCE

- 1 large onion, finely chopped
- 1 tablespoon canola oil
- 1-1/2 cups ketchup
- 1 cup cider vinegar
- 3/4 cup water
- 3/4 cup sugar-free maple-flavored syrup
- 4-1/2 teaspoons Worcestershire sauce
- Sugar substitute equivalent to 1 tablespoon sugar
- 2 teaspoons reduced-sodium beef bouillon granules
- 1 teaspoon salt
- 1/4 teaspoon pepper
- 1/4 teaspoon hot pepper sauce

In a large nonstick saucepan, saute onion in oil until tender. Stir in the remaining ingredients. Bring to a boil. Reduce heat; simmer, uncovered, for 45 minutes or until sauce is thickened and reduced to 2-1/2 cups. **YIELD: 2-1/2 CUPS.**

Cider vinegar and maple syrup lend a unique touch to this easy barbecue sauce. Vary the hot pepper sauce to your liking.

—Lynn Sawyer, Two Rivers, Wisconsin

ALL-SEASONS MARINADE

- 3/4 cup soy sauce
- 1/2 cup canola oil
- 1/2 cup red wine vinegar
- 1/3 cup lemon juice
- 1/4 cup Worcestershire sauce
- 2 tablespoons ground mustard
- 2 tablespoons minced fresh parsley
- 1-1/2 teaspoons pepper
- 1 teaspoon salt
- 2 garlic cloves, minced

This mixture is so versatile, it can be used to marinate just about anything. I like to mix up a batch in a jiffy and keep it in the fridge for grilling beef, pork, chicken or even shrimp.

—Joan Hallford
North Richland Hills, Texas

In a small bowl, whisk all the ingredients. Cover and refrigerate until ready to use. Use as a marinade for beef, pork, chicken or shrimp. **YIELD: 2 CUPS.**

At my wits end with grating zucchini from my garden, I was determined to make something other than zucchini bread and zucchini cake. I found this recipe and altered it to our taste. Now we use it for many dishes!

—Taren Weyer, Hudson, Wisconsin

GARDEN CHUTNEY

6	cups chopped seeded zucchini (about 7 medium)
2	medium tart apples, peeled and chopped
1-1/2	cups raisins *or* dried currants
1-1/2	cups white vinegar
1	cup honey
1	medium sweet red pepper, chopped
1	small onion, chopped
1/3	cup thawed orange juice concentrate
2	tablespoons lemon juice

In a Dutch oven, bring all ingredients to a boil. Reduce heat; simmer, uncovered, for 45-55 minutes or until thickened.

Serve warm or cold. Refrigerate leftovers. **YIELD: 4 CUPS.**

RHUBARB BARBECUE SAUCE

1	cup chopped fresh *or* frozen rhubarb
2/3	cup water
1	medium onion, finely chopped
1	teaspoon canola oil
1	garlic clove, minced
1	cup ketchup
2/3	cup packed brown sugar
1/2	cup dark corn syrup
2	tablespoons cider vinegar
2	tablespoons Worcestershire sauce
1	tablespoon Dijon mustard
1-1/2	teaspoons hot pepper sauce
1/4	teaspoon salt

This tangy rhubarb sauce tastes outstanding served over turkey, chicken or pork. Fresh garlic and several seasonings give it a nice flavor boost!

—Carol Anderson
Coaldale, Alberta

In a small saucepan, bring rhubarb and water to a boil. Reduce heat; simmer, uncovered, for 5-6 minutes or until tender. Remove from the heat; cool slightly.

Place rhubarb in a blender or food processor; cover and process until smooth. Set aside.

In the same saucepan, saute onion in oil until tender. Add garlic; saute 1 minute longer. Add the remaining ingredients.

Whisk in rhubarb puree until blended. Bring to a boil. Reduce heat; simmer, uncovered, for 5 minutes. Use as a basting sauce for grilled meats. Store in the refrigerator. **YIELD: 2-1/3 CUPS.**

CHERRY BARBECUE SAUCE

You can use fresh or frozen cherries to make this flavorful barbecue sauce. It tastes great on ribs and chicken!

—Ilene Harrington
Nipomo, California

1	medium onion, chopped
2	tablespoons butter
2	garlic cloves, minced
2	cups fresh *or* frozen dark sweet cherries, pitted and coarsely chopped
1	cup ketchup
2/3	cup packed brown sugar
1/4	cup cider vinegar
1	tablespoon Worcestershire sauce
2	teaspoons ground mustard
1/2	teaspoon pepper
1/8	teaspoon Liquid Smoke, optional

In a large saucepan, saute onion in butter until tender. Add garlic; cook 1 minute longer. Stir in the remaining ingredients. Cook, uncovered, over medium-low heat for 20 minutes or until cherries are tender and sauce is thickened, stirring occasionally. **YIELD: ABOUT 3-1/2 CUPS.**

PINEAPPLE PEPPER SALSA

1   can (8 ounces) crushed pineapple, drained

1/3   cup sweet red pepper jelly

1/2   cup chopped red onion

1/2   cup chopped sweet red pepper

1   teaspoon minced fresh cilantro

1/8   teaspoon coarsely ground pepper

In a small bowl, combine all the ingredients. Serve immediately or refrigerate until serving. Use as a condiment with grilled meats or as a dip with tortilla chips. **YIELD: 2 CUPS.**

The contrast of sweet and spicy makes this a flavorful topping for grilled meats. For a hotter variety, use jalapeno jelly instead of sweet red pepper jelly.

—Sandy Stark
  Amherst, New York

ROASTED TOMATO 'N' GARLIC MAYONNAISE

4   plum tomatoes

3   teaspoons olive oil, *divided*

1   teaspoon *each* dried basil, oregano and rosemary, crushed

1/4   teaspoon coarsely ground pepper

1/2   teaspoon salt, *divided*

1   whole garlic bulb

3/4   cup reduced-fat mayonnaise

Cut tomatoes in half lengthwise; drizzle cut sides with 1-1/2 teaspoons oil. Combine the herbs, pepper and 1/4 teaspoon salt; sprinkle over tomatoes. Place cut side down on a baking sheet coated with cooking spray.

Remove papery outer skin from the garlic bulb (do not peel or separate cloves). Cut top off garlic bulb. Brush with 1/2 teaspoon oil. Wrap bulb in heavy-duty foil; place on baking sheet with the tomatoes. Bake at 425° for 15 minutes.

Turn tomatoes; drizzle with remaining oil. Bake 20-25 minutes longer or until garlic is tender and tomatoes are softened. Cool for 10 minutes.

Squeeze softened garlic into a small bowl; chop tomatoes and add to garlic. Stir in mayonnaise and remaining salt until blended. **YIELD: 1-2/3 CUPS.**

We love to use this versatile mayo on any sandwich, but it's especially good on grilled hamburgers. I usually make a big batch on the weekends and use it as leftovers to dress up any evening meal.

—Cindie Haras, Boca Raton, Florida

GRILLING HERB MIX

This is a no-fuss seasoning blend that's especially good for flame-broiled chicken or pork.

—Karyn Fischer, Decatur, Michigan

- 2 teaspoons *each* dried basil, oregano and rosemary, crushed
- 1 teaspoon rubbed sage
- 1 teaspoon dried mint
- 1 teaspoon dried thyme
- 1 teaspoon pepper

In a small bowl, combine all the ingredients. Store in an airtight container for up to 6 months. **YIELD: 8 TEASPOONS.**

BUFFALO BURGER TOPPING

Blue cheese lovers will come out of the woodwork for this zesty, full-flavored sauce.

—Michael Cohen, Los Angeles, California

- 2 tablespoons butter, softened
- 2 tablespoons brown sugar
- 3/4 cup mayonnaise
- 1/4 cup Louisiana-style hot sauce
- 1 celery rib, finely chopped
- 6 tablespoons crumbled blue cheese

In a small bowl, beat butter and brown sugar until light and fluffy. Beat in mayonnaise and hot sauce until smooth. Chill until serving. Spoon onto cooked burgers. Top with celery and cheese. **YIELD: 6 SERVINGS.**

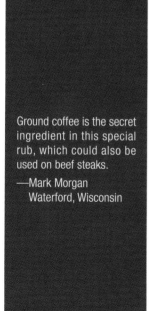

Ground coffee is the secret ingredient in this special rub, which could also be used on beef steaks.

—Mark Morgan
Waterford, Wisconsin

JAVA-SPICE RUB FOR PORK

- 1 tablespoon finely ground coffee
- 1 teaspoon kosher salt
- 1 teaspoon brown sugar
- 1 teaspoon chili powder
- 1/2 teaspoon ground cumin
- 1/2 teaspoon ground cinnamon
- 1/2 teaspoon pepper
- 1/4 teaspoon garlic powder

ADDITIONAL INGREDIENTS (for *each* batch):
- 1 pork tenderloin (1 pound)
- 1 tablespoon canola oil

In a small bowl, combine the first eight ingredients. Transfer to a small spice jar. Store in a cool dry place for up to 2 months. **YIELD: 3 BATCHES (3 TABLESPOONS TOTAL).**

TO PREPARE PORK TENDERLOIN: Brush pork with oil; rub with 1 tablespoon seasoning mix. Cover and refrigerate at least 2 hours or overnight.

Prepare grill for indirect heat. Grill pork, covered, over indirect medium-hot heat for 25-30 minutes or until a meat thermometer reads 160°. Let stand for 5 minutes before slicing. **YIELD: 4 SERVINGS PER BATCH.**

11
DESSERTS

PG. **241**   **GRILLED**
POUND CAKE WITH
BERRIES

IT'S TRUE! YOU CAN PREPARE AN ENTIRE MEAL ON THE GRILL, INCLUDING A LIP-SMACKING DESSERT THAT'S SURE TO EARN PLENTY OF PRAISE. WHETHER YOU PREFER CHOCOLATY SURPRISES, BITES WITH FRUITY APPEAL OR A LITTLE OF BOTH, YOU'RE SURE TO SATISFY THE SWEET TOOTH WITH THE ITEMS IN THIS COLORFUL CHAPTER.

PEANUT BUTTER S'MORES

This is what I depend on when dessert is a last-minute thought. It's a decadent take on campfire s'mores.

—Lillian Julow, Gainesville, Florida

- **8**   **large chocolate chip cookies**
- **4**   **teaspoons hot fudge ice cream topping**
- **4**   **large marshmallows**
- **4**   **peanut butter cups**

Spread the bottoms of four cookies with fudge topping.

Using a long-handled fork, grill marshmallows 6 in. from medium-hot heat until golden brown, turning occasionally. Carefully place a marshmallow and a peanut butter cup on each fudge-topped cookie; top with remaining cookies. Serve immediately. **YIELD: 4 SERVINGS.**

★

GRILLING TIP

THESE S'MORES are a fun take on the traditional campfire confection, but don't be afraid to get even more creative. Replace the fudge topping with caramel topping, and substitute your favorite bite-size candy bar for the peanut butter cups.

These rich and creamy custards are the perfect ending to any holiday menu. Grilled and served in a pumpkin shell, they're sure to impress your guests.

—Taste of Home Test Kitchen

GINGERED PUMPKIN CUSTARD

6	small pie pumpkins (4- to 6-inch diameter)
2	tablespoons all-purpose flour
2	tablespoons crystallized ginger
1/2	teaspoon ground cinnamon
1/4	teaspoon salt
1/4	teaspoon ground cloves
1-1/4	cups heavy whipping cream
1-3/4	cups canned pumpkin
3/4	cup packed brown sugar
1/4	cup orange juice
3	eggs, lightly beaten
1	teaspoon grated orange peel

TOPPING:

1/4	cup all-purpose flour
1/4	cup packed brown sugar
1/4	cup chopped pecans
3	tablespoons cold butter

Prepare grill for indirect heat. Wash pumpkins; cut a 2-in. circle around each stem. Remove tops; scoop out seeds and loose fibers (save seeds for another use if desired). Set pumpkins and tops aside.

In a large saucepan, combine the flour, ginger, cinnamon, salt, cloves and cream until smooth. Add pumpkin, brown sugar and orange juice. Cook and stir over medium heat until bubbly. Remove from the heat. Stir a small amount of hot filling into eggs; return all to the pan, stirring constantly. Cook and stir until bubbly. Stir in orange peel.

Fill pumpkins with hot filling to within 3/4 in. of top. Grill pumpkins, covered, over indirect medium-hot heat for 30 minutes.

For topping, combine the flour, sugar and pecans in a small bowl; cut in butter until crumbly. Sprinkle over filling. Grill 30 minutes longer or until a thermometer inserted in filling reads 160°.

If desired, grill pumpkin tops over indirect heat during the last 30 minutes of grilling. Remove pumpkins and tops from grill; cool for 10 minutes before serving. Place tops on pumpkins if desired. **YIELD: 6 SERVINGS.**

GINGER-GLAZED GRILLED HONEYDEW

1/4	cup peach preserves
1	tablespoon lemon juice
1	tablespoon crystallized ginger
2	teaspoons grated lemon peel
1/8	teaspoon ground cloves
1	medium honeydew, cut into 2-inch cubes

In a small bowl, combine the first five ingredients. Thread honeydew onto six metal or soaked wooden skewers; brush with half of the glaze.

Coat grill rack with cooking spray before starting the grill. Grill honeydew, covered, over medium-high heat for 2-3 minutes on each side or just until melon begins to soften and brown, basting frequently with remaining glaze. **YIELD: 6 SERVINGS.**

If you've never grilled fruit like this before, you're in for a real treat! I love the idea of cooking everything from appetizers to desserts on the grill. This is sweet and really light. It's a great way to end a meal.

—Jacqui Correa, Landing, New Jersey

Give this impressive fruit treat a try as dessert or just a simple snack on a breezy summer night.

—Janet Schroeder
Strawberry Point, Iowa

WARM FRUIT KABOBS

1	medium apple
1	medium banana
1	medium peach *or* nectarine
1	medium pear
2	slices fresh pineapple (1 inch thick)
2	tablespoons brown sugar
2	tablespoons lemon juice
2	tablespoons canola oil
1	teaspoon ground cinnamon

Cut all of the fruit into 1-in. chunks. Alternately thread onto 16 soaked wooden skewers (using two skewers side by side for each kabob so the fruit doesn't turn). In a small bowl, combine the brown sugar, lemon juice, oil and cinnamon.

Grill kabobs, uncovered, over medium heat for 6 minutes or until heated through, turning often and basting frequently with brown sugar mixture. **YIELD: 8 SERVINGS.**

GRILLED PEACH CRISPS

2 tablespoons sugar

1 teaspoon ground cinnamon

4 medium peaches, halved and pitted

4 cups reduced-fat vanilla ice cream

1 cup reduced-fat granola

In a small bowl, combine sugar and cinnamon; sprinkle over cut sides of peaches. Let stand for 5 minutes.

Coat grill rack with cooking spray before starting the grill. Place peaches cut side down on grill rack. Grill, covered, over medium heat for 8-10 minutes or until the peaches are tender and begin to caramelize.

Place peaches in dessert bowls. Serve with ice cream and granola. **YIELD: 8 SERVINGS.**

Most of the fat and sugar is eliminated from this grilled version of peach cobbler. A perfect finish to a summer barbecue, this dessert always impresses our guests.

—Michelle Sandoval, Escalon, California

APPLE SKEWERS

4 medium apples, peeled and quartered

4 teaspoons sugar

1-1/4 teaspoons ground cinnamon

If grilling the apples, coat grill rack with cooking spray before starting the grill. Thread apples on four metal or soaked wooden skewers. Lightly spray with cooking spray. Combine sugar and cinnamon; sprinkle over apples.

Grill, covered, over medium heat or broil 4 in. from the heat for 6-8 minutes on each side or until golden brown and apples are tender. Serve warm. **YIELD: 4 SERVINGS.**

We enjoy these flavorful grilled apples with a lightly spiced coating all year. Best of all, they're a cinch to grill, and cleanup's a breeze.

—Doris Sowers
Hutchinson, Kansas

SCREAM FOR ICE CREAM

WHEN IT COMES to grilled dessert, you can nearly always jazz up individual servings with vanilla ice cream. Add a scoop or two to any fruit skewers or even grilled cake wedges. There are a few recipes in this chapter for grilled crisps and cobblers. Ice cream is a perfect match for these timeless treats.

POT OF S'MORES

1	package (14-1/2 ounces) whole graham crackers, crushed
1/2	cup butter, melted
1	can (14 ounces) sweetened condensed milk
2	cups (12 ounces) semisweet chocolate chips
1	cup butterscotch chips
2	cups miniature marshmallows

Prepare grill or campfire for low heat, using 16-18 charcoal briquettes or large wood chips.

Line a Dutch oven with heavy-duty aluminum foil. Combine cracker crumbs and butter; press onto the bottom of the pan. Pour milk over crust and sprinkle with chocolate and butterscotch chips. Top with marshmallows.

Cover Dutch oven. When briquettes or wood chips are covered with white ash, place Dutch oven directly on top of six of them. Using long-handled tongs, place remaining briquettes on pan cover.

Cook for 15 minutes or until chips are melted. To check for doneness, use the tongs to carefully lift the cover. **YIELD: 12 SERVINGS.**

Mom's easy Dutch oven version of the popular campout treat is so good and gooey. The hardest part is waiting for the s'mores to cool so you can devour them. Yum!

—June Dress
Boise, Idaho

CAKE & BERRY CAMPFIRE DELIGHT

2	cans (21 ounces *each*) raspberry pie filling
1	package (18-1/4 ounces) yellow cake mix
1-1/4	cups water
1/2	cup canola oil

Vanilla ice cream, optional

Prepare grill or campfire for low heat, using 16-20 charcoal briquettes or large wood chips. Line a Dutch oven with heavy-duty aluminum foil; add pie filling. In a large bowl, combine the cake mix, water and oil. Spread over pie filling.

Cover Dutch oven. When briquettes or wood chips are covered with white ash, place Dutch oven directly on top of 8-10 of them. Using long-handled tongs, place remaining briquettes on pan cover.

Cook for 30-40 minutes or until filling is bubbly and a toothpick inserted in the topping comes out clean. To check for doneness, use the tongs to carefully lift the cover. Serve with ice cream if desired. **YIELD: 12 SERVINGS.**

EDITOR'S NOTE: This recipe does not use eggs.

This warm cobbler is one of our favorite ways to end a busy day of fishing, hiking, swimming or rafting. Many times, Mom tops each serving with a scoop of ice cream.

—June Dress
  Boise, Idaho

FRUIT GRILLING CHART

Grilled fruits are tasty, nutritious finales to meals throughout the year. Before grilling fruit, wash it under cool, running water and use a vegetable brush if needed. Remove any blemished areas. Grill fruit until tender. Turn halfway through grilling time.

TYPE	WEIGHT OR THICKNESS	HEAT	APPROXIMATE COOKING TIME (IN MINUTES)
APPLES	1/2-in. slices	medium/direct	4 to 6
APRICOTS	pitted, halved	medium/direct	6 to 8
BANANAS	halved lengthwise	medium/direct	6 to 8
PEACHES	pitted, halved	medium/direct	8 to 10
PEARS	halved	medium/direct	8 to 10
PINEAPPLE	1/2-in. rings	medium/direct	7 to 10

GRILLED POUND CAKE WITH BERRIES

1   cup sliced fresh strawberries
1   cup fresh raspberries
1   cup fresh blueberries
5   tablespoons sugar, *divided*
1   tablespoon minced fresh mint
1   cup heavy whipping cream
1   tablespoon lemon juice
1   teaspoon grated lemon peel
3   tablespoons butter, softened
6   slices pound cake (about 1 inch thick)

The toasty flavor of lightly grilled pound cake makes it the perfect accompaniment for summertime berries. Lemon-kissed whipping cream is a delightful finishing touch.

—Taste of Home
   Test Kitchen

In a large bowl, combine the strawberries, raspberries, blueberries, 2 tablespoons sugar and mint; set aside.

In a small bowl, beat cream until it begins to thicken. Beat in remaining sugar. Add lemon juice and peel; beat until soft peaks form. Cover cream mixture and refrigerate until serving.

Spread butter over both sides of cake slices. Grill, uncovered, over indirect medium heat for 1-2 minutes on each side or until light golden brown. Serve with berry mixture and whipped cream. **YIELD: 6 SERVINGS.**

CAMPFIRE COBBLER

1-1/4 cups biscuit/baking mix

1 envelope instant maple and brown sugar oatmeal

1/4 cup cold butter, cubed

1/3 cup milk

2 cans (21 ounces *each*) blueberry pie filling

3/4 cup unsweetened apple juice

Prepare grill or campfire for low heat, using 12-16 charcoal briquettes or large wood chips.

In a large resealable plastic bag, combine biscuit mix and oatmeal. Add butter; squeeze bag until mixture resembles coarse crumbs. Gradually add milk; knead to form a soft dough. Spread into a greased ovenproof Dutch oven. Combine pie filling and apple juice; pour over dough.

Cover Dutch oven. When briquettes or wood chips are covered with white ash, place Dutch oven directly on top of 6-8 of them. Using long-handled tongs, place 6-8 briquettes on pan cover. Cook for 15 minutes or until filling is bubbly.

To check for doneness, use the tongs to carefully lift cover. If necessary, cook 5 minutes longer. **YIELD: 6 SERVINGS.**

At your next campfire, try preparing this wonderful dish for a dessert. It is so quick and simple.

—Taste of Home
Test Kitchen

HONEY-RUM GRILLED BANANAS

2 tablespoons rum

2 tablespoons honey

1 teaspoon ground cinnamon

4 medium firm unpeeled bananas

Vanilla ice cream

In a small bowl, combine the rum, honey and cinnamon; set aside. Cut bananas in half lengthwise, leaving the peel on.

Place bananas cut side down on grill. Cover and grill over medium heat for 3 minutes. Turn and brush with honey mixture. Cover and grill 5-6 minutes longer or until tender. Peel bananas. Serve immediately with ice cream. **YIELD: 4 SERVINGS.**

Here's a perfect dessert following a cookout. My family was skeptical at first, but everyone tried it and they all agreed it was delicious. I use coconut rum from the Bahamas.

—Lori Wendt, Mahomet, Illinois

CITRUS-GLAZED FRUIT KABOBS

1	cup (8 ounces) vanilla yogurt
1	tablespoon chopped fresh mint
1/4	teaspoon ground ginger
3/4	cup packed brown sugar
1/4	cup lime *or* orange juice

Dash ground cinnamon

2	kiwifruit, peeled, halved and thickly sliced
1/2	cup *each* fresh peach, apricot, plum and nectarine wedges
1/2	cup thickly sliced ripe banana
1/2	cup cubed fresh pineapple
1/2	cup cubed peeled mango

For sauce, in a small bowl, combine the yogurt, mint and ginger; cover and refrigerate for 30 minutes.

For glaze, in a small saucepan, combine the brown sugar, lime juice and cinnamon. Cook and stir over medium heat until sugar is dissolved. Remove from the heat.

On eight metal or soaked wooden skewers, alternately thread the fruit; brush with half of the glaze. Grill, uncovered, over medium-low heat for 12-16 minutes or until lightly browned, turning occasionally and basting frequently with remaining glaze. Serve warm with yogurt sauce. **YIELD: 8 SERVINGS.**

What could be sweeter, simpler and more perfect for alfresco dining than grilled seasonal fruit?
—Agnes Ward
Stratford, Ontario

BAKED APPLES ON THE GRILL

  4   **medium tart apples, cored**

1/3 **cup raisins**

1/3 **cup flaked coconut**

1/4 **cup packed brown sugar**

1/2 **teaspoon ground cinnamon**

Place each apple on a piece of heavy-duty foil (about 12 in. square). Combine the remaining ingredients; spoon into center of apples. Fold foil over apples and seal tightly.

Grill, covered, over medium heat for 20-25 minutes or until apples are tender. Open foil carefully to allow steam to escape. **YIELD: 4 SERVINGS.**

Sweet coconut provides the delicious difference in this grilled great. Our two children enjoy helping me stuff the yummy filling into the apples. It's so easy that sometimes we don't even bother to do the measuring!

—Jodi Rugg, Aurora, Illinois

FRUIT 'N' CAKE KABOBS

1/2 **cup apricot preserves**

  1   **tablespoon water**

  1   **tablespoon butter**

1/8 **teaspoon ground cinnamon**

1/8 **teaspoon ground nutmeg**

  3   **medium nectarines, pitted and quartered**

  3   **medium plums, pitted and quartered**

  3   **medium peaches, pitted and quartered**

  1   **loaf (10-3/4 ounces) frozen pound cake, thawed and cut into 2-inch cubes**

In a small saucepan over medium heat, combine the apricot preserves, water, butter, cinnamon and nutmeg until blended.

On eight metal or soaked wooden skewers, alternately thread the nectarines, plums, peaches and cake cubes.

Grill, uncovered, over medium heat for 1-2 minutes on each side or until cake is golden brown and fruit is tender, brushing occasionally with apricot mixture. **YIELD: 8 SERVINGS.**

You can even grill dessert using this delicious idea. A neighbor served these kabobs at a family picnic and brought some over for us to sample. I was pleasantly surprised at the tasty toasted cake and juicy grilled fruit.

—Mary Ann Dell
   Phoenixville,
   Pennsylvania

PEACHES WITH LEMON CREAM

1/4   cup heavy whipping cream

1   tablespoon brown sugar

1   teaspoon vanilla extract

1/2   teaspoon grated lemon peel

3   medium peaches, halved

2   tablespoons canola oil

This is a great treat from the grill. It's easy to prepare, and everyone will ask for seconds. My family looks forward to this dessert all summer long!

—Carole Fraser
North York, Ontario

In a small bowl, beat cream until it begins to thicken. Add the brown sugar, vanilla and lemon peel; beat until stiff peaks form. Cover and refrigerate until serving.

Brush cut sides of peaches with oil; place cut side down on grill rack. Grill, covered, over medium heat for 10-12 minutes or until the peaches are tender and begin to caramelize.

Place peaches on dessert plates; fill with lemon cream mixture. **YIELD: 6 SERVINGS.**

GRILLED PINEAPPLE WITH LIME DIP

1   fresh pineapple

1/4   cup packed brown sugar

3   tablespoons honey

2   tablespoons lime juice

LIME DIP:

1   package (3 ounces) cream cheese, softened

1/4   cup plain yogurt

2   tablespoons honey

1   tablespoon brown sugar

1   tablespoon lime juice

1   teaspoon grated lime peel

Peel and core the pineapple; cut into eight wedges. Cut each wedge into two spears. In a large resealable plastic bag, combine the brown sugar, honey and lime juice; add pineapple. Seal bag and turn to coat; refrigerate for 1 hour.

In a small bowl, beat cream cheese until smooth. Beat in the yogurt, honey, brown sugar, lime juice and peel. Cover and refrigerate until serving.

Coat grill rack with cooking spray before starting the grill. Drain and discard marinade. Grill pineapple, covered, over medium heat for 3-4 minutes on each side or until golden brown. Serve with lime dip.
YIELD: 8 SERVINGS.

This fruity dessert was created by our home economists. If desired, the pineapple wedges can be rolled in flaked coconut before grilling.

—Taste of Home Test Kitchen

INDEXES

ALPHABETICAL RECIPE INDEX

Refer to this index for a complete alphabetical listing of all the recipes in this book.

GENERAL RECIPE INDEX

Refer to this index for a complete general listing of all the recipes in this book.